Visit
B

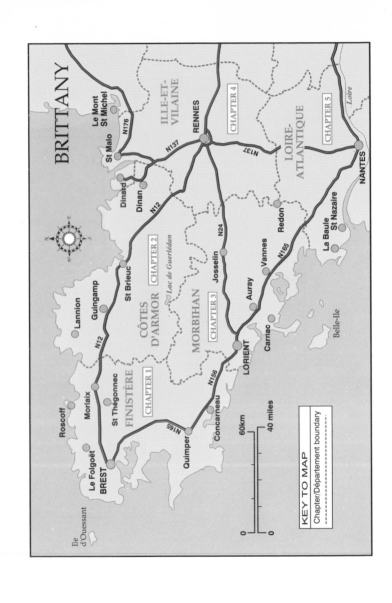

VISITOR'S GUIDE
Brittany

RICHARD SALE

MPC

HUNTER

Published by:
Moorland Publishing Co Ltd,
Moor Farm Road West,
Ashbourne,
Derbyshire DE6 1HD
England

ISBN 0 86190 434 6

Published in the USA by:
Hunter Publishing Inc,
300 Raritan Center Parkway,
CN 94, Edison, NJ 08818

ISBN 1 55650 574 4 (USA)

British Library Cataloguing in
Publication Data:
A catalogue record for this book is
available from the British Library.

Colour origination by:
P. & W. Graphics Pte Ltd, Singapore

Printed in Hong Kong by:
Wing King Tong Co., Ltd.

Cover photograph: St Servan-sur-
Mer (International Photobank).

Illustrations have been supplied as
follows: Richard Sale; pp 19, 26, 34,
35, 46 (lower), 50, 54, 55 (lower), 63
(lower), 66 (top), 67, 71, 74 (both),
94, 103, 106, 107, 114, 115, 118, 134
(lower), 138, 142 (top), 147, 151, 162
(lower), 215 (lower), 222 (top), 226,
Yuon Boëlle 142 (lower), John
Lioyd 183, all other pictures
supplied by the CDT (Comite
Départemental du Tourisme).

MPC Production Team:
Editorial: Tonya Monk
Design: Daniel Clarke
Cartography: Alastair Morrison
Typesetting: Christine Haines

Acknowledgements
The author would like to thank all
those who helped with the
preparation of this book, but
especially Isabelle Touffet of the
Brittany Chamber of Commerce in
London, Angelika Le Brun in
Quimper, Annoïck Gouereou in
Vannes, Veronique Abriou in St
Brieuc, Jean-Paul Dorie in Nantes
and Sylvain Le Clerc. He would
also like to thank Brittany Ferries
for their help throughout the
project, especially Clair O'Connell
of the London Office.

CONTENTS

Key to Symbols Used in Text Margin and on Maps

木	Recommended walk	⌂	Church/Monastery
♣	Parkland	⊞	Building of interest
✴	Garden	Π	Archaeological Site
⛫	Castle/Fortification (*Château*)	🏛	Museum/Art gallery
✳	Other place of interest	🏞	Beautiful view/Scenery, Natural phenomenon
⏣	Caves	⇁	Aquatic interest
🦌	Animal Interest/Nature reserves	△	Watersport facilities
		🐦	Birdlife

Key to Maps

═══	Motorway		City
────	Main Road		
═══	Minor Road	◯	Town /Village
`····`	Département Boundary		River/Lake

How To Use This Guide

This MPC Visitor's Guide has been designed to be as easy to use as possible. Each chapter covers a region or itinerary in a natural progression which gives all the background information to help you enjoy your visit. MPC's distinctive margin symbols, the important places printed in bold, and a comprehensive index enable the reader to find the most interesting places to visit with ease. At the end of each chapter an Additional Information section gives specific details such as addresses and opening times, making this guide a complete sightseeing companion. At the back of the guide the Fact File, arranged in alphabetical order, gives practical information and useful tips to help you plan your holiday — before you go and while you are there. The maps of each region show the main towns, villages, roads and places of interest, but are not designed as route maps and motorists should always use a good recommended road atlas.

INTRODUCTION

Brittany arouses an affection in those who visit it that is difficult to capture in words. Scenically, it cannot compare with the Alps and its climate is less dependable than that of the Mediterranean coast, yet it has an array of undeniable charms. The coast is ruggedly beautiful in parts, but also dotted with superb sandy beaches, while the villages along it are both visually delightful and historically interesting. The mysterious megalithic sites — of which Brittany has the highest concentration, and the best, in Europe — are a constant source of wonder. The Bretons, with their charming costumes and their *pardons*, are an endearing people, and the line of strong castles strung out along the landward side of the region's rectangle, speak of an independence of mind from the French that still means that a holiday in Brittany is not quite the same as a holiday in France.

The old Brittany, the medieval land of the Breton dukes, had the Loire as its southern border, the eastern border being less well-defined. Today, the region technically encompasses four *départements*, the land close to the Loire forming part of the *département* of Loire-Atlantique in the Pays de Loire. For the purposes of this book we roll back the years, covering not only Finistère, Côtes d'Armor (a *département* that, until recently, was called Côtes-du-Nord), Morbihan and Ille-et-Vilaine, the four *départements* of the 'new' Brittany, but that part of Loire-Atlantique that lies north of the Loire.

Geography

The land that is now Brittany was formed some 600 million years ago when the earth movement known as the Hercynian Fold forced a huge, V-shaped mass of rock above the sea that, at the time, covered France. This V-shaped mass had the Ardennes and Brittany at the tops of its arms, and the Massif Central at its base. The rocks thrust up by the fold were hard and crystalline, granites and gneisses, and these remain the basis of the Breton countryside.

In Brittany the upthrust resulted in two parallel, east-west ridges of hills, that were gradually worn down by erosion, so that today's visitor could be forgiven for overlooking them. The ridges are still visible, but only just, the northern one forming the Monts d'Arrée, and the upland areas that head east towards Menez Bré and Guingamp, and then on to Loudéac, the southern ridge forming the Montagnes Noires, but soon becoming lost in the Breton heartland, only to re-appear as the Landes de Lanvaux, north of Vannes. After millions of years of erosion, in part assisted by the Ice Ages, the highest point of the hard ridges does not quite reach the 400m (1,312ft) contour, though as a result of the underlying hard rock much of Brittany is a plateau that lies above 175m (574ft).

The Ice Ages that helped erode the granite peaks also chiselled at the Breton coastline, producing the *abers*, the fjord-like inlets of the north Finistère coast. The rise in sea level that followed the melting of the ice also altered the landscape, creating deep inlets and transforming some inland crags into sea cliffs. The battering of the Atlantic on the new coastline and cliffs then produced the spectacular seascapes that are now so prominent a feature of Brittany. The best areas are, of course, a matter of personal choice, but the 'Coasts of Pink Granite' and Emerald, on the northern shore, and the Crozon and Raz peninsulas to the west will be high on the lists of all visitors.

The sea was the source of food for the earliest inhabitants, and still provides work for a large number of Bretons, the coast having deep-sea ports, its trawlers fishing for tuna in the Bay of Biscay and off Africa, or for cod in the North Atlantic, as well as those whose fleets work closer to home. The local boats specialise in fishing for crustaceans, of which the langoustine is the most traditional. In addition to these boat-based industries, there are also the shore-based oyster and mussel fisheries, the shell-fish being grown in tidal bays and harvested for both local and export markets.

The coast was *armor* to the Bretons, the land of the sea, while inland was *argoat*, the land of forests. Before man arrived in the region it is likely that virtually all of the inland plateau was covered by oak and beech woods, and pockets still exist, most notably near Huelgoat, in central Finistère, and close to Paimpont, to the west of Rennes. The Forest of Paimpont is the ancient Broceliande, a forest linked with King Arthur and Merlin, the Round Table and the Holy Grail. Clearing of the inland forest started as soon as ancient man changed from being a hunter-gatherer to a farmer. Today the cleared land supports a varied agriculture, with apple orchards in Ille-et-Vilaine, vegetables in Finistère and cereal production between the two. Dairy farming is the most important aspect of stock raising, Brittany producing around 20 per cent of the French output.

With fishing and agriculture being so important to Brittany's economy, it is no surprise to find that almost one-third of Breton industrial workers are engaged in food processing. Another third are engaged in the 'modern' industries of electronics and telecommunications that have recently moved into the 'green field' sites of Brittany.

History

The first tangible reminder of man's presence in Brittany are the megaliths. About 4,000 years BC the first of these were erected, their erection/construction continuing from that time — the late Neolithic period — through the Bronze Age, a period of about 2,000 years. The megaliths themselves are dealt with later in this Introduction: from an historical point of view it is worth noting only that the folk who constructed them remain as much a mystery as their reasons for doing so.

As the Bronze Age folk were replaced by those of the Iron Age — and here, as elsewhere, it is not clear whether the replacement was a gradual one, by assimilation, or a bloody one, by conquest — the stage was set for the arrival of the Celts who are now most clearly associated with the area. The first Celts to arrive in the peninsula named it *armor*, the land of the sea, a name still used to describe the coastline, and the name recently given to the *département* of Côtes d'Armor, once called Côtes-du-Nord.

When the Romans invaded Gaul, as Celtic France was called, they moved steadily northward, subduing the various tribes that held it. One of the last tribes to be conquered, and one that gave them a great deal of trouble, was the Veneti, who lived close to what is now the town of Vannes, a town named in their honour. In 56BC the Roman fleet of Julius Caesar defeated the fleet of the Veneti either in the Gulf of Morbihan or on the sea close to it. After the defeat the Romans took control of Brittany, and the rest of France, coaching the locals in the Roman way and bringing a peace and civilisation that lasted 400 years.

When the Romans retreated from northern Gaul to defend Rome from the barbarian hordes, Roman Brittany continued much as it had at first, but in the middle of the fifth century it was invaded. The invasion was not, surprisingly, from France, but from Britain. In Britain the Roman withdrawal had been followed by an invasion of Angles and Saxons. These landed in the east of the country, but

Brittany is renowned for its fantastic beaches

A large proportion of Brittany's industrial workers are connected with the fishing industry

gradually spread westward. Ultimately they reached the Severn, cutting off the Celts of the south-west peninsula from those of Wales. The Saxons pushed on down the peninsula, forcing the Celts into Cornwall. Eventually the Celts were left with nowhere to go, so they sailed south to reach the land their cousins had settled all those centuries ago. The new Celts transformed the land. They gave it new names: the whole peninsula they called Little Britain (because the land they had left was Great Britain) a name that was soon shortened to Brittany. Those who took over the south-western tip of the peninsula named it after Cornwall the land they had left, so similar were the seascapes and plateaux, even to the number of megalithic remains. Today the area is still called Cornouaille.

These new Celts brought with them their tales of a heroic leader who had routed the Saxons before being betrayed and killed. He was called Arthur, and soon the Breton landscape, just like the British landscape, was dotted with places that tied them to the Arthurian legends. Megalithic tombs became Arthur's tomb, the forest near Paimpont became Broceliande, complete with a valley in which Merlin had been held by Morgan-le-Fay, and the legend of Tristan and Iseult was transferred to an island near Douarnanez. The settlers also brought their language, Breton, that is still spoken and bears very marked similarities to Welsh, the language of the Celts left behind in Britain.

The new Bretons were a fiercely independent people who distanced themselves from the rest of France. When the Franks rose to power under Charlemagne, Brittany was invaded and subjugated, but when Nominoé, a nobleman from Vannes, was made Duke of Brittany by a later Frankish king, he immediately threw the Franks out and turned Brittany into the independent state. It maintained its independence for another 700 years, though that period was not entirely one of peace and tranquillity. In the early tenth century Norse invaders ravaged Brittany, only being ejected when Alain Barbe-Torte, the Breton king who had taken refuge in Britain, returned and raised an army. Strangely, Barbe-Torte (Crooked Beard) was the last Breton king, his successors calling themselves dukes.

The Breton nobility were involved in the Norman Conquest of England in 1066, the links between the two being crucial some 300 years later when the death of Duke Jean III resulted in a power struggle in Brittany. Duke Jean was childless, and indicated that he wished the Duchy to pass to his niece Jeanne de Penthièvre, the wife of Charles de Blois, whose claim was supported by the French. This inheritance was disputed by Duke Jean's nephew, Jean de Monfort, who was supported by the English. The dispute lead to the War of

Succession, a war that lasted 23 years and in which many of the castles that the visitor sees today saw action. It was during this war that the Battle of the Thirties, one of France's most famous acts of chivalry, took place near Josselin.

The War of Succession ended when Charles de Blois was killed and his army defeated at the Battle of Auray in 1364. Brittany had been ravaged, but under the Montfort dukes it rose to even greater heights, maintaining a steadfast independence from France, an independence secured with the aid of a string of impressive castles along the border between the two, a border that now forms the eastern boundary of the Breton province. Ultimately the power of the Breton duke began to frighten the French crown. In 1483 the 13-year old Charles VIII became King of France, though real power rested with his sister Anne de Beaujeu. In 1486 another Anne, the 11-year old daughter of the Breton Duke François II, was betrothed to Maximilian, the Hapsburg prince who was heir to the crown of the Holy Roman Empire. This possibility of an alliance between Brittany and Rome so frightened Anne de Beaujeu that she invaded in 1487. The invasion was repulsed, but a second, stronger army in 1488 was successful, the Breton army being defeated at St Aubin-du-Cormier. The Treaty of Verger, signed after the battle, all but ended Breton independence giving the French Crown, amongst other things, the right of consent in the marriage of François' daughters. Two weeks after signing François died, it is said, of a broken heart.

He was succeeded by his daughter Anne, the famous Duchess Anne, or Anne of Brittany, whose name is encountered all over the province. To save her people at the siege of Rennes Anne agreed to marry Charles VIII rather than Maximilian, and when Charles died suddenly, she further united Brittany and France by marrying his successor Louis XII. Though the formal unification of the Duchy with France did not take place until 1532, almost 20 years after her death, Anne must take credit for the bloodless way in which it came about.

In the years between unification and the Revolution, Brittany was often at the forefront of the development of France. Jacques Cartier sailed from St Malo to discover Canada, the Treaty of Nantes gave religious freedom to all citizens (in theory at least) and the St Malo corsairs brought wealth to the kingdom. Brittany welcomed the Revolution (but did not anticipate the excesses of Carrier at Nantes) though the revolt of the Chouans showed that the old Celtic desire for a king still had a hold on many.

During the 1939-45 war Brittany played a sadly prominent role, the great ports of Brest and St Nazaire being so important in the North Atlantic War that they were heavily defended by the Germans, and frequently attacked by the Allies. In each case the towns were all but destroyed by the time peace came in 1945. Since that time Brittany has continued to play an important role in the development of France. The Rance barrage was the the world's first tidal power station, and the first trans-Atlantic television programme was transmitted from Pleumeur-Bodou.

Aspects of Brittany

THE MEGALITHS

The standing stones of Brittany are one of its greatest wonders, the concentration of sites, the size of the stones involved, and the sheer power and beauty of some of the monuments, being without equal in Europe.

Surprisingly little is known about the builders, remains other than the stones themselves being limited and fragmentary. It is known that they were farmers, and that their civilisation was sufficiently well advanced to have allowed them the considerable free time necessary to move multi-ton stones across the countryside. They believed in an after-life, as some of the monuments were definitely tombs and were stocked with simple grave-goods implying that the soul of the departed would need them in the next life. The existence of pottery — of a particular form known as bell-beaker, which has led to them being called Beaker People — and of early forms of bronze, implies that the megalith folk covered the period from the late Stone to the early Bronze Ages. They also worked gold for jewellery, so they had both skilled craftsmen and a developed sense of art. Of the reasons for the erection of those megalithic monuments that are not tombs, the alignments and the single standing stones for instance, nothing is known. As a result of this absence of knowledge many theories have evolved. From earliest Celtic times the monuments were woven into local legend: the stones were boys and girls who danced on the Sabbath and were turned to stone for their blasphemy; stones had been thrown by giants or the Devil, usually after having been found in a shoe; they were Arthur's cave, or look-out stone, or tomb. Later, in the European romantic era (the nineteenth century), the stones were ascribed to the Druids, the little understood Celtic priesthood. This is now known to be nonsense, the Breton Druids existed over 2,000 years after the last stone was erected, but the idea lives on in the occasional name — Druid's altarstone, Druid's table. Most recently, after the discovery of the probable astronomical alignments at Stonehenge in England, it has been conjectured that the stones were forms of solar or astronomical observatories used for predicting mid-winter or eclipses. The arguments on both sides of this debate have been an odd mixture of the profound and the acrimonious, and all that can be safely said at this stage is that some of the monuments may have had astronomical significance.

In Brittany the most frequently seen megalith is the single standing stone or menhir (from the Celtic *maen hir*, long stone). The largest of these was that at Locmariaquer, which stood about 20m (66ft) high and probably fell only 200 years ago when it was struck by lightning. Of those that remain standing there are several at 8 to 9m (26 to 30ft), the most impressive being that at Champ Dolent near Dol-de-Bretagne. That of Men-Marz near Brignogan-Plage is interesting for having been 'Christianised'. Such was the power of these monuments on the imaginations of local folk that they felt the need to placate or de-mystify them. The former took the form of an annual anointing with honey and beeswax, a custom that was certainly alive 50 years ago and may still go on in some remote areas. The latter involved the chiselling of Christian symbols on the pagan stone. At Men-Marz a crucifix has been added to the stone.

The next form of monument is the alignment. In this many stones would be erected to form a shape. In Britain the usual shape is a circle, but in Brittany, though there are circles, the usual form is a straight line (or lines) of regularly spaced stones. The alignments of Carnac are among the wonders of the world, with thousands of stones in dozens of lines. The alignments are baffling as they are neither parallel, nor continuous, nor do they all point the same way. At Avebury, near Stonehenge in England, there is a similar, though smaller, alignment in which alternate stones are columnar and triangular, implying phallic representations and, it is assumed, some form of fertility rite. There is evidence for a similar pattern at Carnac, but here the alignments are much more elaborate than Avebury's double row 'avenue', and they do not always lead, as they do at Avebury, to a specific circle or other monument.

Megalithic tombs fall into two forms. The dolmen (from the Celtic *dol men*, flat or table stone) is a flat slab of stone supported on a number of uprights. Some of these dolmens may have been covered by earth mounds to form long burrows, though it is conjectured that some remained uncovered. The dolmen was the simplest form of tomb, later forms including a passage to the grave site, several grave sites, or a long gallery tomb. Of the passage graves the most impressive are at Barnenez in Finistère, and the tumulus of St Michel at Carnac, each of which involves elaborate dry-stone walling to retain the earth mound that covered the tomb. The gallery grave, or *allée couverte* as it is known in France, at Le Mougou is among the most beautiful of all the monuments. The tombs of the Merchants' Table at Locmariaquer and that on the Ile de Gavrinis in the Gulf of Morbihan deserve special mention as they have been carved with a variety of geometric designs. As granite is the hardest of all rocks, and the carvings are both precise and elaborate, the effort required to produce them was phenomenal.

A final monument type is best represented by the Roche aux Fées, the Fairies Stone, south of Rennes. This looks like a large version of an *allée couverte*, but many experts now believe that it was not a tomb, but a form of ritual temple. As with the alignments, it is probable that we will never know with any certainty.

Breton costumes are elaborately designed

COSTUME

Despite the postcards on sale in virtually every town, and the words written in every local guide book, the visitor will actually be very lucky to see a Breton costume outside of one of the many costume museums dotted about the province. The reason is both cost and fashion: the costumes are very expensive because of the labour intensive embroidery and the elaborate designs, coupled with the decline in the number of women skilled in costume making; and the young Breton folk are not as enthusiastic about wearing a costume that is so markedly different from the modern fashion. Today, the costume is likely to be seen only at *pardons* or, perhaps, at a wedding, baptism or first communion.

The costume is not one, but many, the areas, and even the towns, of Brittany each having their own special version, though the basic form is usually similar. Men wear black trousers, occasionally baggy trousers known as *bragoubras*, short black jackets with wide lapels, waistcoats, and felt berets, usually with ribbons. The women wear dark, sometimes tiered, skirts, black bodices, aprons and a *coiffe*, or hat. The amount of lace, embroidery or brocade on the outfit would usually indicate the wealth and status of the wearer's family.

Though it sounds a straightforward costume, the differences between towns were significant. In Quimper the men's jacket was pale blue, while in the Bigouden, the country around Pont l'Abbe, the waistcoats were long and richly embroidered. Similar differences were seen in the women's costumes, usually in the apron and *coiffe*. The Pont-Aven apron was small, that of Quimper was bib-less, while that of Lorient has a bib to the shoulders. Similarly, the Douarnenez *coiffe* was small, that of Huelgoat just net over the hair, while that of Plougastel was lace-free white linen, with many long ribbons. The most beautiful *coiffe* is found in Pont-Aven, an elaborately winged lace creation matched by winged shoulder pieces on the red bodice. But the most remarkable *coiffe* is that of the Bigouden area where it has grown almost as tall as the local menhirs, a tower of lace.

PARDONS

The Breton *pardon* is in part religious, in part secular, consisting of a procession, sometimes accompanied by saintly relics, to an old chapel and church, followed by a fair with Breton music and dancing. It is believed that *pardons* may have their origins in Brittany's Celtic period. The Celts believed that the gods occasionally co-habited the real world and held festivals at which, they therefore believed, the gods were present. From these festivals the *pardons* developed. The name itself is medieval, the annual procession offering those who followed it the chance to seek forgiveness for their sins. Some of the events also offered the possibility of a miraculous cure, many of the saint's reliquaries being believed to offer a cure for a specific ailment. One of the best examples was the *pardon* to the church of St Jean-du-Doigt, the finger of the name — said to be that of John the Baptist — being claimed to cure eye disorders if the eye was bathed in water into which the finger had been dipped. Annually at the time of the *pardon* the saintly relic was immersed in water, the event drawing folk with eye problems from all over Brittany.

Today the secular part of the festival is usually just a fun fair, perhaps with a rock band and a great deal of drinking. Many Bretons regret this, believing that the *pardons* of yesteryear, where the *biniou* (bagpipes) and *bombarde* (a form of oboe) played and men and women in full costume danced, were greatly superior, and that the decline is symptomatic of a general decline in Breton cultural values. It is likely that this, in part at least, is true, and is a cause for regret. But the old *pardons* were not always the beautiful festivals they are now made out to be. Once at St Servais the menfolk of the four local dioceses fought for possession of a wooden statue, the winning diocese being thought to gain better crops. At first the rivalry was largely symbolic, but eventually groups of thugs fought each other with clubs and broken limbs and serious head injuries were commonplace. Eventually the *pardon* was banned.

Many of the towns and villages in Brittany have their own *pardons*, so many in fact that only the most famous or unusual are mentioned in the text. If your holiday village is not among them, it is worth contacting the local Tourist Information Office to see if there is to be a local *pardon* during the time of your stay. If there is it will be worth attending, not just to see the local costumes and *coiffes*, but to be part of a tradition that may well be more than a thousand years old.

PARISH CLOSES

The *Enclos Paroissial*, the Parish Close, is the most typical of all Breton religious buildings, a celebration of life and a memorial to the dead. In its earliest form the centrepiece of the Close was the village cemetery, though many of today's examples are no longer so grouped. In its more usual form the Close is a walled enclosure reached through a triumphal arch and completed by an ossuary and Calvary. The arch signifies the triumph of the Christian life in attaining immortality. Some arches look very similar to the classical triumphal arch, though others are far more elaborate, the best of these being the triple span topped by a long gallery at Sizun.

Festivals play a major role in the cultural activities of Brittany

Mont St Michel, the gateway to Brittany

The ossuary chapel became necessary when the relatively small size of Breton cemeteries meant that new burials invariably involved the exhumation of the bones of those who had died generations ago. The exhumed bones would be stored in the chapel, the chapel also being used for funeral services. Today most of the chapels are empty and little used.

The Calvary seems to have been an extension of the idea of 'Christianising' a menhir, the tall granite structures seeming to echo the ancient standing stones. In essence the Calvary was a representation of the Crucifixion, but as time passed they grew more elaborate, depicting various scenes from the Passion, from the Bible stories or from the lives of the saints, particularly the saint associated with the village. For the priest the Calvary was a visual text, especially useful because most of his parishioners were unable to read, and he

Crêpes *are synonymous with Breton cuisine*

would preach from below it, pointing out the scenes as he described them. Local villages competed with each other for possession of the richest, most elaborate Calvary and Close, the richness not only indicating the premier village, but reflecting the wealth of its inhabitants. Consequently some of the Calvaries are superbly carved and have dozens of figures in their scenes. That at Guimilau has over 200, that at Plougastel-Daoulas almost as many. The latter Calvary also has a depiction of a moral tale, the story of Catell-Gollet (Catherine, or Kate, the Lost) which was doubtless used as the theme for many a sermon.

The church that formed the final part of the Close also had distinctive features, many of which can be seen, often elaborated, in churches that do not form parts of a Close. Breton churches have large entrance porches, often filled with statuary, and slender towers or spires. The towers were greatly loved by the parishioners as they also reflected the wealth and standing of the village. Indeed, such was the civic pride attached to the tower that occasionally the Breton Duke, or the French King, would order its destruction to show his disfavour of a village or a local lord, the act being a cause for genuine dismay.

Inside the church the most noticeable feature is usually the rood screen, the carving of some of these rivalling the Calvary's of other villages. Many of the screens were carved in wood, but occasionally, as for instance at Le Folgöet, the screen would be carved in granite.

FOOD AND DRINK

To most visitors Brittany means crêpes, the thin pancake which can be eaten both savoury and sweet being synonymous with the area. In most *crêperies* the visitor will be offered a choice between *crêpes* and *galettes*, the difference being unclear, even to the extent that it is not always (though usually) the *galette* which is savoury, being offered with ham, cheese, mushrooms, seafood or any combination of them. *Galettes* are normally made from buckwheat, with *crêpes* — the desert pancake, usually served with butter, sugar, lemon or jam — being from wheat and lighter (both in colour and texture). However, these distinctions are now being lost, especially in eastern Brittany. In the west, the visitor may still be offered traditional forms of *crêpe*, such as Quimper's *crêpes dentelles*, a rolled form that is so thin it almost becomes a biscuit.

The other joy of Breton cuisine is its seafood, no surprise for a province with such a long coastline. Pride of place must go to *Homard à l'Armoricaine*, Breton lobster in a rich sauce, the ingredients of which usually include cream, tomatoes, onions and brandy. There is a story that the name is wrong, and should read *l'Americaine*, the dish having been invented in a Parisian restaurant at the request of an American, but the Bretons counter this by denying the tale, and pointing out that even if it were true then it was because the American in question learned the recipe from a Breton who had emigrated to the USA.

Other seafoods which are worth sampling are *langoustines*, a crayfish that is served whole to the diner, and the eating of which results in a larger pile of shells on the plate than were there when the waiter brought it, *moules* (mussels) and of course, *huîtres* (oysters). The Bretons also have their own version of bouillabaise, called *cotriade*, a fish stew usually based around conger eel, but also including several other local fish.

On the meat menu a Châteaubriand steak will be required eating for all visitors with a sense of literary history. The other great delight is *pré-salé* lamb or mutton, from the flocks reared on the saltmarshes of Mont St Michel Bay.

The only Breton wines are Muscadet and Gros Plant which are produced around Nantes. A sweet wine is also grown on the Rhuys Peninsula, but though of legendary strength it is deemed not to travel well and most is turned into an excellent brandy. Of longer drinks, cider is the most traditional, though most people maintain that the ciders of Normandy are superior to those of Brittany. For a real change try *chouchen* or *hydromel* a mead of fermented honey. But be cautious, it is deceptively strong and has caught out many a visitor.

1

FINISTÈRE

The most westerly of the four *départements* of Brittany is named for its position, for this is *Finis Terre*, Land's End in Latin, the name given to the area by the Romans when they reached the extremity of Gaul. In Breton the area is called *Penn ar Bed*, a name which also translates as Land's End. Finistère is the most Breton of all the *départements*, the one with the highest concentration of speakers of the Breton language, with the best of the Parish Closes, the most famous of the *pardons*, the most remarkable of the *coiffes*. It is also a land that portrays most exactly the contrast between the *armor* and the *argoat*. The coastline is as ruggedly beautiful as could be wished by the most ardent lover of seascapes, while the forest around Huelgoat, though smaller than Paimpont and less well endowed with Arthurian legends, is every bit as attractive. The town's and villages too are a delight: Quimper has a beautiful old quarter, Concarneau a splendid walled section.

Because of its size, and the number of interesting sites it has to offer, Finistère will be considered in three sections. First the northern coast, the Breton fjord coast, the Coast of Legends. Next we move south to the *argoat* and the land of the Parish Closes. Finally the south of the *département* is covered, an area that includes not only some of the best coastal scenery in Brittany, but some of the best holiday beaches, together with Quimper, the *département's* capital.

Northern Finistère

For many visitors, their first view of Brittany is of **Roscoff** from the dock of a Brittany Ferries boat as it nears the elaborate breakwater complex of the port. This is appropriate, Brittany Ferries having had their origins in Roscoff, though in the early years the ships carried cauliflowers rather than people. In the 1950s the local farmers,

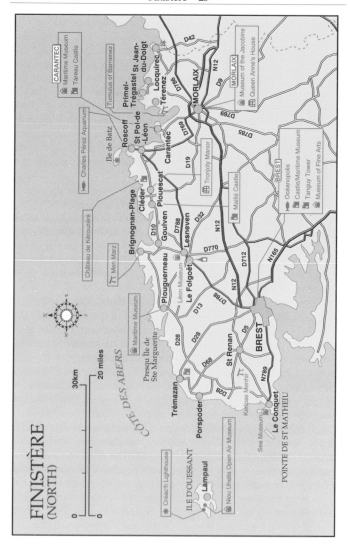

growing tired of the limited market for their vegetables in France — a problem caused by the poor road system heading west and the perishable nature of cauliflowers and artichokes, their chief crops — decided to look for a market in Britain, a mere 8-hour boat trip away. When the farmers' leader, Alexis Gourvennec, approached British carriers about the possibility of shipping from Roscoff to Plymouth he was told that they had no interest in dealing with Russia! This unlikely story may well be apocryphal, but it is a fact that Gourvennec was unable to find any shipping line to carry his wares. He therefore badgered the French Government into financing port improvements at Roscoff and assisting SICA (the Societé d'Intérêt Collectif Agricole), the local farming organisation, to set up a shipping line. The trade was wildly successful, several French vegetable types soon rivalling the bicycling Johnny Onion-man's stock. Eventually the company realised that with a bigger ship people and cars could be carried along with the cauliflower lorries, and Brittany Ferries was born.

The ferry port is close to the town, but despite this the town is rarely visited, the arriving visitor usually being anxious to be away to his holiday destination. The town is almost always as badly served by the returning visitor, the more so now that the facilities at the port have been improved. Roscoff, if noted at all, is usually seen as a fleeting glimpse of the curious church tower. That is sad, Roscoff being a neat seaside town with a fine old quarter and several points of real interest.

The glimpsed tower is the remarkable tiered belfry of the church of Notre-Dame de Kroaz-Batz, a sixteenth-century Gothic building. The belfry is a masterpiece in Renaissance style and is certainly the most distinctive in Finistère. Inside the church there are a fine series of alabaster carvings, worked in the fifteenth century, with scenes from the Passion. Other decorations include ships and cannons, reliefs that hint at the basis of the town's prosperity. Roscoff has always been a trading port, though the cannons imply that the memorial is to the men who carried on the more prosperous, but illegal, trade of the corsair. Corsairs (the name is romantic, and is usually used in preference to the more mundane, but equally valid, name of pirate) operated from the port in the sixteenth and seventeenth centuries, preying on ships in the English channel and bringing their loot back to swell the town's coffers. Some of the most interesting houses in Roscoff date from this period: those in Place Lacaze-Duthiers close to the church and those in Rue Amiral-Reveillére that lead from it towards the port. One house in the latter street is named for Mary Stuart commemorating, or so it is said, the night she spent in the town when she landed from Scotland on her way to meet here husband-to-be, François the Dauphin. At the time of her landing in August 1548 Mary was only five years old, though she was still two years older than her betrothed. The young Queen — she had become Queen of Scots at the age of five days when her father, James V, had been killed at the battle of Solway Moss — stayed in France until her marriage in 1558. François became king in 1559, but he was a sick young man and died six months later leaving Mary a widow at 16. A turret and plaque on the seafront commemorate Mary's landing. No such memorial having been erected to the arrival in Roscoff of the less than bonny Prince Charles, the Young Pretender, after the failure of the 1745 rebellion. It is said that English ships chased the prince's vessel to the very threshold of the harbour.

Close to Notre-Dame de Kroaz-Batz is the Charles Pérez Aquarium, the highspot of a visit to Roscoff. The aquarium consists of one large tank and several smaller ones that hold many of the fish and other sea creatures found in the Channel. There is also a study centre for marine biology and oceanography.

Roscoff's harbour is enclosed by pincer-like headlands, one crowned by Notre-Dame de Kroaz-Batz, the second, the Pointe de Bloscon, being a fine viewpoint with a panoramic table set close to the old chapel of Ste Barbe. From the Pointe, reached by walking along Rue des Capucins, where a fig tree in the Maison des Capucins, planted in 1625 by Capucin monks, is now enormous, covering over 600sq m (372sq ft) and yielding ½ ton of fruit annually — the eye is drawn towards the **Ile de Batz** a small — 2½ mile (4km) by ½ mile (1km) — inhabited island about ½ mile (1km) offshore across a vicious tidal channel. The island, pronounced 'Ba', has a lighthouse that can be visited (200 steps to the top at 145ft , 44m) a village with a fine old church and, on the east side, a ruined chapel. The island was occupied in the sixth century when a Welsh saint, St Paul (St Pol in Brittany) arrived to establish a hermitage cell. St Paul rid the island of a fearful dragon who had terrorised the local fisherfolk, the dragon being hauled into the sea at the Trou de Serpent (Dragon's Hole) when the saint used his cloak as a leash. The hole can be visited by a short walk that goes past the lighthouse and then takes the path to the right, reached beyond a ruined house. The ruined chapel, in Romanesque style, was built on the site of St Paul's original cell and hosts a *pardon* on the closest Sunday to 26 July.

The village church houses St Paul's cloak, the saint having died on the island in AD573, though it is likely that the 'cloak' actually dates from the eighth century and is oriental in origin. Elsewhere, the village is a delight, the menfolk carrying on their long tradition of fishing, the women collecting seaweed from the beaches to act — with added ground shells — as fertiliser on their vegetable gardens. In the village bicycles can be hired for a more comprehensive exploration of the island.

St Paul is also commemorated in the name of the town a little way south of Roscoff, **St Pol-de-Léon**. Appropriately, the town's cathedral contains the skull, a finger and an arm bone of the saint, who is said to have lived to the great age of 104. The saint's bronze reliquary can be found in a chapel off the chancel. In the chancel itself, in niches in the walls, are the skulls of thirty-four other early Christians, each in a wooden casket. The cathedral — it is no longer technically, a cathedral, the bishopric (the first in Brittany, with St Pol as Bishop) having long since moved elsewhere — is largely fifteenth century though the twin towers, 50m(164ft) high, are older. Perhaps the best feature is the superb rose window in the south transept, a fifteenth-century masterpiece, though the sixteenth-century carved stalls in the chancel are also excellent.

South of the cathedral, Rue Géneral-Leclerc, with an array of fine

Roscoff's church tower dominates the skyline

houses, some dating from the seventeenth century, runs down to the Kreisker Chapel, the tower of which has dominated the drive from Roscoff. The tower, a magnificent and intricate assembly of ribs and columns, is 77m (253ft), tall and can be climbed for an expansive view of the down and the surrounding country. This country, known as the **Ceinture Dorée** (Golden Belt) is the most fertile area in Brittany, a patchwork of vegetable fields. The chapel below the tower was built in the fourteenth century and was once used to house meetings of the town council.

Going east instead of south from the cathedral the visitor reaches Maison Prebendale, the fine sixteenth-century residence of the canons, and Rue de la Rive, beside it. The road gives access to two short, but excellent, walks. One visits the Champ de la Rive, taking a surfaced path to the right to reach the crest of a hill where a panoramic dial points out places in the bay to the east and south. The second follows the road and then Rue de l'Abbé-Tanguy to reach Rocher Ste Anne (St Anne's Rock) a lower, but equally good, viewpoint close to a small harbour.

South from St Pol-de-Léon the D769 cuts across the fields of the Golden Belt to reach the deep incut of the La Penze river, following the river to the village of Penze, then heading east for the Morlaix river and the town of the same name. North of the road is a triangle

Ile de Batz

of land sandwiched between the two estuaries. At the triangle's tip is **Carantec**, a pleasant village with several very good beaches. The village is famous for its *pardons*. On the third Sunday of July the *pardon* of St Carantec is held at the church, where a fine seventeenth-century processional cross can be seen. More interesting are the *pardons* held on Whit Monday, the Sunday after 15 August and at New Year, at the chapel of Our Lady on the island of Callot. This island can be reached for long periods at mid-tide by car as well as on foot and is visited for its fishing as well as for the chapel, which houses a sixteenth-century statue of the Virgin.

Also in Carantec there is a small maritime museum with exhibits on oyster breeding, the estuary's sea and bird life, and the local privateers. Close by, at Pen-al-Lann Point, there are fine views of the estuary, and from the Point the Château du Tareau can be visited. The castle was built in the mid-sixteenth century to protect the estuary and river, and therefore the town, from attacks by the English pirates. Later it became a prison.

Morlaix is reached after the D769 has crossed the base of the triangle of Carantec and reached the Morlaix river. The river is then followed into the town, the view of which is dominated by a vast two-tier viaduct that carries the Paris-Brest railway line high over the river. The viaduct, 60m (197ft) high and 285m (935ft) long, is hardly great architecture, but the busy little estuary port, alive now with pleasure rather than commercial craft, at its base seems to ignore it completely. Anciently the craft would have included corsair ships, and a number of these sailed across the Channel in 1522 to attack Bristol. In reprisal, Henry VIII sent a large fleet to attack Morlaix. The fleet arrived on a day when most of the town was away at a festival. The soldiers and sailors pillaged the town, but before sailing away with their booty they raided all the wine cellars and after a convivial afternoon lay down to sleep it off. The Morlaix folk arrived back soon after and slaughtered many of the English, an event which caused the town's fathers to adapt the motto *S'ils te mordent, mords-les*, '*If They Bite You, Bite Them*'. They also adopted a coat-of-arms with a leopard facing a lion. Later, the old enmity was put to one side when Morlaix became the destination for English smugglers carrying tobacco and snuff. The cause seems to have been less the money to be made from contraband than the Morlaix folk's dislike of a local tobacco factory, run by the India Company, which had a monopoly of sales and charged a high price for its products. The tobacco industry has a long history in the town, and a cigar factory is still operating.

Morlaix is famous for being the birthplace of Jean-Victor Moreau, one of the Revolutionary army's most successful generals. So successful was he that he was offered the country ahead of Napoleon, declined and continued to win battles for Bonaparte. Eventually Napoleon, who disliked the public's adulation of Moreau, brought a trumped-up charge of conspiracy against him, and forced him into exile. Outraged, Moreau joined the Russians and fought against Napoleon, dying of wounds at Dresden. He is buried at St Petersburg.

Within the town there are two interesting churches. That of St Mathieu, in the southern part of the town, near the D9, has a sixteenth-century tower, but was rebuilt in the nineteenth century. Inside is a very unusual fourteenth-century wooden statue of the Virgin and Child which opens to reveal a statue of the Trinity. The church of St Mélaine, which lies below the viaduct, is fifteenth-century Gothic and has some fine modern stained glass and an interesting wooden panel painted with Biblical scenes.

Close to St Mélaine is Rue Ange-de-Guernisac with rows of superb half-timbered houses. Following this fine street the visitor reaches Place des Viarmes. Ahead now, Rue des Vignes reaches the Musée des Jacobins, a museum housed in an old Jacobin church with a magnificent fifteenth-century rose window. The museum houses exhibits on the history of Morlaix, including a cannon from an old corsair ship, and items of local furniture. There is also a fine collection of early religious statuary, and a number of contemporary paintings.

If, instead of going straight on to the museum, the visitor turns right in Place des Viarmes, he soon reaches the Grand Rue, now a pedestrian-only street, allowing better viewing of the excellent fifteenth-century houses. Some of these houses are *maisons à lanterne*, houses in which a central hall was lit by a roof skylight, the upper rooms being reached by spiral staircases supported by intricately carved newel posts. One of the best of these houses is the Maison de la Reine Anne, Queen Anne's House. It is named for Queen Anne, the Duchess of Brittany who visited the town in 1505 as part of a pilgrimage to saintly relics during the illness of her husband, Louis XII. Morlaix, rich on the booty of its corsairs, gave the Queen a gold ship set with diamonds, and a live ermine wearing a diamond collar. The ermine was the Duchess of Brittany's emblem. These items are not on show in the house, but it is an almost perfect example of a *maison à lanterne*, the spiral staircase being especially good. Despite being 11m (36ft) high it was created from a single trunk, and has a beautifully carved newel post.

North-east of Morlaix, Finistère thrusts a final square of land out into the Channel before ending at the estuary of the Douron river.

This is a section of the Côte de Granit Rose, the Pink Granite Coast, though in truth it is not until Côtes d'Armor is reached that the coastline becomes ruggedly memorable. Here, in Finistère, the coast is characterised by long sandy beaches — good holiday country. A road along the eastern bank of the Morlaix river reaches this coast from the town, passing through **Ploujean**, birthplace of France's first man in space, and with a church that houses Marshall Foch's pew, the great soldier having had an estate nearby. After crossing the Darduff, a tributary of the Morlaix, the road heads north through Plouézoch to reach Plougasnou. But before reaching that village a minor road leads off left to reach a conical headland topped by one of Brittany's finest megalithic remains, the **Tumulus of Barnenez**. This Neolithic tomb, or long barrow, is 75m (246ft) long, about 25m (82ft) wide and up to 8m (26ft) high. It was constructed of dry-stone walling and into its southern edge were cut 11 passages, up to 12m (39ft) long, leading to burial chambers constructed of drystone or rock slabs. The tumulus is a remarkable construction, the more so when it is considered that it is at least 5,000 years old, perhaps older, and should be visited, even if no other Neolithic tomb is on the itinerary. There is also a small museum to the finds from the tumulus.

Beyond the turn-off to Barnenez is **Térenez**, a very pleasant little port, and a good section of coastal driving from the Pointe de Diben, a fine viewpoint, to the Pointe de Primel and Primel-Trégastel. The coast here is locally known as the Heather Coast, though below Primel Point the rock jumble is most definitely pink. The point is also a very fine viewpoint. **Primel-Trégastel** has several good sandy beaches, with occasional pink rocks, while Plougasnou is a pleasant small town grouped around a square and sixteenth-century church. Close by is the oddly-named village of **St Jean-du-Doigt**.

The village is named for a finger of St John the Baptist held in a reliquary in the church. The finger is said to have been brought to a local chapel in the early fifteenth century, the church having been raised to house the relic a few years later. The legend has it that the finger was brought inadvertently by a young Frenchman returning home to Plougasnou. It was revealed when church bells rang of their own accord, and trees bowed to him all along his route. In addition to the finger, it is actually the first joint of an index finger, there is a fine processional cross and a silver Renaissance chalice. The cross is used in the *pardon* held on the last Sunday in June which is attended by folk with ophthalmic problems, recalling an old legend. Outside the church there is a sacred fountain, water from which was captured in a basin into which St John's finger was dipped at regular intervals.

Eyes bathed in the water were said to have been cured of a variety of ailments.

The coast can be reached only intermittently beyond St Jean-du-Doigt, until the road rejoins the water at **Locquerec**. This small fishing port has recently been turned into a marina and resort, though it retains much of its old charm. The church, once 'owned' by the Knights of Malta has a Renaissance turret and a splendid altar-piece. From the village a short walk, about ½ hour for the return journey, visits the Pointe de Locquerec for where there are fine views of Lannion Bay and the Douron estuary. Inland from Locquirec is **Lanmeur** a small market garden town whose church has an eighth-century crypt making it one of the oldest religious buildings in Brittany.

Westward from Roscoff to the Pointe-de-St Mathieu the coast is known as the Côte des Abers, usually translated as the Coast of Estuaries, as *aber* is a Celtic word, frequently met in Wales, meaning a joining of waters, usually a river and the sea. On this northern coast of Finistère these *abers* are often deeply incut producing excellent scenery, but necessitating lengthy detours for anyone trying to stay close to the sea.

Travelling west on the D10 from St Pol-de-Léon the visitor soon reaches the Château de Kérouzéré, built in the early fifteenth century from local granite. Originally this solid castle had four embattled corner towers, but following a prolonged siege at the end of the sixteenth century one was demolished. Inside, the castle offers a glimpse of the far from romantic life of the medieval soldier, the castle having three floors each with large barrack rooms, though the edge has been taken off by small collections of seventeenth-century tapestries and Breton furniture.

Further along the D10 reaches **Cléder**, where a turn to the right leads to the Manoir de Traonjoly, a sixteenth- to seventeenth-century manor house made even more beautiful when Renaissance-style dormer windows were added. The manor stands in fine grounds and has a courtyard enhanced by a terrace complete with stone balustrade, an elegant touch. Sadly, only the exterior is open to the public.

Plouescat has a fine covered market dating from the seventeenth century, the roof held aloft by huge oak beams. Northward, the coast offers several sandy coves that are usually empty, while local villages serve the local delicacies of *cotriade*, and *caillebottes*, a thick cream. South of the town, on the D30, are two interesting castles, the Château de Maillé, more stately home than castle and built in granite in the sixteenth century with a Renaissance style wing being added a century later, and the Château de Kergarnadeac'h, claimed to have been the last castle built in France, in 1630. It is now ruinous, but enough survives to be of interest.

South from the two castles is a third, the Château de Kerjean, an altogether more splendid building. It was built in the sixteenth century by Louis Barbier who had inherited a fortune and vowed to construct the finest château in Brittany. His version has been called the 'Versailles of Brittany', but that is a gross exaggeration even if the half-castle, half-mansion building is visually splendid. Although Kerjean would be recognised by Barbier today it is not as he built it, having been badly damaged by fire and war in the eighteenth century. It was painstakingly, but not completely, renewed during this century. A visit to the château should include a walk in the fine parkland around the house, though most visitors will naturally be drawn to the castle's interior, entered from a courtyard reached by drawbridge, with its superb collection of seventeenth- and eighteenth-century Breton furniture. The kitchen, with many old utensils, is also fascinating.

Continuing along the D10 the visitor catches glimpses of the sea before arriving at **Goulven**, a tiny village whose church has a belfry that is claimed to be the finest in Brittany, a masterpiece of Renaissance architecture. From Goulven the main road bends south to **Lesneven**, a town that has taken full advantage of its crossroads position to become an important local centre. There are several old granite houses, but little else to detain the visitor, though the Musée de Léon, housed in a seventeenth-century convent and dealing with the history of the local area, is interesting. The original decree of Louis XIV (the Sun King) setting up the convent is on show.

Close to Lesneven is **Le Folgoët**, where the basilica commemorates one of the most popular of Breton legends. The village's name means 'Fool's Wood', named for a fourteenth-century half-wit called Solomon who lived beneath a tree begging alms and continuously repeating 'Lady Virgin Mary', the only words he knew. When he died a lily grew from his grave bearing the words 'Ave Maria' on its petals. Local men excavated the grave and found that the lily grew from Solomon's mouth. The Breton Duke, Jean de Montfort, had just won his victory at Auray and decided to raise a church to the miracle. Later Anne, Duchess of Brittany, gave money to decorate the building. The basilica is Le Folgoët's treasure, a wonderful building whose north tower is frequently said to be the finest in Brittany. Water from a spring under the altar flows from the east wall and is drunk by pilgrims. Inside there is rood screen carved from granite, one of the great masterpieces of Breton art, as well as much else to admire.

Following the miracle of Solomon's lily the village became a place of pilgrimage, a tradition that still exists, the Le Folgoët *pardon*, being called the Great Pardon and attracting thousands of spectators from all over Brittany and France. The *pardon* is held on the first Sunday in September (or on the eighth if the first of September is a Sunday). Finally, the village inn holds a small museum of medieval statues and furnishings.

Those visitors who do not wish to continue to Lesneven and Le Folgoët can turn right in Goulven to reach the road heading north for **Brignogan-Plage** and the coast. Brignogan as a village has little to detain the visitor, but it does have a superb beach, a wide sweep that also continues into several small caves made private by curiously shaped rock piles. The walks to the granite headlands on either sides of the beach are short but interesting, the views excellent. On the west side the walk reaches Chapelle Pol, built in surprising fashion on a couple of boulders, in the last century. Also close by is Men Marz, one of Brittany's tallest menhirs (standing stones), though one badly served by local planners as both the road and a house have been allowed too close. The granite menhir is 9½m (30ft) high and has been 'Christianised' by a summit cross. Whether the cross was chiselled or glued would require inspection from a long ladder.

West from Brignogan the coast becomes increasingly rugged and beautiful, with heather edges to impressive granite cliffs. The shore line is not followed by a road, visits being made by out and back journeys along narrow lanes through fine country. L'Aber Wrac'h is the most incut of the *abers*, extending so far inland that it would enjoy the name fjord if its edges were a little steeper. Perhaps sea loch is a better name. **Plouguerneau**, a little north of the *aber*, is a pleasant little village with a church that houses a collection wooden statues carved by the villagers in thanks for their escaping the plague. Here, too, is a small museum dedicated to the maritime traditions of the *abers*. Seaward of the village are cliffs that look out to the lighthouse on the Ile Vierge, at 77m (253ft) the tallest *phare* in France. Lights of a very different sort are said to have been displayed from headlands closer to the mouth of the *aber*, for anciently this was wrecking country. Today, the visitor to the tiny port of **L'Aber Wrac'h**, on the southern side of the *aber*, will find a more civilised place with a sailing school and rows of elegant yachts. Some of the locals here, and on the Aber Benôit to the south, still make a precarious living collecting seaweed from the shoreline, selling it for the manufacture of potash-based fertilisers.

Separating the two *abers* is a finger of land that ends at the Presqu'ile de Ste Marguerite. A *presqu'ile* is, literally, a 'nearly island' a dot of land separated from the mainland by little more than a causeway. The dunes of Ste Marguerite offer an interesting walk, with piles of seaweed drying on the sand and a fine view to the rocks off-shore. On those to the south, the Roches de Portsall, the *Amoco Cadiz* ran aground in 1978 releasing its oil cargo with disastrous results for the local fishermen and birdlife.

Aber Benôit is crossed close to its head by a road that reaches the village of Portsall and a better view of its notorious rocks. Close by is the village of **Trémazan** and the castle of the same name. Legend has it that the castle was once a temporary shelter for Tristan and Iseult. More definitely it was the birthplace of Tanguy du Châtel whose reckless killing of the Duke of Burgundy as he talked peace with the French Dauphin is credited with prolonging the Hundred Years' War. Today, the castle is ruinous.

South of Trémazan the coast road becomes a real joy, staying closer to the shoreline and offering several stopping points from which short walks reach magnificent viewpoints. **Porspoder**, a neat little village, is reputedly the spot where Budoc, one of the early Celtic saints and later the Bishop of Dol-de-Bretagne, landed. South again the best local viewpoint is reached, the Rocher du Crapaud overlooking the Aber Ildut, a candidate spot for where the English Channel ends and the Atlantic Ocean starts. Inland of Aber Ildut is the

A favourite place for mooring yachts is at the small port of L'Aber Wrac'h

Château de Kergroadès, a well-restored early seventeenth-century castle with a courtyard surrounded by a elegant gallery. The interior is not open to the public.

Continuing south the visitor passes the 37m (121ft) Trézien lighthouse to reach Pointe de Corsen, a 50m (160ft) cliff that is the most westerly point in France, despite the prominence given to the Pointe de Raz further south in Cornouaille. Corsen is the other candidate point for the demarcation between the Channel and the Atlantic, and is a spectacular viewpoint. There is a car park close to the point, and from it a very good walk of 2½km (1½ miles) reaches another car park tucked into the Anse de Porsmoguer to the south. Return can be made along quiet lanes, or by reversing the walk. The latter is more fun than it seems as the walk is short, and the view quite different, but just as good, on the return trip. Off shore here is the **Ile d'Ouessant** and other, smaller, islands that make up part of the Armorique Nature Park.

Access to the island, known locally as Ushant, is by boat from Brélès, at the head of Aber Ildut, Le Conquet or Brest. The journey takes about 2 hours, the landing being at Lampaul, the island's capital, or at Stiff. The islanders have existed on subsistence farming

The tallest lighthouse in France can be seen at Ile Vierge

for centuries, the climate, which is distinctly warmer than the mainland in winter because of the Gulf Stream, allowing a reasonable harvest from thin soil. Only when an Atlantic gale blows in during the winter months does Ushant become inhospitable, though occasional sea fogs give the place an eerie feel, especially with the fog horns wailing mournfully. Traditionally the island's menfolk have fished or been sailors, with the women tending the fields and herds. The importance this work bestowed on the women was such that island tradition has it that they propose marriage.

Lampaul is a pleasant village with a mix of new and old, some ruinous houses. Be sure to look out the memorial in the cemetery that holds the *Proëlla* crosses. Another Ushant tradition was the modelling of these wax crosses as memorials for men lost at sea. After a night's vigil around the cross at the man's house, the cross was placed in the church. The word *proëlla* is an ancient one, meaning the homecoming of the soul.

Bicycles can be hired in Lampaul, and these can be used to explore the island which measures only 7 x 4km (4 x 2½ miles) and has few roads. West from Lampaul the cyclist (or walker) soon reaches an open-air museum in the tiny village of **Nion Uhella** where a pair of traditional Ushant houses have been authentically restored and furnished. Originally such houses would have been built from the timbers of shipwrecked ships: the blue and green colours are also traditional. There is also an exhibition to the geology of the island chain. Further on, just beyond the restored mill of Karaes, a turn off to the right leads to the Créac'h lighthouse. This light, together with that on the Bishop's Rock in the Scilly Isles, marks the start of the Channel for shipping. In one room of the lighthouse there is an exhibition to the history of lighthouses, from coal-fired lamps to modern automatic lights, with special emphasis on the life of the keepers. The lighthouse can only be visited by appointment ☎ 98 488093. Below the Créac'h light the jagged rocks of the island's tip are excellent, the seascape magnificent, especially if a sea is running. Close by are the old chapel of Notre Dame de Bon Voyage, built in the fifteenth-century on the site of a fifth-century Celtic hermitage, and Pern Point, another fine viewpoint. Elsewhere, the points of Port Duin and Arlan are also excellent, while the Stiff lighthouse offers a fine view of the mainland.

South of Crosen Point the village of **Le Conquet** lies on the edge of another *aber*, protected by the hooked nose of the Pointe de Kermorvan. Le Conquet is a fishing village — its old traditions being explored in the Sea Museum — the chief catch being lobster and crab, and is one of the start points for trips to Ushant. From Le Conquet the visitor can drive on to Brest by way of the main road, the D789, that drifts inland from the sea, though detours can be made to the headland of **Pointe de St Mathieu**, one of the most evocative sites in Brittany. Here are the salt-splashed and wind-lashed remains of a Benedictine monastery that has its origins in the sixth century. The first monastery was founded by St Tanguy, but took the name of St Matthew when a boat bringing the head of the Apostle to Europe from Ethiopia was caught in a terrible storm, but was saved when a channel of calm water appeared as the head was held aloft. The monastery was destroyed at the time of the Revolution.

At the very tip of the headland is a memorial to all the French sailors who died in the 1914-18 war. The lighthouse can be visited, a climb to the top revealing a superb panorama which includes the Pointe du Raz, the Crozon Peninsula and Ushant.

Instead of following the coast the visitor can reach Brest by going inland to St Renan and then down the D5. West of **St Renan**, a town of no particular interest, though the museum to local history has some features of interest, is the menhir of Kerloas, Brittany's tallest standing stone (though there is a fallen menhir that was once taller in Morbihan) at 10m (33ft). The stone, which weighs over 150 tons, was dragged at least 2½km (1½miles) and at least 100m (328ft) uphill to this spot, a phenomenal achievement.

Whichever route is taken the visitor soon arrives in **Brest**, Finistère's largest city. A thumb of land sticks up from the western end of the Crozon Peninsula, reaching to within about 1½ km (1 mile) of the coast near Brest. The narrow channel of water between these two parts of Finistère is the Goulet de Brest, and it leads to the Rade de Brest, a deep water roadstead that is the finest natural harbour in Europe, if not the world. The advantages of the Rade were probably apparent as soon as the Brittany folk wanted to sail in search of fish or trade, and were being exploited by the English throne in its strivings to conquer France from the fourteenth century onwards. During the War of Succession the English supported Jean de Montfort against his sister Jeanne, and in 1341 Jean asked them to protect Brest for him. This they did, enthusiastically. After Jean had won the Duchy he asked the English to leave but found as many before him had that invited armies often decline the invitation to leave. The English stayed for more than fifty years, only agreeing to return the town to the Duchy when Charles VI of France asked Richard II of England personally. Charles was Richard's father-in-law. This 'incident' between the French and the English over Brest was followed by others as the town became increasingly important to the French navy. One particularly famous incident occurred on 10

August 1513, the feast day of St Lawrence. On shore there were celebrations throughout the town, the guests of honour, some 300 of them, being entertained on the *Belle Cordelière*, a warship that Anne of Brittany had given to her Duchy. When the festivities were in full swing an English fleet was spotted off shore, heading for Brest. The Breton fleet sailed out, the *Belle Cordelière* joining them without disembarking the guests. Unfortunately the fleet commander was not up to the task: he panicked and headed back to shore. The *Belle Cordelière*'s captain, Hervé de Portmuguer, immediately attacked the lead English shop, hoping to buy time for the retreating Breton fleet. In the battle that followed, which was doomed to failure, the *Belle Cordelière* and one of the English ships caught fire, and each exploded with great loss of life. De Portmuguer and all of his guests died.

By the seventeenth century Brest's importance to French naval power had been recognised at government level and Colbert, the Navy Minister, made it the home of the Navy, setting up the *Inscription Maritime*, an office that ensured excellent crews by providing a package that gave reasonable pay and training, and a pension for life to all sailors. Colbert also set up colleges for marine gunners and engineers, as well as several marine-based institutes that were ahead of their time. The naval dockyards were improved and fortified, and Brest became a formidable European power base. It remained so until, and throughout, the 1939-45 war, when the German navy used it as a battleship and U-boat base. *Scharnhorst* and *Gneisnau* were based here, and Brest was the *Bismark*'s destination on her final voyage. The U-boat pens, huge concrete structures at Laninon across the River Penfeld from central Brest, prompted heavy Allied bombing raids which devastated the city. To this devastation further destruction was added after the Normandy landings when there was intense fighting for control of the city and its port.

The destruction explains the modern look of Brest, all that concrete and glass being a very far cry from the normal Breton town. The city is still a major naval base, and the new developments have created a strong commercial presence. Neither of these aspects are highly 'touristy', and as a consequence Brest is not a tourist centre. Nevertheless there are sites that are of interest to the visitor, who may well find that a day's exploration will be rewarding. High on the list of sites to visit is Océanopolis in the Moulin Blanc Marina (the Port de Plaisance du Moulin Blanc) to the east of the Port de Commerce. This sea world centre is housed, somewhat appropriately, in a crab-shaped building and has huge aquaria holding many species of the maritime life that can be found off Brittany's coast. There is a replica sea cliff with specimens of local seabird life and frequently changed exhibits on other aspects of the marine-based ecosystems. There is also an auditorium for lectures on related topics.

The Port de Commerce dates from the nineteenth century, and has a dry dock for ships of 500,000 tons. It is one of Frances biggest ports, with cargo rates of several million tons annually. On the other side of the Port de Commerce from Océanopolis is Brest castle, one of very few reminders of the city's past. The castle site, defending the entrance to the River Penfeld, has been fortified since Roman times at least, though what is seen today is a twelfth-century castle modified and extended continuously through to the seventeenth century. Visitors to the site have limited access as the Port Authority occupies much of the building, but the fifteenth-century guard towers, one of which houses the Musée de la Maritime, and part of the ramparts are open to the public. The museum, in the Paradise Tower, has many model ships, a collection of prints of old sailing ships and other memorabilia from Brest's maritime heritage. On the opposite side of the Penfeld from the castle is the Tour Tanguy, a fourteenth-century tower built to complete the fortification of the Penfeld's mouth. It house the Musée du Vieux Brest, with exhibitions on incidents in Brest's eventful past. To the right of the tower is the Pont de Recouvrance: with a central span of nearly 90m (295ft) weighing more than 500 tons this is the biggest drawbridge in Europe. It is raised to give access to the River Penfeld and the Naval dockyard (the Port de Guerre), tours of which are allowed, but only for French nationals.

From the castle a walk along Cours Dajot passes the Port de Commerce to reach the best viewpoint of the anchorage of the Rade. A panorama dial here points out the components of the roadstead's Crozon backdrop, from Menez-Hom to the left to the Pointe des Espagnols (on the Crozon) and Pointe du Portzic (west of Brest) to the right. The Rade itself could be argued to be the least interesting aspect of the view, but it is such an impressive piece of water that it forces itself on the visitor. It covers over 150sq km (about 59sq miles or 37,500 acres) and is, on average, about 15m (50ft) deep. It is no surprise that occupation of it has frequently been considered an essential requirement to control of the seaways to Europe.

The visitor who turns left off Cours Dajot soon reaches Brest's Musée des Beaux-Arts in Rue Emile Zola, which has nineteenth-century paintings on the ground floor, and seventeenth- to eighteenth-century works on the first floor. The earlier works includes paintings by Crespi and Canaletto, while the later works include paintings by Monet and Fromentin.

Now walk along Rue Emile Zola, away from the castle, and turn left into Rue Macé to reach, to the right, the church of St Louis in Place St Louis. Much of Brest's rebuilding has been in a style that would not receive the approval of even the most modern of architects but the church, and Place de la Liberté, to the east, are excellent. The church was completed in 1957 and is well set in a huge square. Inside there are good contemporary stained glass windows and tapestries. Place de la Liberté, with its gardens and cenotaph is a fine, airy place.

Central Finistère

In this section we shall visit that band of Finistère which lies south of the Elorn river, which is closely followed by the N12, the main road from Morlaix to Brest. The southern border of the band is equally arbitrarily defined by the River Aulne, and includes the Crozon Peninsula. These definitions allow the broad sweep of the Armorique Regional Park to be wholly included.

From Brest this part of Finistère can be entered across the Pont Albert-Louppe, an elegant bridge, but one whose name commemorates nothing more than the chairman of the Finistère Council who approved it. Across the bridge is Plougastel an indented peninsula of land that forms one section of the shoreline of Brest's Rade. The peninsula is one of the leading Breton centres for strawberries and early vegetables and flowers, which can make a visit at the right time — in May and June especially, when the roadside strawberry sellers compete for trade — a delight. The peninsula offers several good viewpoints of the Rade, the Pointe de Kerdeniél, reached by a 10-minute walk from the road end beyond the delightful fishing and sailing hamlet of Lauberlach, is especially good, though that from Kéramenez, across the Anse de Lauberlach from the hamlet, has the advantage of a helpful panorama dial. **Plougastel-Daoulas** is famous for its Calvary, a visit being a good introduction to the superb parish closes that lie to the east. The Calvary was carved to give thanks at the end of the Plague epidemic of 1598 and is of local granite with details in lighter ochre. It comprises 180 separate figures and illustrates the story of Catell-Gollet, Catherine the Lost. This young servant girl frequently failed to confess all of her sins and eventually this came to the notice of the Devil, who, sensing a soul for the taking, appeared to her in human form, and become her lover. He persuaded her to steal consecrated bread from the church which she did. Her damnation complete, Catell (Catherine or Kate), was condemned to an eternity of misery, and is depicted as being torn apart by demons. The story is not found outside Brittany, but was frequently used by Breton priests as a text to frighten village girls away from pre-marital relationships. It also forms the basis of the Guimiliau Calvary. The Plougastel-Daoulas calvary has most of the typical Breton elements: below the Crucifixion are Roman horseman, while to either side are the T-shaped crosses of the thieves. Below the horseman there is a *Pietà* (the Virgin carrying the dead Christ). The rendering of Kate's story may be less vibrant than that at Guimiliau, but is still a magnificent achievement. The village church seems dull by contrast, though its vividly coloured interior does have its charm.

At a bridge over the Daoulas river, a few miles east of Plougastel-Daoulas is a village that shares its name with the river, and with half the name of its neighbour. **Daoulas** also has a fine Calvary, and several of the other elements of parish close. The ossuary is sixteenth century, while the church is older, perhaps twelfth century. Nearby is a twelfth-century Augustinian abbey, now an official building of the Finistère *département*. Three sides of the abbey's cloister square, built in the mid-twelfth century in fine Romanesque style, remain standing. Elsewhere, the village has some beautiful houses dating from the fifteenth century. The best are in Rue de l'Église, and from it a short walk leads to a fountain dedicated to the Virgin. The fountainhead is sixteenth century and has a relief carving of St Catherine of Sienna. The nearby chapel is probably contemporary, but with later additions.

South of Daoulas two more inlets cut into the Plougastel peninsula. At the head of the second **Le Faou**, on the river of the same name. The town is beautifully positioned on the river, though it looks far nicer when the tide is in rather than out, and is very picturesque with its slate-faced houses. There is a fine sixteenth-century covered market. The Vielle Renommée hotel really is as old and famous as its name implies, for its accommodation and Breton menu, and the church is interesting.

Defining the northern end of the peninsula is **Landerneau**, a gem of a place where the old bridge over the Elorn river carries intact terraces of sixteenth-century houses. Most of the houses have now been converted into shops, and some of the shop fronts are too modern for the scene, which is sad, but the bridge is still a fine sight. North from the bridge there are several superb seventeenth-century houses in Place de Général-de-Gaulle and Rue de la Fontaine-Blanche which lead to the church of St Houardon which dates from the same period.

To the east of Landerneau are the most famous of the Breton parish closes. The Circuit de Trois Enclos visits St Thégonnec, Guimiliau and Lampaul-Guimiliau, but it misses several fine sites, so our route moves westward from Landerneau towards Morlaix visiting several

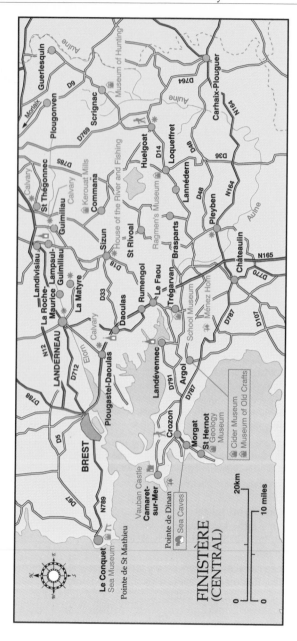

A fine slate-faced house in Le Faou

Sixteenth-century houses span the Elorn river at Landerneau to form the old bridge

✳ more villages. The first is **Pencran**, just a mile south of Landerneau, where there is a sixteenth-century ossuary, a seventeenth-century arch and an unusual Calvary set in a wall. The village church is a fine building with a nicely carved porch decorated with Old Testament scenes and the Apostles. On the D712 that links Landerneau and
✳ Landivisiau is **La Roche-Maurice**, a village set below the ruins of an old castle. The finest item in the close here is the ossuary, a very large building dating from 1640. Above the external font is a relief carving of Death, shown as a skeleton clutching an arrow. The figure is obviously Ankou, the common representation of Death in Breton legends. Normally Ankou is depicted with a scythe and is sometimes driving a cartload of bodies, the cart hauled by an emaciated horse. Tales of Ankou abound in local legends, all testifying to his implacable nature. One especially appealing one tells of a blacksmith who stayed up all night sharpening Ankou's scythe when he arrived in the village, only to find that the following day it was he, the blacksmith, that Death sought. The church beyond the font has a finely carved porch and, inside, a fine rood screen and excellent, and large, sixteenth-century stained glass window.

✳ The parish close at **La Martyre**, to the south, is a personal favourite. It is the oldest in the area, dating from the fifteenth century, and has been suggested as the original of all such closes. The best feature is the triumphal arch which manages to be solid and graceful at the same time. The Calvary is set on the arch and the ossuary has interesting carvings. The church has another fine porch, good wood carvings and some excellent sixteenth-century glass windows. In medieval times La Martyre held an annual fair at which the produce of southern France, wine and fruit, and that of the north, wood and vegetables, were sold. Today it is a quieter place, so much off the beaten track that it is frequently bypassed, and the visitor will usually find he has the close to himself. *Pardons* are held at La Martyre on the second Sunday in May, and the second Sunday in July.

✳ South-east of La Martyre is **Sizun** whose close has a triple arch complete with Corinthian columns and capitals, the arch be completed by the Calvary, here set on a decorative gallery. Both the arch and the superb twin-arched ossuary chapel date from the late sixteenth century. The chapel now houses a local museum with examples of Breton furnishings and costumes. The church has a rebuilt seventeenth-century organ, though this is rather inconspicuous in an interior which is lavishly gilded and painted, a sharp contrast to the granite exterior. Beyond the church, Sizun is a pretty place, and anglers will be entertained by the extravagantly named

Maison de la Rivière, de l'Eau et de la Pêche, an old mill with a museum to the art of freshwater fishing. There are also aquaria with specimens of Breton freshwater fish.

North-east of Sizun lie the three closes of the famous circuit. The first reached is **Lampaul-Guimiliau**, which has the least impressive close, but the most impressive church. At one time the church had a 70m (230ft) spire, but this was struck by lightning in the early nineteenth century and has never been rebuilt. The entrance porch has a fine collection of statues, but the real treasures are inside. Chief among these is the rood-beam (rood-beams being forerunners of rood-screens), its faces carved with scenes from the Passion and bearing an anguished Crucifixion between the figures of the Virgin Mary and John the Baptist. Elsewhere, there are other examples of superb wood carvings, especially the choir stalls, several altar pieces, and a sixteenth-century *Pietà* with no less than six figures, but carved from a single trunk. There is also a superb stoup depicting a pair of devils writhing painfully as a result of being immersed in Holy Water. The parish close itself has a good arch, though the Calvary, which is very old, dating from the early sixteenth century, is quite plain.

It is certainly plain in comparison to that at the nearby village of **Guimiliau** whose Calvary is one of the finest of all, a masterpiece of Breton religious art and, with over 200 figures, also one of the largest. As at Plougastel-Daoulas, part of the statuary retells the story of Catell-Gollet. The figures here are more life-like, perhaps less stylised would be a better description, than at Plougastel-Daoulas, and depict scenes from the life of Christ and the Apostles, as well as Kate's sad end. The church beside the Calvary also has much to admire. The south porch has statuary as fine as that of the Calvary while inside there is superb woodwork, especially in the seventeenth-century oak baptistery in the north aisle. The pulpit, carved in 1677, with its four corner statues and panels depicting the Virtues, is also excellent.

North-east of Guimiliau is **St Thégonnec**, the last of the great trio of Closes, and the one which vies with Guimiliau as the finest of all. The close is entered through a solid, rounded arch completed by elegant lanterns. Inside, the ossuary is chapel-like, with a fine carved and painted Holy Sepulchre. The Calvary is superb, for although there are many fewer figures than at Guimiliau they are more vibrant: Christ and the Apostles are calm and dignified, those inflicting torture and death are pinch-faced, the very essence of mean-minded evil. St Thégonnec himself is depicted, along with his wolf-cart, legend having it that when his donkey was eaten by

The Calvary at Guimiliau is a masterpiece of Breton religious art

A detail of the Calvary at St Thégonnec

wolves he took one of them to haul his cart. Finally, there is the church with its Renaissance tower and a pulpit that is acclaimed as another masterpiece of Breton art, with its statuary of the Virtues and panels of the Apostles. Elsewhere, there are other fine wood carvings from the seventeenth century.

North of the parish close villages is **Landivisiau**, a town that boasts the largest cattle market in France, but little else to detain the visitor, though the fifteenth-century granite fountain to St Thivisiau, the town's patron saint and after whom it is named, is worth a visit. The fountain, reached by a short walk along Rue St Thivisiau, an interesting, if narrow, street, is decorated with relief carvings.

Eastward from St Thégonnec, beyond Pleybier-Christ where there is another parish close, is a section of the Parc Naturel Régional d'Armorique. This large park covering over 35,000 acres, is named for the *armor*, the land by the sea, though it mostly covers an area of the *argoat*, the land of the wood. It is a disjointed park, split into three large areas and two small ones that cover the essential Breton scenery from Ushant, the rugged, sea-swept island, through the estuarine land of the Aulne, to the Monts d'Arrée, an upland moor. The park was created in 1969 with the intention of preserving these last remnants of the historical Breton landscape, complete with its flora and fauna, and also its human activity. The latter is aided by the setting up of craft co-operatives which maintain the old traditions, and by the creation of museums to local culture, such as the open-air museum already mentioned on Ushant and the House of the River in Sizun. South of the parish close villages is the section of the park that covers the last upland moor in Brittany, the wild and beautiful **Monts d'Arrée**. The rocks that underline the moor are the same hard granites and gneisses that form the building material of the churches and parish closes we have visited. Though the rocks are hard and impermeable, the weathering of eons has created a series of rounded hills (*ménez*) covered with a thin, poor soil in which only moorland plants thrive. Occasionally the underlying rocks do poke through this smooth landscape, creating upthrusts similar to the tors of Dartmoor, though here the folded nature of the strata means that there are no 'cheesewring' tors but, rather, towers and spires of tortured rock known as *roc'hs*. The highest point of the Arrée is usually quoted as Toussaines Beacon, at 383m (1,256ft), though the excellent maps of the French IGN are at odds with this view, giving a height of 387m (1,269ft) for an un-named rounded *ménez* to the east of the D785 some 3km (2 miles) north of the Beacon. These high points are reached on the D785 from Pleybier-Christ, or on the D752, a minor road from Commana. There is a parish close at **Commana**, the better part of which is the church itself with its fine porch. More interesting is Eco-Museum of Moulins de Kerouat, a little way west on the Sizun road. Here the old water mills have been restored as working museums, together with parts of the old village — the miller's house, communal bread oven, farm buildings etc. It is an interesting glimpse of nineteenth-century Brittany. South of Commana is another interesting item, the *allée couverte* just beyond the hamlet of Le Mougau. This Neolithic gallery grave is almost complete and very impressive.

The D785 follows the summit ridge of the Arrée closely and so offers excellent views, but those can be improved still further if the Roc'h Trévezel is climbed. The Roc'h, one of the most picturesque of the outcrops, is close to the road and easily ascended, though children should be accompanied as some parts are steep and the ground would make for a very unpleasant landing. The view is excellent: to the north-east and south-west is the high Arrée ridge with its heather and gorse covering, and the chapel of St Michel-de-Brasparts in the distance; to the north is the gentler landscape in which are set the parish close villages, while to the south is the St Michel reservoir and the domes of the Brennilis nuclear power station. Before the creation of the reservoir the hollow it now fills was an impenetrable swamp known locally as the Mouth of Hell. The reservoir's fringes are still marshy, and will be of interest to the lover of bog plants. A waymarked route — watch for the orange signs — goes around the reservoir, a variant of it (one that requires a whole day) taking in the ridge of Ménez Kador, south-west of our viewpoint.

The road also follows the Ménez Kador ridge to reach the base of the hill topped by St Michael's chapel. The peak, somewhat extravagantly called the Montagne St Michel, reaches 380m (1,246ft) and rises about 110m (360ft) above the road. The chapel was built in the seventeenth century, though it has been much restored. There may have been an earlier building as a local legend claims that the site was originally occupied by a temple to Bénélos, the Celtic sun-god. Stranger is the suggestion that there was competition for the site between early Christians and the pagan followers of the Celtic god. If this is true, then it is an extraordinary example of the persistence of folk memory.

South of the chapel is the Maison des Artisans, a local craft centre set up to promote the aims of the regional park. Here there are a fine collections of paintings, sculpture and pottery, gold and silverwork and much more.

South again, a road off right, the D30, reaches St Rivoal and the western Arrée, but for the moment we continue on the D785 to reach the village of **Brasparts**, another village with a Parish Close. Here, on the Calvary, St Michael is shown killing a dragon, a link with the chapel on the Arrée ridge. South again is **Pleyben** where there is another superb Calvary. Originally created in 1555, it was moved two centuries later and re-assembled. In the years that followed new figures were added so that the Calvary, which follows the incidents of Christ's life in an anti-clockwise direction, is an evolving, a living, monument to Breton Christianity. The church beside it has a fine tower and some excellent carved and painted panelling. It is the site of a large and important *pardon* on the first Sunday in August. Also within the village there is a fine *crêperie* where visitors can watch the manufacturing process, and enjoy the end product.

To move east it is best to start from Brasparts, following the edge of the regional park through **Lannédern**, where there is a small parish close, to **Loqueffret** where the main attraction is the Maison des Pilhaouerin, a small museum dedicated to the history of the Arrée ragmen, a group of semi-nomadic peasants who made a precarious living buying and selling rags, rabbit skins and scrap metal. East again is **St Herbot** where the church is dedicated to the patron saint of horned cattle. Beside the rood screen are two stone tables on which the local farmers place hairs pulled from their cattle's tails during a service held each year in May.

The next Finistère village is **Huelgoat**, one of the finest of Breton villages, not only for its own sake, pretty though it is, but for its position, beside a lake and close to one of the most beautiful remaining sections of *argoat*. The village itself offers a very pleasant stroll, a walk along the lake edge — the lake is famous for its carp and is a mecca for anglers — being followed by a walk down the wide main street. The main delights are in the forest, however, and those are reached from the end of the lakeside road (Rue du Lac). Cross the road ahead to reach a lane along which several picturesque jumbles of granite boulders are soon reached. These have fanciful names — the Grotte du Diable (The Devil's Cave), which is reached by a ladder descent, Ménage de la Vierge (The Virgin's Kitchen) — but despite that are excellent. One of the best features is the Roche Tremblante, a logan stone weighing over 100 tons. The stone has been disfigured by having the name painted on it, but is still a wonder of nature. Logans are boulders so delicately poised that despite their weight the slightest touch in the correct place will cause them to rock. Legend has it that the rocking foretold the future to anyone who could 'read' the movement. A walk of 800m covers these sites, but the walk can be extended to create a round trip of about 3km (2 miles) if the Grotte d'Artus, a cave created from a large jumble of boulders, and the Mare aux Sangliers (Boars' Pool) are visited. The pool, fed by two small waterfalls and enclosed in trees, is named for its boar's head shape and is extremely beautiful. The woods, a marvellous mix of oak, beech and conifer, offer numerous other possibilities for walks of all lengths: the Allée Violette follows the Argent river that flows into Huelgoat's lake, a river that occasionally flows below boulder heaps, while the Sentier des Amoureux, the Lovers' Path, seems determined to get its followers lost in secret hollows. Longer walks are also possible, the woods being crossed by GR37/380 as well as the Promenade du Canal, a 2 hour walk that starts and ends at Huelgoat and follows a canal dug in the nineteenth century to provide water to the ore washing tanks of silver mines located in the woods. These mines, which gave the river its name, were worked from Roman times until the late Middle Ages.

To the north of Huelgoat is **Scrignac**, a village with a museum devoted to hunting, a curious idea in these days of conservation, though the museum does also have sections on animal behaviour. North again, an isolated section of the regional park, long and thin, points northward towards **Guerlesquin**, a neat little town with a good number of delightful granite houses, some of which date from the fifteenth century. Close to the centre, in Place Prosper-Proux, is

The forest at Huelgoat offers pleasant walks

the town's seventeenth-century prison, a building in which the prisoners occupied the ground floor, with their guards living on the floor above. Close to the town is **Plougonven**, a village with a good parish close, the best part of which is the two-tiered Calvary.

Heading south from Huelgoat the visitor crosses the infant Aulne in order to reach **Carhaix-Plouguer** famous as the birthplace, in 1743, of La Tour d'Auvergne, one of France's best-known soldiers. Théophile-Malo Corret, the son of a Carhaix lawyer, wanted to join the army from an early age but was denied entry to the École Militaire because of his lowly origins. He joined the ranks, but was so able that he rapidly became a sub-lieutenant, the highest rank the son of a professional man could achieve. However, Théophile discovered that one of his female ancestors had been the mistress of a Prince de la Tour d'Auvergne, and was allowed to take the surname and to use it to claim access to higher ranks. He served with bravery and shrewdness in the Franco-Spanish War, spending his spare time studying Celtic history on which he became an expert. Following the Revolution La Tour d'Auvergne became the epitome of the Republican ideal, a gallant soldier-philosopher, a man marching into battle with a bagful of books on Celtic history. It is in this guise that he is portrayed in *Le Départ de la Tour d'Auvergne* in Quimper's Fine Arts Museum. At fifty, with the rank of Captain (but having turned down further promotion) La Tour d'Auvergne retired, but travelling home from Napoleon's Spanish campaign he was captured by the British and held prisoner in Cornwall. He was released as part of a prisoner exchange and returned to Carhaix to continue his study of the Celts. There, the story goes, he found his Celtic teacher in tears because his son had been called for enlistment. La Tour d'Auvergne volunteered in the lad's place, serving with distinction and earning the title 'Defender of the Fatherland and First Grenadier of the Armies of the Republic' from Napoleon, a title that embarrassed him considerably. He remained a soldier for the rest of his life, dying from a lance wound received during a battle with the Austrians in Bavaria in 1800. Each year the town, which maintains a lock of his hair in the Town Hall, holds a festival in his honour.

The church of St Trémeur has a statue of the saint of the dedication holding his head in his hands, not in despair, but literally, legend having it that he was beheaded as a youth by his father, Commorre, who had been told that he would be killed by one of his sons. The story of Commorre will be told when we reach his castle near Quimperlé.

St Rivoal, the village reached by turning right off the D785 south of Montagne St Michel, is a tiny village and would be easily ignored if it were not the site of one of the Eco-museums of the Armorique Regional Park. The Maison Cornec is a farmhouse dating from the late 1600s and is preserved for its architectural style. It has a covered external stairway to a hayloft, while the living area was divided between the family and their animals, the family claiming the part closest to the fire. Outside there are turf-covered bread ovens and contemporary farm implements.

Now follow the D30 out of St Rivoal to St Cadou, bearing left there on to the D130, then forking left on to the D342 to head south. This road covers a lower, but equally delightful, section of the Arrée moorland, and soon reaches the Domaine de Ménez-Meur, an estate that covers over 400 hectares (about 1,000 acres) and which is one of the most interesting centres for the Armorique Regional Park. The estate house is an information centre for the park, with audio-visual shows and craft displays, while the park has large enclosures stocked with park animals such as deer, sheep, wild boar and horses.

Turn right beyond Ménez-Meur on to the D42 to reach Pen-ar-Hoat-ar-Gorre, a farm beneath of a prominent hillock. The climb to this hillock takes about 30 minutes and is very worthwhile for the view, which covers not only the moorland, but the Cranou forest to the south, a beautiful stretch of beech and oak wood which has a road running through it and several good picnic sites. West of the forest is **Rumengol** famous for its *pardons* on Trinity Sunday and 15 August. Gradlon, the King of Brittany who lived on the legendary island of Is, is said to have founded a chapel in the village in the sixth century though there is no evidence of an earlier building in the sixteenth-century village church. It is not to the church that the village *pardons* process, the centre for those being a small chapel with a fifteenth-century Calvary that stands by the conifers next to the village 'green'.

From Rumengol the road heads for Le Faou. From there turn south on the main road, the N165, bypassing several small villages, and exiting on the N164 for **Châteaulin**. The town stands just above the tidal reach of the Aulne and is a centre for salmon fishing. At one time Châteaulin was a port of some importance, but today trade has all but ceased, leaving the quays as picturesque reminders of former times. Nothing remains now of the castle of the name, though its chapel can still be visited. Chapelle Notre-Dame dates from the thirteenth century and houses a medieval sculpture of the Virgin and Child with St Anne. Châteaulin is the starting point for explorations of the Crozon Peninsula, but before going there the visitor should take the opportunity of climbing Ménez-Hom, arguably the finest viewpoint in Brittany. Ménez-Hom is reached by driving west from

Châteaulin on the D887. Just before the turn off to the peak is the chapel of Ste Marie-du-Ménez-Hom, set among trees. Just south of here, at Plomodiern, is the spot where legend has it St Corentin, first Bishop of Quimper, was given the self-healing fish by God. In keeping with the holiness of the area there has been a chapel on this spot for centuries, even though the present one is less than 300 years old.

Ménez-Hom, reached by a short road beyond the chapel, stands only 350m (1,148ft) above sea level, but because of the low-lying nature of much of Finistère is a phenomenal viewpoint. A panorama dial helps the visitor with aspects of the view which, on a good day, includes the whole of the Crozon Peninsula and the southern edge of Douarnenez Bay, and, inland, the Monts d'Arrée. A Breton festival is held on top the peak on 15 August.

North of Ménez-Hom, **Trégarvan** is a pretty village close to the Aulne: nearby there is another of the Armorique Park's Eco-museums. This one, the Musée de l'Ecole, is a restored school from the early years of this century, and is complete with the teacher's rooms. From Trégarvan go west towards the peninsula's tip, turning right at Argol, where the parish close includes a statue of King Gradlon on horseback, to reach **Landévennec**, one of the last villages in this part of the Armorique Park and, as it stands on the western edge of the Aulne estuary, one of the first coastal villages on the Crozon Peninsula. Landévennec stands at the tip of a hook of land that creates the final meander of the Aulne and is famous for a view and a pair of abbeys. The view is obtained from above the village, taking in both Landévennec and the estuary. The abbeys lie in the village itself. The first abbey here was built in the fifth century by St Guénolé, a saint of Welsh origin, though it was rebuilt several times before being finally abandoned in the eighteenth century. Today little remains: the basic foundations of the abbey, the ruins of its church and the ruins of some of the monastic buildings. Legend has it that King Gradlon was buried here, and one monument has been fancifully identified as his tomb. There is a small museum on the site. The new abbey was built by the Benedictine order in 1956. The church has a painted wood statue of St Guénolé, dating from the fifteenth century, an exhibition centre (with audio-visual show on the abbey's history) and a shop.

From Landévennec Crozon can be reached through **Argol**, a village with a museum to cider, and another to the equipment of the peninsula's old carftsmen. **Crozon**, is the village which gives its name to the peninsula, has little to detain the visitor, though the altarpiece in the church, with about 400 carved and painted wooden

Countryside scenery at Morgat

(Opposite) The awesome rock scenery at Pointe de Dinan

The harbour at Camaret-sur-Mer

figures representing the martyrdom of the Theban Legion in Armenia, is exquisite. However it does make an excellent centre for those wishing to explore the area's seascapes at a leisurely pace. It is not easy to tour the headlands west of Crozon, except on foot, but the tips of the oddly-shaped peninsula are reached by good roads. South from Crozon is the Cap de la Chevre, easily reached by a magnificent coastal walk, though as with other such walks the return is along the outward route unless minor roads are used to regain Crozon. At the tip of the Cape is a French Navy signal station, the remnants of a German observation post and a telescope. The view, with or without the use of lenses, is expansive. On the return journey to Crozon the visitor can stop to see the collection of geological samples from the peninsula in La Maison des Minéraux at **St Hernot**. The tour could then end with a visit to the caves at **Morgat**, a very pretty and well-sheltered port. From the port boats take visitors to the sea caves known as Les Grandes Grottes. These are in two groups and are worth viewing to marvel at their size — the cave known as L'Autel (the Altar) is 15m (49ft) high and 80m (262ft) deep — and colours. A smaller set of caves known, not surprisingly, as Les Petites Grottes can be reached on foot at low tide. They lie between Morgat and Le Portzic.

Pointe de Dinan is the closest peninsular tip to Crozon, reached by a 30 minute walk from the car park at the road's end. The view is tremendous, especially of the awesome rock scenery. One of the most impressive of these rocks is the Château de Dinan, a huge mass complete with a natural rock arch that really does look like a castle and can be reached by a 30 minute (round trip) extension to the walk. Be careful on this walk: the rocks can be very slippery and are very unpleasant to land on.

The northern tip of the Crozon Peninsula is the **Pointe des Espagnols**, the Spaniards' Point, which received its name in the late 1590s. In 1590 Philip II of Spain sent a fleet to Brittany with the aim of capturing Brest prior to a full scale invasion. As a prelude to an attack on Brest the Spaniards captured this northern tip of the Crozon Peninsula, and stayed there for four years, resisting all attempts to dislodge them. Finally, in 1594, the French, with the help of 2,000 English soldiers, Elizabeth I being concerned about the possibility of another Spanish Armada if Brest fell, ousted the Spaniards. From the Point the Spaniards had a good view of their projected target, which must have been very frustrating.

South of the point is **Camaret-sur-Mer**, a village that was heavily fortified in 1689 after a succession of invaders had followed the Spaniards. The defences proved their worth in 1694 when an Anglo-

Dutch invasion force was badly mauled by the batteries. Several ships were sunk and the men put ashore were decimated. Those that survived were put to flight by the Breton militia, a sort of home guard armed with scythes, pitchforks and righteous indignation. During the fight a cannonball knocked the top off the church belfry, and it has still not been repaired. Visitors can get closer to this history by touring the Château Vauban, named for Sébastien Le Prestre de Vauban, the military architect in charge of the main 1689 buildings, a massive castle built on the end of the Sillon, a natural breakwater that protects Camaret's harbour. Also at the end of the Sillon is the chapel of Notre-Dame-de-Rocamadour built in the seventeenth century, but restored after a disastrous fine in 1910. Inside, there are numerous model ships donated by local sailors who have escaped drowning against all odds. The chapel is on the site of an earlier one, Camaret having been a stop on the pilgrimage route to Rocamadour in Quercy, with pilgrims using the chapel as a prayer point. An important *pardon*, which ends with a blessing of the sea, is held to the chapel on the first Sunday in September. The sea is still important to the economy of the village, despite its now being a holiday resort, Camaret being one of the leading ports in France for langoustine and lobster fishing.

In 1801 the bay off Camaret was the scene for a significant advance in the history of warfare. In that year Robert Fulton, an American who had moved to France in 1797, demonstrated a submarine called *Nautilus*. The boat was oar-powered by a crew of five and could travel at 2 knots when submerged, staying down for up to 6 hours. The idea of Fulton's demonstration, held in front of several senior French naval officers, was to fix a 45kg bomb to the hull of a British frigate that had conveniently anchored off Brest. However, after *Nautilus* had submerged and headed off for its quarry the frigate weighed anchor and sailed away, at considerably more than 2 knots. The frigate did not realise it was a target, *Nautilus'* crew returned exhausted, the navy was unimpressed and Fulton returned to America disillusioned. Later events, especially at the time of the Battle of the Atlantic when watchers on the Crozon Peninsula would have seen the comings and goings of the German U-boat fleet, were to prove that Fulton's basic idea was sound.

Close to Camaret are a whole array of headlands. Those of the Pointe du Gouin and Pointe du Toulinguet are rarely visited in comparison to the Pointe de Penhir, but deserve to be more popular. That said, though, it has to be admitted that the **Pointe de Penhir** is a stupendous place. From the car park at the end of the road from Camaret there is a short walk to the cliff top and a view straight down the sheer, 60m (about 200ft) cliffs. The view across to the coast of Finistère west of Brest, and south towards the Pointe du Raz is equally breathtaking. The cliff top has a fine memorial to the Breton contingent of the Free French Forces which fought in the 1939-45 war.

The intrepid can descend from the cliff edge, using an airy path to reach the Chambre Verte, the green bedroom, an exotically titled piece of grass that offers a good view of the cliffs and of the Tas de Pois, a cluster of sea-etched granite rocks off-shore, whose name translates as the heap of peas.

Close to the car park is an array of three menhirs, and those interested in such monuments should also visit the alignments of Lagatjar which lie beside the road back to Camaret. The alignments consist of about 140 stones set in three lines, but unlike those we shall see at Carnac, the lines are not parallel, but aligned such that they would intersect if extended.

Southern Finistère

The southern section of Finistère, as defined here, covers a very large area and includes many of the better known Breton holiday resorts, as well as Quimper, the most interesting of Breton cities. We shall start by exploring the country to the west of Quimper.

Heading south from the Crozon Peninsula the casual visitor usually follows the D63 which hurries past the coastal edge. That edge is taken by GR34, a fine footpath, though the coast here is much less spectacular than that to the north or south. There are a couple of places of interest however. **St Côme** is a tiny village with a neat chapel renowned for its seventeenth-century woodcarvings, thought to be among the finest in Brittany, while further south is the chapel of **Ste Anne-la-Palud** where the most famous of all Breton *pardons* is held on the last Sunday in August. The *pardon*, which is preceded by a torchlight procession on the Saturday, is attended by thousands and includes hundreds of folk in Breton costume. On both the Saturday and Sunday Mass is celebrated outside, and traditional costume is also worn again at the Masses on the following Sunday and Tuesday. The chapel itself is nineteenth century, but stands on an ancient site and houses a painted granite statue of Ste Anne which is held in high esteem.

Inland of the chapel is **Locronan**. In the fifth century the Irish saint Ronan came to this area living in a hermit's all in the woods that still surround the town which now bears his name. Nothing remains of St Ronan's original cell or any chapel he had built, though there is a chapel on the Montagne de Locronan, a hillock a short distance to the

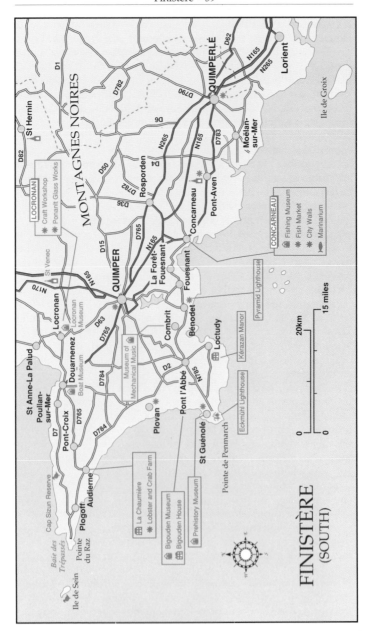

FINISTÈRE
(SOUTH)

east from where there is a superb view of the town, and of Douarnenez Bay beyond. In the seventeenth and eighteenth centuries Locronan was a prosperous place, its folk having secured a large part of the work to keep the French Navy in sailcloth. This prosperity caused a sustained upsurge of building, so that when the need for sailcloth declined, and Locronan's fortunes with it, the town was preserved as a wonderful example of late medieval French architecture. The result is one of the most picturesque town centres in Brittany, with beautiful and elegant granite houses in the main square, and narrow streets full of houses of great character, some leaning forward so that they almost touch those opposite, as fine an arch as you could hope to see. Perhaps the only criticism that could be levelled is that with its excess of craft and tourist shops, Locronan is trying just a bit too hard.

In addition to its architecture, the town is famous for its *pardons*, which here are called *troménies*, a word which derives from the Breton *Tro Minihy* or 'Walk of Retreat'. The Grande Troménie takes place on the second and third Sundays in July of every sixth year, the procession taking a 12km (7 mile) route which circles Locronan Mountain, following the boundaries of an eleventh-century monastic retreat. In the remaining five years there is the Petit Troménie, held on the second Sunday in July, and climbing the mountain. Those wishing to know more about the *pardons* should visit the Locronan Museum, a two-storey building whose upper floor is devoted to the events. The lower floor has collections of local pottery and costumes.

In the town, the church of St Ronan is a beautiful place with a fine decorated pulpit and fifteenth-century stained glass windows. The tower offers a good view of the town. Nearby there is a small fourteenth-century chapel, Notre-Dame-de-Bonne-Nouvelle, with a Calvary and fountain. The best of the local craft works can be seen in the Atelier St Ronan, which specialises in fabrics, and the Maison des Artisans where a variety of crafts are displayed. At the Verriere du Ponant on the road to Châteaulin visitors can watch glassblowing and see a range of finished articles.

Westward from Locronan is **Douarnenez**, the town that gives its name to the huge bay of Atlantic water between the Crozon Peninsula and the Pointe du Raz. Douarnenez is the the site of two of the most enduring of all Breton legends. One version of the story of the island city of Is places it off-shore here (though another version places it further west). It was the home of King Gradlon, said to have ruled Brittany in the sixth century, and was the most beautiful city in the world. The island was protected from the sea at high tide by lock gates which could only be opened by a key which the king always carried with him. Sadly, the king's daughter, Dahut, fell in love with a handsome young man who was the Devil in disguise. Pained by the beauty of Is the Devil wished to destroy it, and persuaded Dahut to prove her love for him stealing her father's key. She did so, and the Devil opened the lock gates to flood the island. King Gradlon fled the city on his horse, with Dahut riding behind him, but the sea had soon risen up to cover the causeway to the mainland. At that point a heavenly voice told Gradlon that to save himself and his people he must throw the demon on his back into the water. Realising what had happened, Gradlon was torn between love for his daughter and the survival of his people. Finally he threw Dahut into the sea, and it retreated to allow safe passage. Gradlon made his new capital in Quimper, his people settling on the *douar nenez*, the new land. Is was drowned for ever, though its fame lives on, for when the French built their capital city they decided to make it as beautiful at Gradlon's city. They believed they had succeeded, so they named it *Par-Is*, like Is. Dahut was turned into a mermaid, known as Marie-Morgan, whose beauty lures sailors to their deaths. It is said that only when a Good Friday Mass is celebrated in a church on Is, beneath the waves, will the island rise again. Then, too, Dahut will be saved from the eternal anguish of causing men to drown.

The island off Douarnenez is the **Ile de Tristan**. A second legend has it that Mark, the King of Cornouaille, had his palace here and sent Tristan, his nephew, to Ireland to bring back Iseult (or Isolde), the daughter of the Irish king, who was betrothed to Mark. Mark gives Tristan a magic potion that Iseult must drink on her wedding night so that her love for Mark will be boundless. Tristan and Iseult drink the potion by mistake and fall madly in love. Up to this point all versions of the story are the same, but from here there are several different endings. In one Tristan and Iseult stay together and are happy. In another Iseult is forced to marry Mark, Tristan goes off to Cornwall and marries, but lives unhappily, finally dying of heart-break when he hears that Iseult has refused to see him again. The story is untrue, however, Iseult being on a ship bound for Cornwall. When she finds Tristan dead she, too, dies. In a final version, Mark kills Tristan, and forces himself on an unhappy Iseult. The plethora of versions results from the story being an old Welsh myth which has evolved into an Arthurian legend by a variety of routes, some British, some Breton.

In the sixteenth century the island was the home of an unpleasant pirate know as La Fontenelle, who used the excuse of being a Catholic rooting out Protestant 'heretics' to wage a cruel and bloody

Colourful characters can be seen at Locronan on troménie day

Cycling in Brittany is a popular pastime and a pleasant way of taking a holiday

The most famous of all Breton pardons, *Ste Anne-la-Palud*

The town of Douarnenez at the head of its huge bay

war against the locals, looting and burning whole villages before retreating to his island lair. Eventually the French king, Henri IV, agreed that if La Fontenelle disbanded his private army he could stay on the island, a remarkable decision in view of the destruction the man had caused. However in 1602 La Fontenelle was found to have been plotting against the king and was executed.

Douarnenez, the town that forms the base for these stories, is surprisingly workmanlike, the deep water harbour meaning that fishing and fish processing is still more important than tourism, except at Tréboul, once a separate town, but now a relaxed suburb of Douarnenez. There are several points of interest, however, the main once being the Musée du Bateau, the boat museum in Place de l'Enfer. The museum is housed in an old fish canning factory and has a quite remarkable collection of boats, both French and foreign, sail and motor driven, wooden and metal. There are also exhibits on boat building. In 1993 the museum is to be extended by the creation of a floating museum of a further twelve boats, a number that will extend to around forty within a few years. The museum afloat will start with a lightship and steam tug, and several different forms of small sailing craft. Elsewhere in the town, the visitor should see the Rosmeur harbour where the real work of the town is carried on, fishing boats tying up here and the fish auction being a noisy, smelly, delightful place. Northward is the new harbour with its 750m (2,460ft) jetty and, a little way west, the Plage des Dames, the town's main beach from where there are fine views of Tristan's isle.

Other fine views are offered from the Sentiers des Plomarc'hs, a walk that starts from the seaward end of Rue des Plomarc'hs at the southern end of Rosmeur harbour. This fine walk reaches Plage du Ris: allow about 2 hours for the return journey — return must be along the same path, but does have the advantage of a stunning view of the town. A shorter walk reaches Pointe de Leydé, another good vantage point, from the car park at the end of the road from Tréboul.

From Tréboul a minor road stays close to the coast all the way along the Sizun, or Cornouaille, Peninsula to the Pointe du Raz. That is where most travellers are heading, but there are a couple of interesting spots off the road that tend to be less crowded than the famous point. A turn off left at **Poullan-sur-Mer**, a pleasant, but somewhat optimistically named village about 1½km (1 mile) inland, allows two interesting chapels to be reached. Notre-Dame-de-Kérinec, the first reached, has a fine tower, built in the seventeenth century, but rebuilt as an exact copy in 1958 after the original had been struck by lightning. The second, Notre-Dame de Confort, has sixteenth-century stained glass windows, one depicting a Tree of

Jesse. Note, too, the carillon of twelve bells rung as a request to the Virgin to help a child with speech difficulties.

To the right of the road the headlands of Pointe du Millier and Pointe de Beuzec, each a good viewpoint, can be reached, though the better site is **Cap Sizun**, which is, in part, an ornithological reserve. The cliffs here are about 70m (230ft) high and during the spring and early summer are alive with cormorants, auks and gulls. There are no rarities, but the sight and sound of the seabirds is a delight.

Ahead now the last headlands of the Cornouaille Peninsula enclose the Baie des Trépassés is a pincer-like grip. To the north is the Pointe du Van, close to which stands the fifteenth-century chapel of St They. The view here is less spectacular than that at Pointe du Raz, but excellent nonetheless. **Pointe du Raz** itself is a place of extraordinary beauty — provided the souvenir shop cluster beside the car park is avoided: it is to be demolished in 1994 — a wild and rugged headland which, when a high sea is running, is also one which typifies the immense power of nature. At the headland there is a statue of Notre-Dame-des-Naufragés, the Virgin of the Shipwrecked, an apt dedication as the tidal race between Raz and the Isle de Sein off-shore is notoriously dangerous. A local saying has it that on one can venture into this tidal race without fear or sorrow. From the statue a walk goes around the headland: it is not for the fainthearted, a fixed line being needed at one point to aid the visitor past the Enfer de Plogoff, the Plogoff Inferno, where the sea crashes in at the bottom of a sheer rock wall.

Many guides refer to Pointe du Raz as the most westerly point of Europe. That ignores Spain and Portugal, and also the fact that Raz is not even the most westerly point of France, but it does have the feel of being at the end of the world, and is justifiably popular with the French and foreign tourists alike.

The **Baie des Trépassés** is famous for the legends that have grown up around its name which was thought to derive from the French version of the Breton *Boe an Anaon*, the Bay of Souls. One story has it that when the Druid religion flourished in Brittany, the dead of the priesthood were buried on the Ile de Sein, the bodies being put on board ship in the bay. A second story has it that Is, the legendary capital of King Gradlon stood not off Douarnenez but in this bay. A final story is based on fact, the bodies of shipwrecked sailors tending to be washed ashore in the bay. Either of these tales can give the place an eerie feel, particularly on a misty day with the sea crashing on the rocks of Raz, and this feeling does not evaporate when the modern, explanation of the bay's name — that it derives from a mistranslation of *Boe an Aon*, the bay of the stream — is remembered.

The rugged beauty of Pointe du Raz

Many islands on the Finistère coast owe their livelihood to fishing

The **Ile de Sein**, across the vicious channel from Pointe du Raz, can be reached from Audierne or, in summer months, from Bestrée, a small port on the southern side of Pointe du Raz. It is a tiny, low, bare island occupied by fishermen whose wives work the wall-enclosed fields. Anciently the island folk were left alone, the mainlanders fearing the tidal race between Raz and Sein, and fearing, too, the old legends of Druidic burials. Today Sein is less secret, though it is still isolated for long periods by winter storms. The islanders are a proud people, with a history of bravery in rescuing sailors from ships in distress. But the main source of their pride is 18 June 1940 when, following de Gaulle's speech to the nation, all 130 men of combat age on the island sailed for Britain to join the Free French forces. In 1946 de Gaulle came to Sein in person to award the island the Liberation Cross.

On the island the birdwatcher will be delighted by the seabird population, and also, perhaps, by a visit to the village house which has been turned into a museum of the island. The lighthouse off the island's western tip is France's final outpost: because of its position and the difficulty of getting supplies to the tiny rock on which it is set the light of Ar Men took fourteen years to build.

To continue a tour of the peninsula, take the road for Audierne.

Loctudy's port is transformed into a hive of activity when fishing vessels return in the evening

This soon reaches **Plogoff** where there is a museum to the legends and facts about Pointe du Raz. The road now passes close to **St Tugen**, with a fine sixteenth-century chapel inside which there is a statue to St Tugen himself. This early Celtic saint had the somewhat unusual, even bizarre, habit of carrying a pair of keys, one in each pocket which when touched together had the power to keep mad dogs at bay. **Audierne** is a very picturesque lobster fishing port in a sheltered position just above the estuary of the River Goyen. It has a good beach, and is also a resort centre with several fine beaches. It is also home to a lobster and crab farm, opposite which the beautiful old thatched cottage known as La Chaumière is seventeenth century and is furnished with Breton furniture and kitchen utensils from the same period. The town has a Michelin-listed restaurant specialising in sea food which is appropriate as Audierne has always attracted the gourmet: the story is told of Sarah Bernhardt visiting the area and staying with a local priest whose dining table had a semi-circular cutout to accommodate his midriff. As an aside here, the same story goes on to describe the actress' visit to Pointe du Raz where her wealthy appearance, she travelled with a maid and butler, and curiosity value attracted a horde of local children whom she chased off with a pearl-handled, loaded revolver.

From Audierne the Goyen can be followed to **Pont-Croix** where it is bridged, or bridged immediately into Plouhinec. Pont-Croix is a very pretty village which rises in terraces from the river. At its heart is the church of Notre-Dame-de-Rosaudon, part thirteenth-century Romanesque, part fourteenth-century Gothic, the latter most clearly shown in the elegant, if flamboyant, south porch. The steeple, at 67m (220ft) was the model for the pair on the cathedral at Quimper. The church has two famous *pardons*, the Grand Pardon on 15 August, and the Petit Pardon on the first Sunday of September. On the evening of the second Saturday of August there is a torchlight procession through the town.

Beyond Plouhinec the visitor reaches Plozevet where there is a sacred fountain, and then has a choice of routes. Ahead is the direct route (the D784) for Quimper, southwards is the D2 for the Pointe de Penmarch. The coast on this part of the peninsula is curious, a shingle band some 20km (12 miles) long separating the sea from a series of *etangs*, brackish water lagoons. This is wild country, despite the number of farms, and offers difficult, but certainly secluded, walking. Several roads reach the shingle, and two journeys are definitely worthwhile even if you are not contemplating a walk. The chapel of Languidou near **Plovan** is now a forlorn ruin, though enough remains to be of interest. The rose window, probably thirteenth century, is superb. Closer to Pointe de Penmarch is the chapel of Notre-Dame de Tronoën whose Calvary is the oldest in Brittany, dating from 1450. The Calvary is wonderfully elegant, the story of the Passion being depicted in two relief panels below a Crucifixion. Though the hundred or so carved figures here have been battered by time they are still vigorous enough to be a delight.

South of the Calvary are the villages of St Guénolé and Penmarch which, together with Pont l'Abbé, form the heartland of the Bigouden, an area which is now famous for the *bigoudène*, a very tall, and the most stylised, version of the Breton *coiffe* or head-dress.

The first sign of **St Guénolé** is the Musée Prehistorique Finistèrion, devoted to the pre-Roman history of the *département*. On show in the open-air section the museum are a series of megaliths displaced from other sites, while inside are other megalithic finds, chiefly carved stones from burial chambers and a reconstruction of a complete Iron Age burial, together with stone arrowheads and axes from earlier, Stone Age, cultures and pottery from the later, Celtic, Finistère folk. For good measure there are several 'authentic' dolmens nearby, one at the Pointe de la Torche, and another closer to the museum. St Guénolé, which is also famous for a series of off-shore rocks, close to the port which offer great entertainment when reasonable seas are running, is a charming place grouped around an old tower, a last remnant of its earliest church.

Following the coast road from the village the visitor reaches the **Pointe de Penmarch** on which stands the Eckmühl lighthouse. Pointe de Penmarch is not as good as Pointe du Raz: the seascapes are less rugged, and because of the closeness of the villages of Penmarch and Kérity there is a less wild feel. But a visit is still worthwhile, especially for the view from the lighthouse. It is 65m (213ft) high and from the top there is a tremendous view which includes the Ile de Sein, Pointe du Raz and the Cornouaille Peninsula, and the coast eastwards towards Concarneau.

Neither Kérity, a small fishing port, or the town of Penmarch detains the visitor long. From Penmarch the coastline can be followed, passing Lesconil, a very picturesque fishing port, to reach **Loctudy**, another interesting fishing port. The boats here, as at the other local ports, tend to arrive in the early evening giving the place a bustle that is really attractive. Loctudy's fleet bring in sole and sea bass. The village church has an superb interior in Breton Romanesque style and close to it stands a stele, an inscribed upright slab of rock, dating from Brittany's Gallic period and standing about 2m (6½ft) high. From the village Ile Tudy, not an island at all, but a thin isthmus of land, can be reached by ferry. The ferry does not carry cars, which might be an advantage for a quiet morning in another pretty fishing port. Also reached by boat from Loctudy are the **Iles de Glénan** a small group of islands about 1½ hours sailing time away. Ile de St Nicholas, the island reached from Loctudy — the same island is also reached from Bénodet, while Ile de Penfret is reached from Concarneau — has a sub-aqua school. Several of the islands are uninhabited bird sanctuaries which the keen ornithologist might consider visiting for their tern and gull colonies.

From Loctudy the road to Pont-l'Abbé passes the Manoir de Kérazan, a largely nineteenth-century house with a sixteenth-century wing set in a large and beautiful park. The house was given to the Institut de France in 1928 by Joseph Astor (no relation to the Anglo-American Astors) and is now open to the public. It is decorated in impressive style, with Louis XV panelling (not all of it original), excellent furniture and a fine collection of paintings of Brittany.

Pont-l'Abbé is named for the bridge built by monks from an ancient monastery at Loctudy. Today the town sits on both sides of the inlet of the sea which that ancient bridge crossed. The town is the 'capital' of Pays Bigouden, and the visitor is guaranteed to see the famous *coiffe* at the Fête des Brodeuses, the Embroidery Fair held on the second Sunday of July. At the fair all types of embroidery, for which the town is famous, are exhibited, as are dolls, the making of which is also a town speciality. The dolls are dressed in traditional costume, some in the costumes of other provinces of France, and exhibit the same skill in embroidery. Interestingly, one of the reasons for this cottage industry was an embroidery school set up in Kérazan Manor by Joseph Astor. The visitor interested in the *coiffe* can follow its evolution into today's stovepipe creations at the Musée Bigouden where the development is shown alongside examples of the full Bigouden traditional dress. There are also items of Breton furniture and other unconnected exhibits, for instance a collection of model ships. The museum is housed in the keep of the town's ancient castle, dating in part from the fourteenth century. From other parts of the castle there are fine views of the town and inlet.

An equally interesting spot for those interested in the Bigouden area is the Maison du Pays Bigouden, about 2km (1 mile) from the town centre on the Loctudy road. This old farm has been restored, together with its outbuildings, and furnished in authentic style. Finally, the memorial to the Bigouden folk, an impressive work wrought from a granite block by the sculptor François Bazin is worth some time. It stands by the river close to the church of Notre-Dame-des-Carmes, the fourteenth-century former chapel of a Carmelite monastery.

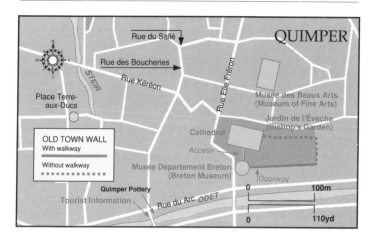

QUIMPER

Rue du Sallé

Rue des Boucheries

Rue Kéréon

STEIR

Rue Elie Fréron

Place Terre-aux-Ducs

Musée des Beaux Arts
(Museum of Fine Arts)

Jardin de l'Évêche
(Bishop's Garden)

Cathedral

Access

OLD TOWN WALL
With walkway

Without walkway

Musée Département Breton
(Breton Museum)

Doorway

Quimper Pottery

Tourist Information

Rue du Arc   ODET

0   100m

0   110yd

One of the most magnificent cathedrals in Brittany is at Quimper

There is a *pardon* to the chapel on the Sunday following 15 July.

North from Pont-l'Abbé is Quimper, Finistère's most beautiful city, though a short detour to **Combrit** is worthwhile to see the Musée de Musique Mécanique, a museum devoted to all forms of mechanical instrument, from barrel organs and pianolas to juke boxes.

For the best entry to **Quimper**, the most complete of Breton cities, it is necessary to go to Bénodet and to take the boat along the River Odet. The boat trip passes through some beautiful country, going past old castles and even crossing a lake at Kérogan where the Odet widens in quite extraordinary fashion. Beyond, the twin spires of St Corentin cathedral came into view as Quimper is reached, a truly magical entry to the city.

The city is named for its position, at the confluence of the Steir and Odet rivers — in Breton the *kemper*. It was founded, according to legend, by King Gradlon after his escape from Is, and he installed Corentin as the first bishop. The king had discovered Corentin on the flanks of Ménez-Hom where the saint lived by slicing a piece from the only fish in his pond, and then throwing the fish back into the water where it miraculously regenerated. Today the first bishop is commemorated in the name of the city's cathedral, a superb building. It was built, in Gothic style, over a 200-year period starting in the mid-thirteenth century and when completed finished at the top of the twin towers, the graceful spires having been added as lately as 1856. Thankfully the stone has how weathered into the rich colour of the older stone, and many visitors do not realise the age difference. Inside, the stained glass of the upper windows is fifteenth century and Breton, a very rare combination. There are also some fine statues and frescoes. Outside, there is a statue of King Gradlon, mounted so as to represent the sad loss of Is. Until the Revolution a festival was held in Gradlon's honour each year, festivities culminating in a city official climbing up on to the statue, to sit on the horse behind the king. He would then put a napkin around the king's neck, pour a glass of wine, offer it to the king, drink it when he declined (as statue's invariably do) and toss the empty glass into the assembled crowd. The city offered a prize to anyone who caught the glass and returned it unbroken to the official. The prize was a very large one, and was never claimed, local wisdom having it that the glass stem was sawn almost completely through before the event. Finally, for a very good view of the cathedral, which is set close to the Odet, climb through the beech trees on Mont Frugy on the far side of the river.

From the cathedral, Rue Kéréon leads into the old town, which straddles the Steir, a river which has a somewhat undignified end, running under a street for the last few metres of its length. Rue Kéréon is beautiful, a cobbled street between rows of half-timbered houses some with double overhangs. The street leads to Place Terre-au-Ducs, a square of half-timbered houses that is equally picturesque. Here, or in one of the equally delightful side streets, you can find a *crêperie* and spend a leisurely lunchtime while the feet recover in time for the afternoon's exploration.

From Rue Kéréon, Rue des Boucheries leads off to Rue du Sallé another quite delightful street. Now cross Rue Elie Fréron to reach the Musée des Beaux-Arts, housed in the town hall, with its collec- tion of paintings from the sixteenth century through to the twentieth century. There are works by Rubens, Fragonard, Picasso and Cocteau, and a room devoted to the work of Max Jacob, Quimper born and a long-time friend of Picasso. Jacob was born in Rue du Parc in 1876, the son of Jewish shopkeepers and left for Paris in 1896 to become a writer or painter. He became both, being a fine poet and a worthy artist. In Paris he shared a room with Picasso, the story being told that Jacob worked during the day and slept at night while Picasso slept all day, in the one bed they shared, and painted all night. In 1907, while he was living in Montmartre Jacob saw a likeness of Christ in one of his paintings and, believing it to be a sign as he had not deliberately painted it, he immediately became a Christian. He was baptised, with Picasso as godfather, and in 1921 moved from Paris to live and work in monk-like seclusion. He tired of this in 1936 and moved back to Paris where he remained until the German occupation. His parents, still living in Quimper, were transported to Auschwitz and killed, Max being taken in early 1944, his conversion to Christianity not saving him from being considered a Jew. His artist friends attempted to save him, but in the cold of winter, with inadequate food and clothing, he died of pneumonia while awaiting transportation to a concentration camp.

Closer to the cathedral is the Musée Departmental Breton, a museum devoted to the local area, with exhibits on its archaeology and Breton culture. The museum is housed in the old bishop's palace and includes furnishings, carvings and costumes. A step away is the Jardin de l'Evêche (Bishop's Garden), at the eastern end of the cathedral, a pleasant spot, worthwhile visiting for the view of the cathedral alone.

A new town museum is to be devoted to pottery. Quimper has been famous for pottery since the late seventeenth century when the first workshop was set up. The earliest potters, one of whom was the Jean-Baptiste Bousquet after whom the road in which the pottery museum stands is named, came from the south and east of France,

Trévarez Park with flowers in full bloom

Pleasure boats moored at Concarneau marina

and their workshop shows influences of the styles of Moustiers-Ste-Marie, in Provence, and of Rouen, but as more of the craftsmen were recruited locally so the designs changed to reflect Breton culture. Today Quimper pottery, which is all hand-decorated, is distinctive. The museum will reflect the history of the local art, and for good measure two of the city potteries allow visitors to watch the process, as well as to buy the end product. The predominant colour of Quimper pottery was, and still is, blue, which explains the Breton nickname for a Quimper resident: *glazik*, little blue.

But though pottery is Quimper's chief contribution to Breton culture, in terms of celebrating that culture its Festival de Cornouaille, held in the week preceding the fourth Sunday in July, is the major cultural festival of the province, featuring music, song and dance.

North-east of Quimper the country is less varied and interesting until the Montagnes Noires are reached. There are, however, several worthwhile places to visit. Near Quéllenec is the Site du Stangala, a rock outcrop standing clear of the fine local woodland and so offering a breathtaking view over a horseshoe band of the Odet river. Northward, the Calvary of the chapel of Notre-Dame-de-Quilinen is interesting for its tapering Calvary. It was carved in the mid-sixteenth century and is the better for being positioned among trees. At

The traditional craft of basket weaving can still be seen throughout Brittany

St Venec, northward again, the chapel has a statue depicting one of the more unusual Breton legends. According to this St Given (also known as St Blanche as the Celtic word *wen* means white) gave birth to triplets — Venec, Guénolé and Jacut, all of whom became saints — and miraculously grew a third breast to cope with nursing. The stone statue shows the family group.

To the east of St Venec are the **Montagnes Noires**. As the name implies, these hills were probably once forested, though little of that woodland cover now remains. Though geologically similar to the Monts d'Arrée, the Noires are lower and have fewer patches of moorland. The high point, Roc de Toullaëron at 326m (1,069ft), stands above a beautiful section of oak woods. It is reached by a short walk, allow 20 minutes, from a car park, and offers an excellent view over the woods themselves, and of the Monts d'Arrée. The Noires form a single east-west ridge, and north of this lies the Nantes-Brest canal which links the Aulne to the Oust. Close to the canal are two small villages which have good Calvaries. That at **Cléden-Poher** is sixteenth century and set next to a fine church, while that at **St Hernin**, a village named for an Irish monk, is delicate and very elegant. To the west, Écluse de Gwaker, Gwaker Lock, is the prettiest of the locks on the canal and stands close to the Laz forest, one of the last sections of wooded Noires. Within the forest the Domaine de Trévarez can be visited, an 80 ha (198 acres) forest park with a ruined château at its heart. In addition to fine woodland there are clusters of camellias, rhododendrons and azaleas. From the park a section of GR38 heads north across excellent country, passing the canal to reach Châteuneuf-du-Faou, a centre for salmon fishing.

The boat ride down the Odet from Quimper starts, or ends, at **Bénodet**, one of the best known of Finistère's resort towns. It has a good number of camp sites, but those, and the crush in the town at the height of the season, cannot detract from its charms, especially the picturesque harbour, with its fine views over the Odet, and the sheltered beach. At the beach end of the town there is a casino, and, close by, the Pyramid lighthouse from the top of which the view is remarkable, extending all the way to the Eckmühl lighthouse at Pointe de Penmarch.

East of Bénodet the coastline softens considerably, a coast for a relaxing visit rather than one of dramatic seascapes. The most interesting spot is **Beg-Meil** — from where boats ply to the Iles de Glénan in summer — once a sea mill, but now a small resort with several excellent beaches. **Fouesnant** is at the centre of an area renowned for apple orchards and is, as a result, a cider making town laying claim to producing the best Breton cider. There is an apple festival on the third Sunday in July each year. Also worth seeing is the *pardon* on the 26 July or the Sunday following, when the women-folk wear their distinctive costume. To see the costume at other times it is only necessary to visit the church where a monument by the porch shows a woman in the dress, complete with *coiffe*. Close to Fouesnant is **La Forêt-Fouesnant**, a little port on an inlet of the sea. The church here has a good parish close with a sixteenth-century Calvary. Across the water, and a little way seaward, is the new marina of Port-la-Forêt. From La Forêt it is just a short drive to Concarneau.

Concarneau is France's third largest fishing port and is an absolute ✳ must for the visitor, both for its historical interest and for the delights of the fish auction and the fish restaurants. Historically it is the Ville Close, the walled city, that is of interest. The city is set on an island in the middle of the wide inlet of the sea that is protected by the hooked beak of Concarneau's headland. Since the fourteenth century the island was protected by granite walls and so good were these fortifications that when the English took control of the city during the Breton War of Succession, as part of the support they gave Jean de Montfort, it took the French thirty years and three sieges to get it back. In the seventeenth century Vauban improved the defences, creating a fortress that was, in its day, virtually impregnable. The city is now linked to the main town by a causeway, though the entry, through a granite arch, is still a step back in time. Inside there is a maze of narrow alleys, the houses now mostly given over to 🚶 souvenirs, but still great fun. The walls are complete and can be walked, the trip is about 1km (½ mile) and takes an hour with pauses for photography, and offer excellent views of the sea and the fishing port. Within the city there is a fine museum devoted to fishing (the Musée de la Pêche), with exhibits on the development of the fishing 🏛 industry and the methods employed to catch different fish. There are some ten boats of different designs, including a whaling boat, and aquaria with live exhibits.

In the town on the mainland the main attraction is the *criée*, or fish ✳ market where the catch of Concarneau's fleet, chiefly deep-sea trawlers catching tuna, is sold. The sights, sounds and smells of the market will accompany the visitor for some time after. The debt the town owes to the fishing industry is remembered each year in the Fêtes des Filets Bleus held in the week that precedes the penultimate Sunday in August. This 'festival of the blue nets' was once a religious event with a blessing of boats and nets, but now (perhaps because most nets are brown rather than blue!) it has become a celebration of the Breton joy of life.

Close to the fishing port is the Laboratoire de Biologie Marine, or Marinaruim, part of the Collége de France's research wing, but with interesting audio-visual displays on marine life, and several aquaria.

From Concarneau the visitor can move inland to **Rosporden**, a neat little town, famous for its Breton *chouchen*, a type of mead. The town is built close to a lake created by a widening of the Aven river. The fine church tower with its four pinnacles and tracery windows is delightfully reflected in the pool. All around the town there are fine places that can be explored at leisure. The same is true closer to the coast where there are several fine spots on the way to Pont-Aven. Among the best is Pointe de Trévignon, where an old castle stands at the very tip of the headland.

Pont-Aven is another beautifully positioned town, set where the Aven river widens almost to an estuary despite the sea still being several kilometres away. Anciently the river's rush to this wider section was used to power waterwheels, of which there were many. Indeed, it was once said that they outnumbered the houses. Only one survives as a working mill, though several are passed during the course of a delightful walk along the Promenade Xavier-Grall, or along the banks of the Aven itself. The promenade is named after a local poet. Within the old section of the town there are houses of the same vintage as the mills, and the whole is so picturesque that it comes as little surprise to discover that Pont-Aven was, and is, popular with artists. The most famous group, the Pont-Aven School, were those who followed Paul Gauguin to the town in the late 1880s. Gauguin's stay at Pont-Aven came after he had left Paris and his office job to become a painter, and from here he made his fateful journeys to Arles, a visit that culminated in Van Gogh cutting off part of an ear, and to Tahiti where he was, eventually, to spend his final years. Gauguin's time at Pont-Aven was as boisterous as might be expected. He lived, for a time, with a woman called Anna who travelled everywhere with a monkey on her shoulder. One day in Concarneau the local children threw stones at the monkey, hitting it. Gauguin hit the children, and in the ensuing fracas knocked down a sailor. The sailor went back to his ship and collected his crew mates who beat Gauguin soundly, breaking his leg. He spent some time in bed as a result, during which time Anna sold everything from his studio and left Brittany for good. A small museum in the town has a floor dedicated to the school, with works by some of its less well-known artists. The museum also has exhibits on the history of the town, on the Pont-Aven School, with items from the Pension Gloanec where the artists stayed, and on the origins of the Fête des Fleurs d'Ajonc, the Gorse-Flower festival. This was first organised in 1905 by the poet and songwriter Théodore Botrel as a celebration of Breton culture, and is still held annually on the first Sunday in August. On that day there are numerous music and dance events.

Those paying homage to Gauguin will also wish to visit the Chapelle de Trémalo, a sixteenth-century Breton chapel that houses the seventeenth-century wooden crucifixion that Gauguin painted in *Le Christe Jaune* (*Yellow Christ*), one of his most famous paintings. At **Nizon**, about 3km (2 miles) north-west of Pont-Aven the Calvary was the model for Gauguin's *Green Christ*.

Between Pont-Aven and Quimperlé the coastal belt is taken over by orchards which produce Breton cider. The Bélon river which flows through this country is famous for its oyster beds, and many of the local restaurants offer the visitor a combination of the two. **Moëlan-sur-Mer** lies at the centre of the area: the first part of the name derives from the *lan*, or hermitage, of Moë, an early Celtic saint. The second part is somewhat optimistic, as the village is about 5km (3 miles) from the sea. St Philibert-et-St Roch, a chapel close to the village, has a fine Calvary. East of the village is the River Laita that forms Finistère's border with Morbihan. The river flows up the edge of the **Forêt de Carnoët**, another remnant of the original Breton beech and oak forest. Once it was the domain of the Count of Commorre who, legend has it, lived at the now-ruinous Château du Carnoët. Having been told by a fortune teller that he would be killed by his son, the Count killed each of his first four wives when they became pregnant. The fifth wife, Trephine, fearing for her safety when she became pregnant, escaped to the forest where she was hunted by the count. She had her son in secrecy, but Commorre found her soon after and beheaded her. There are two versions of the ending to the tale: in one the English saint, Gildas, a genuine sixth-century monk and chronicler, found Trephine, put her head back on and restored her to life, and then went to the count's castle where he threw a handful of soil at the walls. The castle promptly fell down killing the count. A second version has the soil thrown by Trephine's son after he had been beheaded by his father, but had picked up his head and walked to the castle.

Quimperlé, the town at the northern end of the forest, is named, as with Quimper, for its position at the *kemper* (confluence) of two rivers. It is a pretty town, especially near the old cobbled river quays and in the narrow alleys of half-timbered houses. The best of the houses are in Rue Dom-Morice and Rue Brémond-d'Ars each of which is close to the church of Ste Croix. By common consent the apse of Ste Croix is the finest example of Romanesque architecture in Brittany. The church's plan is a copy of the Holy Sepulchre in

Jerusalem, presumably copied from the descriptions of returning Crusaders. Rue Dom-Morice's finest house is number 67, the Archers' House, which is also the town museum with exhibits on its history.

The oldest, and best, section of the town, that section close to Ste Croix, stands on an island between the Isole and Ellé rivers which join at the *kemper* to form the Laita which flows beside the Carnoët Forest. That part of the town across the Isole is less elegant, though the church of Notre-Dame-de-l'Assomption has some beautiful architectural woodwork.

Additional Information

Places to Visit

NORTHERN — FINISTÈRE

Brest
Océanopolis
Port de Plaisance du Moulin Blanc
Open: May to September daily except Monday mornings 9.30am-6pm. October to April daily except Monday mornings 9.30am-5pm (but 6pm on Saturday and Sunday).
☎ 98 344040

Castle/Maritime Museum
Cours Dajot
Open: all year, daily except Tuesday 9.15am-12noon, 2-6pm.
☎ 98 221239

Tanguy Tower and Museum of Old Brest
Open: July and August daily 10am-12noon, 2-7pm. June and September daily 2-7pm. October to May Thursday only 2-5pm, but daily in school holidays.
☎ 98 008770

Museum of Fine Arts
Rue Emile Zola,
Open: all year daily except

Tuesday and Sunday morning, 9.45-11.45am, 2-6.45pm.
☎ 98 446627

Carantec
Maritime Museum
Open: mid-June to mid-September daily except Sunday 10am-12noon, 3-7pm.
☎ 98 670030

Tareau Castle
Opening times variable, depending upon tides and weather.
☎ 98 670043 or 98 670030

Cléder
Tronjoly Manor
Exterior only open: all year, daily 10am-6pm.

Ile d'Ouessant (Ushant)
Niou Uhella Open-Air Museum
Open: June to September daily 10.30am-6.30pm. April, May daily except Monday 2-6pm. October to March daily except Monday 2-4pm.
☎ 98 488637

Créac'h Lighthouse Museum
Open: June to September daily 10am-6.30pm. April, May daily except Monday 2-6pm.

October to March daily except
Monday 2-4pm.
☎ 98 488070

Le Conquet
Sea Museum
Open: June to September daily
10am-6.30pm. April, May daily
except Monday 2-6pm. October to
March daily except Monday 2-4pm.
☎ 98 890427

Le Folgoët
Museum
Open: mid-June to mid-September
daily except Sunday morning
10am-12.30pm, 2.30-6pm.

Lesneven
Léon Museum
Open: May to September daily
except Tuesday 1-6pm. October to
April daily except Tuesday and
Friday 1-6pm.
☎ 98 830147

Morlaix
Museum of the Jacobins
Open: July, August daily 10am-
12noon, 2-6pm. May, June,
September daily except Monday
10am-12noon, 2-6pm. October to
April daily except Monday 10am-
12noon, 2-5pm.
☎ 98 886888

Queen Anne's House
Open: July, August daily except
Sundays 10am-7pm. April, May,
June, September daily except
Sunday and Monday 10am-
12noon, 2-7pm. Tours available.
☎ 98 796385

Plouescat
Maillé Castle
Open: exterior July to mid-

September daily 10am-6pm.
Interior July to mid-September
Tuesday to Thursday by prior
appointment only. Two days notice
required.
☎ 98 614468

Kerjean Castle
Open: July, August daily 10am-
7pm. June, September daily except
Tuesday 10am-12noon, 2-6pm.
May, October daily except Tuesday
2-5pm (Wednesday 2-6pm).
November to March Wednesday
and Sunday only 2-5pm.
☎ 98 699369

Plouézoch
Tumulus of Barnenez
Open: April to September Thursday to Monday 9.30-11.15am, 2-
5.45pm. October to March Thursday Monday 10-11.15am, 2-4.15pm.
Guided tours available.
☎ 98 672473

Plouguerneau
Maritime Museum
Open: mid-June to mid-September
daily except Monday 10am-
12.30pm, 2.30-6pm. Mid-September
to mid-June Saturday, Sunday
10am-12.30pm, 2.30-6pm.
☎ 98 046030

Roscoff
Charles Pérez Aquarium
Open: April to June, September
daily 2-6pm. July, August daily
9.30am-12noon, 2-7pm.
October to March by request.
☎ 98 697230

St Pol-de-Léon
Tower of Notre-Dame de Kriesker
Open: mid-June to mid-September
daily 10am-12noon, 2-6pm.
☎ 98 690115

Kérouzéré Castle
Exterior open at all times.
Interior open: mid-June to mid-
September daily 10am-12noon, 2-
6pm. Guided tours available.
☎ 98 299605

St Renan
Museum
Open: mid-June to mid-September
daily except Monday 10am-
12.30pm, 2.30-6pm. Mid-September
to mid-June Saturday, Sunday
10am-12.30pm, 2.30-6pm.
☎ 98 842254 or 98 849686

CENTRAL FINISTÈRE

Argol
Cider Museum
Open: mid-June to mid-September
daily 10.30am-6pm.
Mid-September to mid-October
daily except Monday 2-6pm.
☎ 98 277326 or 98 273413

Museum of Old Crafts
Open: mid-June to mid-September
daily 10.30am-6pm. Mid-September to mid-October daily except
Monday 2-6pm.
☎ 98 271434

Camaret-sur-Mer
Vauban Castle
Open: Easter, June to September
daily 10am-12noon, 2-7pm.
All other times daily 2-6pm.
Closed mid-January to mid-
Febuary.
☎ 98 279422

Notre-Dame-de-Rocamadour
Open: Easter to October daily 9am-
7pm. November to Easter Saturday, Sunday 9am-7pm.

Commana
Kerouat Mills
Open: mid-March to June,
September, October daily except
Saturday 2-6pm.
July, August daily 11am-7pm.
☎ 98 688776

Daoulas
Abbey
Open: June to September daily
10am-7pm. October to May by
appointment only.
☎ 98 258439

Landévennec
Old Abbey
Abbey Ruins Open: all year
Monday to Saturday 9.30am-
12noon, 2.30-6pm. Sunday 3-6pm.
Site Museum Open: July and
August Monday to Saturday
9.30am-12noon, 12.30-6pm. Sunday
3-6pm.
☎ 98 277334

New Abbey
Open: all year, but access sometimes limited daily 10am-5pm.
☎ 98 277334

Loqueffret
*Maison des Pilhaouerin (Ragmen's
    Museum)*
Open: June to August daily 2-5pm.
☎ 98 264032

Morgat
Sea Caves
Open: May to September daily, but
weather dependent. Trip, by boat
(from the harbour) takes about 45
minutes.
☎ 98 270954 or 98 272250

Pleyben
Crêpes Cozien
Open: all year, daily 9am-4pm.
☎ 98 263269

Scrignac
Museum of Hunting
Open: June to September daily
except Tuesday 10am-12noon, 2-6pm.
☎ 98 958535 or 98 782500

Sizun
Museum
Open: June to September daily
9am-12noon, 1-5pm. October to
May daily 2-5pm.
☎ 98 688776

House of the River and Fishing
Open: June to September daily
10.30am-7pm. May Monday to
Saturday 9am-12noon, 1-5pm.
Sunday 1.30-6pm. October to April
daily 2-5pm.
☎ 98 688633

St Hernot
Geology Museum
Open: mid-June to mid-September
daily 10.30am-7pm. Mid-September to mid-October daily except
Monday 2-6pm.
☎ 98 271973

St Rivoal
Cornec House
Open: July, August daily 1-7pm.
June and 1 to 15 September daily 2-6pm.
☎ 98 688776

Ménez-Meur
Open: June to September daily
10am-7pm. October, November
and February to May Sunday and
Wednesday 10am-12noon, 1-6pm.
Closed January.
☎ 98 688171

Trégarvan
School Museum
Open: June to mid-September daily
1.30-7pm.
☎ 98 688776

SOUTHERN FINISTÈRE

Audierne
Lobster and Crab Farm
Open: July, August daily 9am-12noon, 2-5pm. September to June
Monday to Saturday 8am-12noon,
2-4.30pm. Sunday 8am-12noon.
☎ 98 701004

La Chaumière
Open: Easter to September daily
10am-7pm. Guided tours available.
☎ 98 701320

Bénodet
Pyramid Lighthouse
Open: mid-March to October daily
10am-12noon, 2.30-6pm.
Guided tours available.
☎ 98 572477

Combrit
Museum of Mechanical Music
Open: June to September daily 2-7pm. October to May Sunday 2-7pm.
☎ 98 563603

Concarneau
City Walls
Open: mid-June to September daily
10am-7.30pm. Easter to mid-June
daily 10am-12.30pm, 2-7pm.
☎ 98 970144

Fishing Museum
Open: July, August daily 9.30am-8pm. May, June, September daily
10am-12.30pm, 2.30-7pm. October

to March daily 10am-12.30pm, 2.30-6pm.
☎ 98 971020

Fish Market
Open: all year Monday to Thursday at 7am and 10am.
Marinarium
Open: mid-June to September daily 10am-12noon, 2-6.30pm. April to mid-June daily 2-6.30pm.
☎ 98 970659

Douarnenez
Boat Museum
Place de l'Enfer
Open: June to September daily 10am-7pm. October to May daily 10am-12noon, 2-6pm.
☎ 98 926520

Floating Museum
Open: all year, daily from 10am-7pm.
☎ 98 926520

Ile de Sein
Museum
Open: July to September daily 10.30am-12noon, 2-6.30pm.
☎ 98 709272

Locronan
Museum
Open: July to September daily 10.30am-12.30pm, 2.30-7pm.
☎ 98 917005

St Ronan Studio
Open: Easter to October daily 10am-6pm. Sale room open all year, daily 10am-6pm.
☎ 98 917068

Craft Workshop
Open: mid-June to September Monday to Saturday 9am-1pm, 2-8pm. Sunday 10am-1pm, 2-8pm. October to mid-June Monday

Saturday 9am-12noon, 2-7pm.
Sunday 2-7pm.
☎ 98 917011

Ponant Glass Works
Open: June to mid-September daily 9am-8pm. Mid-September to March daily 10am-6pm.
April, May daily 9.30am-6.30pm.
☎ 98 917439

Loctudy
Kérazan Manor
Open: June to September daily except Tuesday 10am-12noon, 2-6pm.
☎ 98 874040

Odet River Trips
The journey from Quimper to Bénodet, or return, takes about 1½ hours. Departure times vary with the state of the tide. For details contact Vedettes de l'Odet, Bénodet
☎ 98 570088

Plogoff
Pointe du Raz Museum
Open: June to September daily 10am-6pm. October to May daily 10am-12noon, 2-6pm.
☎ 98 706054

Pointe de Penmarch
Eckmühl Lighthouse
Open: all year daily, but for guided tours only and at the discretion of the keepers.
☎ 98 586117

Pont-Aven
Museum
Open: April to September daily 10am-12.30pm, 2-7pm. October, November daily 10am-12.30pm, 2-6pm. December daily 10am-12.30pm, 2-5pm.
☎ 98 061443

Trémolo Chapel
Open: Easter to October daily 9am-7pm.

Pont-l'Abbé
Castle/Bigouden Museum
Open: June to September daily except Sunday 9am-12noon, 2-6.30pm. No admission after 11.15am and 5.45pm.
Guided tours available.
☎ 98 872444

Bigouden House
Open: June to September daily except Sunday 10am-12.15pm, 3-6.30pm. No admissions after 11am and 6pm. Guided tours available.
☎ 98 873563

Quimper
Museum of Fine Arts
Town Hall
Place St Corentin
Open: May to September daily except Tuesday 9.30am-12noon, 2-6pm.
☎ 98 954520

Breton Museum
Rue de Roi-Gradlon
Open: June to September daily except Tuesday 10am-7pm.
October to May daily except Monday and Tuesday 9am-12noon, 2-5pm.
☎ 98 952160

Pottery Museum
14 Rue Jean-Baptiste Bousquet
A new museum. Hours to be announced. Ask at Tourist Information Office or
☎ 98 901272 for details.

Quimper Pottery
Open: all year Monday to Friday 9.30-11.30am, 1.30-4.30pm. No admissions after 3pm on Fridays.

Guided tours available.
☎ 98 900936

Kéraluc Pottery
Open: July, August daily except Sunday 9am-12noon, 2-6.30pm.
September to June Monday to Friday 9-11.30am, 2-5pm.
☎ 98 530450

Post Office and Telecommunications
Boulevard de Kerguèlen
Market Days: every morning in the Market Hall, Saturday street market.

Car Hire: Avis
8 Avenue de la Gare
☎ 98 903134

Europcar
12 Rue de Concarneau
☎ 98 900068

Quimperlé
Museum
Open: mid-June to mid-September Tuesday to Saturday 10am-12noon, 1.30-6pm.
Sunday 10am-12noon, 2-6pm.
☎ 98 960141

St Guénolé
Prehistory Museum
Open: June to September Monday to Saturday 10am-12noon, 2-6pm.
Sunday 10am-12noon. October to May by appointment only.
☎ 98 586035

Trévarez Park
Open: July, August daily 11am-7pm. April to June, September daily except Tuesday 1-7pm.
October to March Saturday and Sunday 2-6pm.
☎ 98 268279

Tourist Information Centres

**Comité Départemental du
   Tourisme du Finistère**
11 Rue Théodore Le Hars
BP 125
29104 Quimper
☎ 98 530900

Bénodet
51 Avenue de la Plage
29950
☎ 98 570014

Brest
1 Place de la Liberté
29200
☎ 98 442496

Châteaulin
Quai Cosmao
29150
☎ 98 860211

Concarneau
Quai d'Aiguillon
29900
☎ 98 970144

Douarnenez
2 Rue Dr Mével
29100
☎ 98 921335

Huelgoat
Place Mairie
29690

☎ 98 997232 (June to September).
98 997155 (October to May).

Landerneau
Pont de Rohan
29800
☎ 98 851309

Morlaix
Place Otages
29600
☎ 98 621494

Pont-Aven
5 Place Hôtel-de-Ville
29930
☎ 98 060470

Quimper
3 Rue Roi Gradlon
29000
☎ 98 530405

Quimperlé
Pont Bourgneuf
29300
☎ 98 960432

Roscoff
Rue Gambetta
29680
☎ 98 611213

2

CÔTES D'ARMOR

Until recently the Breton *département* that included the majority of the Channel coast was called Côtes-du-Nord, but that name has now been changed to the more evocative Côtes d'Armor, a name that includes the wholly appropriate allusion to the ancient Breton concept of *armor*, the land by the sea. The coast is a fascinating one, a coast of contrasts — the rugged cliffs of the Pink Granite Coast, the beauty of the moorland-capped Emerald Coast, and the surprising beaches of pale sands. Historically this is one of the most important coastlines in France, the land of corsairs and explorers. Inland, too, it is an interesting area, with sections of the old *argoat*, and a array of interesting villages and towns.

This exploration of the *département* starts with the *armor*, covering the area north of the N12, before moving inland to reach the *argoat*.

The Channel Coast

The visitor crosses from Finistère into Côtes d'Armor along the Armorique Corniche, the road that hugs the coast from Morlaix towards St Michel-en-Grève. Almost immediately there are places of interest. Seaward is the Lieue de Grève, a magnificent sandy cove, while inland is the Grand Rocher which can be reached by a 30-minute climb from the road end car park. From it there is an exceptional view of the cove. Inland from here, near **Lanvellec**, is the Château de Rosanbo, originally built in the fourteenth-century castle on a rock above the Bo stream. The castle was extended several times and restored in the nineteenth century, a restoration that converted it into a country house. Inside, the rooms are beautifully furnished, and the library houses a collection of very rare seventeenth-century books. Outside, the castle's formal gardens are splendid.

Beyond **St Michel-en-Grève**, a small, but pleasant, resort, the main road (D786) leads inland to Lannion, while a detour to the left reaches **Trédrez**. The village is famous for having had St Yves as its rector from 1284-1292, though he would not have officiated at the church, a delightful place with a fourteenth-century granite font topped by a carved wooden canopy and some fine artwork, as it was not completed until about 1500. Beyond the village is Pointe de Séhor, the final headland, a good viewpoint, being reached by a short walk. From the Pointe the road heads east along the bank of the Léguer river passing Locquémau, a small fishing port, and **Loguivy-lès-Lannion**. In the church here is a seventeenth-century altarpiece depicting the Magi accompanied by shepherds in full Breton costume and carrying Breton bagpipes. Ahead now is Lannion.

Lannion is a fine old port straddling the Léguer river and with a delightful array of houses, some half-timbered and many more built in the local pink granite. The best of the houses are in the Place du Centre and in Rue des Chapeliers and Rue Geoffroy-de-Pont-Blanc that lead off it. Close to the Place is the town church, but a more interesting religious building is the church of Brélévenez, to the north, which is best reached by climbing 142 granite steps from Rue de la Trinité. The church was built by the Knights Templar in the twelfth century, though later remodelled, except for the fine granite spire which is fifteenth century. Inside, look for the stoup, once used for measuring tithes of grain.

Southward from Lannion there are several interesting châteaux, visits to which can be combined to produce a fine tour from the town. Leave Lannion by the D11 to reach **Ploubezre**, and turn left there for the **Château de Coatfrec**, a rarely visited site with the ruins of a sixteenth century fortified mansion half-hidden among the ivy and shrubs.

Rejoin the D11 and head south, then go left again to reach the **Kerfons Chapel**, beautifully set in a chestnut grove. The chapel is fifteenth century and houses an excellent carved rood screen from the same period. South of the chapel is the **Château de Tonquédoc**. The castle was built in the thirteenth century, but in 1395 it was dismantled on the orders of Duke Jean IV who thought its existence threatened his security. It was rebuilt the next century, but suffered the same fate of being dismantled as a threat in 1622, the fearful individual this time being Cardinal Richelieu. The fine ruins are set close to a stream and can be visited. Sections of the old wall can be climbed for a view over the surrounding country. The next castle is the **Château de Kergrist**, a horseshoe-shaped building with façades from the differing architectural periods from the fourteenth to the eighteenth centuries. The castle is furnished as a country house and stands in a formal garden which overlooks a more natural area of parkland. South from the castle is the chapel of **Les-Sept-Saints** an eighteenth-century chapel incorporating a dolmen. The chapel is the centre of the cult of the Seven Saints who were walled up in cave at Ephesus in the third century for refusing to deny their faith, but were still alive when the wall was broken down some 200 years later. A joint Islamic/Christian pilgrimage is held to the chapel on the fourth Sunday in June.

Eastward from Les-Sept-Saints, at **Bégard**, is Armoripark a leisure complex with giant flumes, dry bobsleigh runs, an ice rink, swimming pools, and numerous other attractions.

Heading north from Lannion brings the visitor to the Côte de Granit Rose, where the rugged cliffs and rocks of the sea edge really do have a pinkish tinge, especially at sunset. The coast road here is a fine one, visiting interesting sites and offering superb views. One site that is off the road is **Pleumeur-Bodou** where a white golf ball 64m (210ft) in diameter houses the CNET telecommunications site. From here the first ever trans-Atlantic TV broadcast was made, via the satellite Telstar, in 1962. The dome can be visited on a guided tour, for which a knowledge of French is essential. Ironically, in view of the dome's shape, there is actually a golf course next door! Also close by is the Trégor Planetarium which, in addition to the standard star ceiling, has exhibitions on astronomy and astrophysics, and on Breton natural history and ecology.

Trébeurden, the first village on the Pink Granite Coast, is close to fine beaches and two viewpoints. Le Castel is reached by a 20-minute walk from a car park near the Tresmeur beach and takes in the offshore Ile Milliau, while Pointe de Bihet, south of the village, overlooks the Léguer estuary. To the north, a causeway links the mainland to **Ile de Grande** on which there is a fine *allée couverte* and an ornithology centre that specialises in the care of injured birds as well as providing information on the local seabird populations. On the mainland coast road, known as the Breton Corniche, there is a tall menhir, 'Christianised' by the addition of a crucifix, while north again there is another fine *allée couverte* at Kerguntuil. On from this, after several superb viewpoints have been passed, **Trégastel-Plage** is reached.

This fine resort is one of the best places to see the weird rocks of the Granite Coast. Though granite is a very hard rock which erodes only slowly it does have intrusions of quartz and mica that are more easily weathered. The washing out of these intrusions, which tend to form specific layers, leaves the distinctive 'tor' behind. Here on the coast, the sea has been added to the corrosive forces of the wind and rain

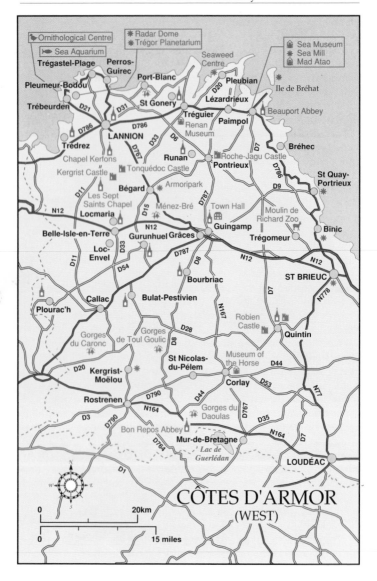

Ornithological Centre
Sea Aquarium
Radar Dome
Trégor Planetarium
Sea Museum
Sea Mill
Mad Atao

Trégastel-Plage
Perros-Guirec
Port-Blanc
Seaweed Centre
Pleubian
Pleumeur-Bodou
D20
Ile de Bréhat
Trébeurden
D21
St Gonery
Lézardrieux
Beauport Abbey
D31
Tréguier
Paimpol
D786
Renan Museum
Trédrez
LANNION
D786
D33
D6
Roche-Jagu Castle
Bréhec
Chapel Kerfons
Runan
Pontrieux
D7
Kergrist Castle
D767
Tonquédoc Castle
D786
St Quay-Portrieux
D11
Bégard
Armoripark
D9
Les Sept Saints Chapel
D15
Ménez-Bré
D787
Town Hall
Moulin de Richard Zoo
N12
Locmaria
N12
Binic
Belle-Isle-en-Terre
Gurunhuel
Grâces
Guingamp
Trégomeur
Loc-Envel
D33
D787
D8
N12
N12
D54
ST BRIEUC
D11
Bourbriac
D7
N778
Callac
Bulat-Pestivien
Plourac'h
N167
Robien Castle
Quintin
Gorges du Caronc
Gorges de Toul Goulic
D26
D8
St Nicolas-du-Pélem
Museum of the Horse
D44
Kergrist-Moëlou
D20
Corlay
D53
N77
Rostrenen
D790
D44
Gorges du Daoulas
D767
D35
D7
D3
N164
Bon Repos Abbey
Mur-de-Bretagne
N164
D790
D764
Lac de Guerlédan
LOUDÉAC
D1

N
W   E
S

0   20km
0   15 miles

CÔTES D'ARMOR
(WEST)

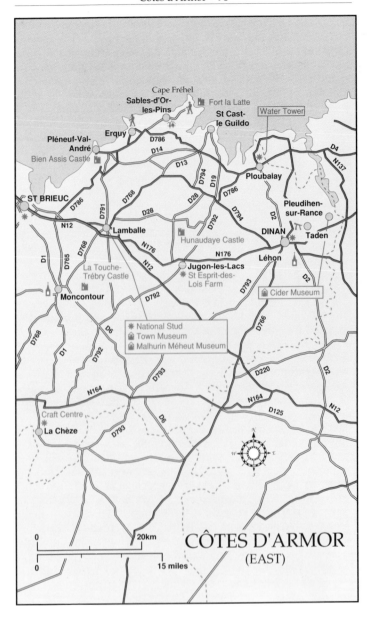

Cape Fréhel

Sables-d'Or-
les-Pins

Fort la Latte

St Cast-
le Guildo

Water Tower

Pléneuf-Val-
André

Erquy

D786

D14

Bien Assis Castle

Ploubalay

D4

N137

ST BRIEUC

D786

D791

D768

D13

D794

D19

D786

Pleudihen-
sur-Rance

D28

D28

D792

D794

D2

Lamballe

N12

D765

D768

N176

Hunaudaye Castle

DINAN

Taden

Léhon

N176

La Touche-
Trébry Castle

N12

Jugon-les-Lacs

St Esprit-des-
Lois Farm

D793

D2

Moncontour

D792

Cider Museum

D6

National Stud
Town Museum
Malhurin Méheut Museum

D766

D1

D768

D792

D1

D793

D220

D2

N164

D793

N164

D125

N12

Craft Centre

La Chèze

D793

D6

D6

N

W   E

S

0   20km

0   15 miles

CÔTES D'ARMOR
(EAST)

and the combination has created some fantastic shapes and fairy-like castles. Some of the best can be seen on the beaches and cliffs of Trégastel-Plage, the very best being on Grève Blanche, the white beach, which is dominated by a huge boulder called King Gradlon. In the town, be sure to visit the Aquarium Marin, a seawater aquarium of fish both local and foreign, the tanks housed in an old series of caves. The stairway near the exit reaches a statue of Père Éternel (Eternal Father), and a fine viewpoint.

From Trégastel boats sail, in summer, for **Les Sept Iles**, a series of island bird sanctuaries where auks, gulls and petrels breed in substantial numbers. There are also some 15,000 gannets on Ile Rouzic. The lighthouse on Ile aux Moines offers a view of the whole island cluster.

Ploumanac'h is a fishing village that is also famous for its curiously-shaped rocks, here gathered together around the headland north of the town. This area forms the Parc Municipal and has a car park and several clear footpaths. The rock clusters have fanciful names (the turtle, the rabbit etc) but are delightful despite that. Some of the best rocks are close to the lighthouse on the headland of Pors Kamor. A much stiffer proposition than the park's strolls, but a really fine walk, is the *Sentiers des Douaniers* which links the park with Perros-Guerec. The walk is name for the customs officials who patrolled the cliffs here on watch for smugglers. In exchange for a walk of about 1½ hours, or 3 hours if the return is on foot rather than by car or bus, there are exceptional seascapes all along the way. The walk passes the Maison du Littoral, a centre set up as a hostel for young people who patrol the local coast tidying it and keeping watch for environmental threats. The centre has frequent summer exhibitions.

At the far end of the customs officials' walk is **Perros-Guirec** a resort and a centre for thalassotherapy, the sea water treatment of medical problems. The use of seawater, and also seaweed, as a treatment is not new, many old Breton remedies including one or the other, but the treatment centres are a new innovation. The resort has several fine beaches, most especially Plage de Trestraou where the *Sentier* ends. The main centre of the resort fronts the beach, though there is an old centre, with buildings grouped around a fourteenth-century church. A more interesting religious building is the chapel of Notre-Dame-de-la-Clarté in **La Clarté**, a village just outside Perros-Guirec. The story is told of a local lord whose ship was endangered by fog and rocks in the sixteenth century and who vowed to build a chapel to the Virgin if his life was spared. It was spared, and he built his chapel at the first spot he saw when the fog lifted, naming it for the Virgin of the Light. An important *pardon* is held to the chapel, which stands at the top of a sharp hill, on 15 August each year. At the town's old harbour is the Musée de Cire, a waxworks that uses full-size figures to recreate important events in the history of Brittany.

Eastward from Perros-Guirec the Pink Granite Coast continues in fine style with several village-ports which can be used as centres for exploring the rugged cliffs. **Port Blanc** is a quaint little place from which a stairway leads to a sixteenth-century chapel with a parish close and a study of St Yves between a rich man and a pauper (see Tréguier). This section of the coast ends at the Pointe de Château, a very fine viewpoint with good beaches on either side. Beyond the point the coast turns south towards the Joudy estuary. Just inland here is the Chapel of **St Gonéry**, an extremely interesting little building, in part tenth century, with a corkscrew steeple. It is believed that St Gonéry himself, a Celtic monk, built the oldest part of the chapel. Inside there is a stone trough that many take for the saint's coffin. In fact it is a ballast trough from the ship that brought him here from Britain, and would have been used for the kitchen fire on the voyage. The saint's skull is kept in the chapel, in a glass-case on what looks like a sedan-chair which is used to carry it in procession. But though these items are interesting it is for its art and wood carvings that the chapel is worthy of a visit. The main chapel was frescoed in the fifteenth century with scenes from the Old and New Testaments. Originally the figures of Adam and Eve, Cain and Abel, were nude, but a later age found this too daring and robes were painted on to the figures. The paintings are wonderfully vibrant, and stunningly realistic in terms of the depiction of the Slaughter of the Innocents, and are well set off by a moving Deposition. The woodwork of note is in a series of friezes executed with typical Celtic flare for savagery.

South of St-Gonéry the road edges closer to the Jaudy, offering a view over its oyster beds, before heading directly for Tréguier. **Tréguier** is one of Brittany's best yachting ports with numerous safe anchorages in the river, and is famous for the cathedral of St Tudwal, a soaring building in pink granite. The cathedral dates from the fourteenth century and is quite magnificent, certainly one of the best two or three in Brittany. Especially good is the open slotted-work spire that rises over 60m (197ft) above the Place du Martray. The open lattice assembly was used to reduce wind-loading, and it has worked successfully enough to have kept the spire intact over the centuries. The cathedral has sixty-nine windows, all of which were once completed by medieval stained glass. Sadly, during the Revolution this was smashed, the windows now having modern glass. However, this modern glass is superb, especially in its use of colours, giving the inside of the cathedral a beautiful colour-glow. To the north of the cathedral, and reached through the elegantly columned Porte St-Jean, are the fifteenth-century cloisters.

The cathedral houses the tomb of St Yves, and a statue to him. Yves Hélari was born into a rich family at Minihy-Tréguier in 1253 and after studying law in Paris he returned to Brittany and became a priest. He did not ignore his legal training, however, specialising in taking the cases of the poor who were challenging the rich. The statue in the cathedral, and several elsewhere, show him between a rich man and a pauper. This grouping represents much of his work, but specifically refers to a case, in which he was judge, brought by a

(Opposite) The weathered rock scapes are a feature along the Granite Coast, especially at Trégastel-Plage

Lannion has a fine array of half-timbered houses

rich man who claimed damages from a poor man who, he said, was living by inhaling the smells from his kitchen. Yves found for the rich man and awarded him, as damages, the sound of a coin rattling in a cup. Every year, on 19 May, the anniversary of Yves' death, lawyers congregate at Minihy-Tréguier and march in procession to the cathedral.

Yves lived an ascetic life, eating only bread and soup, sleeping on a clay bed and constantly wearing a hair shirt that he soaked in water each morning before putting it on. It comes as a surprise to hear that he lived to forty-nine years of age. At his death thousands mourned, and the love of the man is obvious each year at the Pardon of St Yves (Pardon des Pauvres), which is held on the third Sunday in May. Yves was buried in the cathedral and later Duke Jean V decreed that he should be buried beside him. The tombs were destroyed during the Revolution, those that are seen being copies. Finally in the cathedral, the treasury houses several interesting pieces including St Yves skull reliquary, together with some early statues and manuscripts.

Outside the cathedral is the Place du Martray, the heart of old Tréguier. There are good old houses here, and in the steep streets that lead off from it. In the square there is a statue to Ernest Renan, a Tréguier-born nineteenth-century philosopher. Renan described the cathedral as an insane attempt at building an impossible ideal in granite, which seems a little harsh. He also upset the Catholic church by declaring that Christ was a man, albeit an extraordinary one, rather than Son of God. A museum to his life is housed in his birthplace, a sixteenth-century half-timbered house close to the cathedral. Elsewhere, the old town gates at the bottom of Rue Renan, itself filled with half-timbered houses, and the fine woods on Bois du Poète are worth visiting.

South of Tréguier is **Minihy-Tréguier**, birthplace of St Yves and starting point of the Pardon des Pauvres. The church is built on the site of the chapel of the manor house of Ker-Martin, Yves' birthplace, and exhibits his will, written in Latin.

To the east of Tréguier is the Presqu'ile Sauvage, the wild 'nearly island', a magnificent final stretch of the Côte de Granit Rose that is almost cut-off by the fjord-like estuaries of the Jaudy and Trieux rivers. There are good views of these two estuaries at the aptly named Bellevue (for the Jaudy) and at the Bodic lighthouse (for the Trieux). Between the two is the fine viewpoint of Créac'h Maout, at the northern tip of the headland. There, a panorama dial helps the visitor pick out the local coastal features. Chief amongst these is the Sillon de Talbert, a long (3km, 2 miles) and very narrow (mostly about 30m, 100ft) natural spit of shingle that extends in a single sweep out into the channel. The spit, which has been created by the twin currents of the Jaudy and Trieux rivers, can be walked. It offers an extraordinary outing, not only for the views of the Pink Granite Coast, but for the sense of walking out across the sea, and for the salt-resistant plants that grow on it. The spit is also 'farmed', seaweed being collected from its edges and dried on its flat causeway on a commercial basis. Those wishing to know more about the usages of seaweed should visit the Centre d'Etude et de Valorisation des Algues (CEVA), a seaweed study centre near **Pleubian**. Here the industrial and culinary uses of seaweed are presented.

At the base of the Presqu'ile is **Lézardrieux** where the Trieux is spanned by a suspension bridge. South from the village, which has a very elegant belfry of a distinctive local form, with gables and turrets, the Château La Roche-Jagu stands on top of the wooded left bank of the Trieux river. The castle was built in the fifteenth century and was carefully restored in 1968. Not all of the original features were re-instated, however, the west façade showing the corbels and doorways of an external, long-gone walkway. Inside, the wood carving and the sheer craftsmanship of the joinery are a delight. Further up river is Pontrieux, the village at the ancient crossing of the Trieux. Westward from there is **Runan** where there is a Knights Templar church. The fourteenth-century building is very richly decorated, reflecting the wealth of the Templars, and of the Hospitallers of St John of Jerusalem who administered it at a later date. Inside, the figures of the altar, which show five scenes from the life of the Virgin, together with a Christ and a *Pietà*, are excellent.

Across the Trieux from Lezardrieux is Paimpol, while north of the two villages is a headland that forms the first part of a new section of the Côtes d'Armor, the Côte de Goélo. **Paimpol** is a fishing port famous throughout France because of a book, *Le Pêcheur d'Islande* (*The Fishermen of Iceland*), written by Pierre Loti in 1886, and set among the fisherfolk of Paimpol where, at that time, the town's menfolk trawled cod from the waters around Iceland. Those days are gone now, most of the local boats fishing the coasts or farming the local oyster beds. The Musée de la Mer, in Rue de la Bonne, recalls the time of the Icelandic trawlers in models, photographs and exhibits. A second museum that covers the same period is the *Mad Atao*, a boat that has been restored as a floating museum. Paimpol is proud of its maritime heritage, and celebrates it every year in the Fêtes des Terre-Nuevas et des Islandais, the Festival of Newfoundland and Iceland, a day long fair on the fourth Sunday of July. A third museum in the town, the Musée du Costume Trégor-Goélo, has, as the name implies, a collection of costumes in the local style.

Elsewhere, the town has an interesting centre, Place du Martray having some excellent sixteenth-century houses. In one of those lived Gaud, the heroine of Loti's book. Place de Théodore-Botrel commemorates another who helped make the town famous, Botrel being a singer/songwriter who wrote a popular song entitled *La Paimpolaise*. Finally, at nearby Pleudaniel there is an old sea mill which gives a glimpse into the period before electricity.

North of Paimpol, on the road to the Pointe de l'Arcouest are other reminders of the port's past. At **Ploubazlanec** one wall of the cemetery is engraved with the names of local men who died at sea, while at **Porz Even** stands the Croix des Veuves (Widows Cross), a viewpoint of the sea-way approach to Paimpol where women would await the return of their menfolk's boats. Pointe de l'Arcouest is the best local viewpoint, the view seaward dominated by the Ile de Bréhat. The two blocks of pink granite close to the first car park commemorate frequent trips to the area made by the physicists Frédéric and Irène Joliot-Curie. From the Pointe boats cross to the **Ile de Bréhat.**

Because of the short crossing, which takes only about 10 minutes, the fact that it is car free and its climate, the island has become a

(Opposite) St Brieuc, capital of Côtes d'Armor

Paimpol's nautical past makes the harbour well-worth a visit

popular holiday resort. Historically the island was an advanced fortress against invasion and was attacked several times by the English. It was also a provider of good sailors to the French Navy and legend has it that its medieval fisherman visited the waters off America many years before Columbus sailed. One story even maintains that it was a Bréhat man who told Columbus which course to set on his Atlantic crossing. The island's climate, the average winter temperature is about 6°C (43°F), helps a remarkable variety of plants to thrive, which adds interest to a walk from the landing point of Port-Clos.

The walks are of limited length, it being only 3½ km (2 miles) to the Paon lighthouse on the island's northern tip. Closer objectives are the impressive woodland of the Bois de la Citadelle and the viewpoint of the Chapelle St Michel, only 26m (85ft) high and reached by a mere thirty-nine steps, but offering a superb panorama over the island and across to the mainland, with the Sillon de Talbert off to the right. From the island (Port-Clos) one boat trip goes around the island, while another fine trip visits the Trieux estuary and includes time ashore at Roche-Jagu Castle.

South of Paimpol is **Beauport Abbey**, a fine site, one of the most romantic in Brittany, but one that suffers from its closeness to the road. The abbey was built in the thirteenth century by Premonstratensian monks and was wonderfully sited, among trees but overlooking the sea. The monks finally left in 1790 after which the site rapidly deteriorated. Today the refectory (monks' dining room) remains intact, the cloisters mostly so. Of the abbey itself only evocative ruins remain.

South of the abbey the coast is followed by GR34, a car-borne traveller gaining access only intermittently. A good short walk is to follow the GR from Pointe de Plouézec to Pointe de Minard, the latter an excellent viewpoint over St-Brieuc Bay. South of the viewpoint is **Bréhec**, a pretty village that was reputedly the landing point for the Cornish Celts who settled and 'created' Brittany. From Bréhec the main coast road is reached at Lanloup, close to which is the chapel of **Kermaria-an-Iskuit**, a curious name that translates as 'The house of Mary who restores health'. The thirteenth-century chapel is an interesting building, but its finest feature are the fifteenth-century frescoes one of which is a tremendously vibrant Dance of Death in which skeletons and corpses drag the living into their dance. Those depicted include cardinals, lords and peasants, to emphasise the levelling nature of death. The chapel's alabaster and wooden sculptures are also excellent.

St Quay-Portrieux, now a popular Goélo coast resort, is named for a Welsh saint who reputedly made landfall here in the late fifth century. The old harbour, from which fishing boats still leave to catch mackerel and plaice in the bay, is a pretty spot, and the town also has several fine beaches. From one of these, Plage Bonaparte, close to Plouha, a village to the north, and reached by a tunnel bored through the cliff, Allied airmen shot down over France were ferried out to a ship that took them back to Britain. A memorial to the escape route, known as the 'Channel Bus Service' stands close to the car park. The airmen were hidden in houses all over the area, and were assembled at the beach after the BBC gave the signal *Bonjour à tous dans la Maison d'Alphonse.*

On the road to Binic stands **Étables-sur-Mer**, a lively place where there is a fine public park and a chapel with good stained glass windows. **Binic** is another fine port/resort. It was once a deep-sea trawler port and has its own museum to the period. A very different site is the Zoo du Moulin de Richard at **Trégomeur** about 5km (3 miles) inland. The zoo is set in a large park with several small islands and has free roaming herds of deer and goats, as well as more conventionally enclosed lions, tigers, wildebeest, zebra etc. Finally, to the south of Binic is the superb beach of Rosaires, backed by wooded cliffs, which stretches for 3km (2 miles) towards the Pointe des Roslier. Beyond is St Brieuc.

St Brieuc is the capital of Côtes d'Armor, a busy, commercial centre that makes few concessions to the tourist. The city lies on a section of flat land between the rivers Gouet and Gouedic each of which is crossed by heavy, impressive viaducts. It is a modern city, the original town having been badly damaged during the 1939-45 war, as it had been in several wars previously, and rebuilt with an eye to the future rather than the past. Some concessions to older times are made, however, markets still being held in Place du Martray, the square next to the cathedral, and a fair being held in September. There are also some fine old houses dotted about, mostly sixteenth-century half-timbered houses. To see the best take Rue Fardel from Place du Martray. Number 15 Rue Fardel, now a hotel, is the house where James II sought refuge after he had been ousted from the British throne in 1688.

The cathedral of St Etienne (St Stephen) in Place du Martray is a small, heavy building which a quick glimpse could mistake for a fortress. A look at its history reveals that is not far from the truth, several reconstructions since the first work in the thirteenth century having been made to ensure that the cathedral could take on a defensive role. South of the cathedral is St Brieuc's museum which deals with the history of both the city and the *département.*

Gathered around St Brieuc are several satellite industrial villages of no particular interest to the visitor. The coast road dips southward to pass the deep incut cove of the Anse d'Yffiniac named for a village set at the cove's southern extremity. To the east now is the Côte de Penthièvre, the first section of the magnificent Côte d'Émeraude (Emerald Coast), which stretches all the way to Point du Grouin, beyond St Malo. Technically the Emerald Coast — named not for the colour of the water, but for the cliffs which, in summer, are bright green as a result of their covering of heather and bracken fern — starts at Le Val-André. The visitor will concur with this view, there being little to detain him on the section from Yffiniac to Val-André.

Pléneuf-Val-André is now the official name of the resort town that stands in the lee of Pointe de Pléneuf. The town claims to have the best beach on Brittany's Channel coast, a title for which there is stiff competition (and which is, ultimately, a personal opinion). For those who want a change from lying on the beach and discussing its merits there are fine walks in the area. The first, taking around 30 minutes, visits the point with its fine view of the off-shore bird sanctuary island of Le Verdelet. The second, about twice the length, takes the Watchpath, the customs officials' and coastguards' walk between

A colourful corner of Matignon, en route to Cap Fréhel

Val-André and the small port of Dahouet to the south, following a section GR34.

Inland from Val-André is the **Château de Bien Assis**. This fine, moated castle, built of pink sandstone quarried at Erquy, dates from the fifteenth century, but was extended in the seventeenth century when it was also converted into a fortified mansion. It is still inhabited. The castle is reached along a tree-lined avenue across fine parkland. Inside it is exquisitely furnished, mainly in Louis XIV and Breton style, and has an excellent collection of Far Eastern porcelain.

North of the castle is **Erquy**, a fishing port for *coquilles St Jacques* (scallops), and Cap d'Erquy the first highlight of the Emerald Coast. The tip of the cap is reached by a 20-minute walk (through the emerald heather and bracken) from the road-end car park and offers a fine view south along the Côte de Penthièvre. For those looking for

A dramatic view of Fort la Latte

a longer walk, the whole of the seaward edge of the square headland of Cap d'Erquy is followed by GR34: return to Erquy by the minor road through Les Hospitaux.

Nearby, the village of **Sables-d'Or-les-Pins** has one of the most appealing names in Brittany, reflecting its position near golden sands and pine trees. The view of the sands and the Channel through the pine forests is exquisite. Northward, the coast road hugs the cliff edge to reach **Cap Fréhel** one of Brittany's most picturesque headlands and a tremendous viewpoint. The red, black and grey sandstone cliffs of the Cap fall vertically for over 70m (230ft) into the sea and are seen at their best on a walk (allow about 30 minutes) around the headland. The walk starts close to the lighthouse and continues to the headland's tip where there is a foghorn. This sounds twice per minute in foggy weather and looks as though it would seriously damage the ear drums of anyone unfortunate enough to be stood nearby. Close to the horn are the Rochers de la Fauconnière, best seen from the restaurant which is reached by a steep path. The cliffs here are covered with gulls and cormorants in the nesting season. Other birds that can be seen in the area include terns, scoters (a sea duck) and shearwaters.

The view from Cap Fréhel, which is improved if the 145 steps of the lighthouse are climbed, is remarkably expansive, taking in virtually the whole of the Emerald Coast and, on very clear days, the Channel Islands. The view of the cap itself is improved if the boat trip to, or from, Dinard/St Malo is taken, this trip also offering a fine view of the local section of the Emerald Coast. The trip retraces the early part of the journey of St Malo sailors: in their case passing the Cap had an added significance as their wedding vows were suspended until the Cap was rounded again on the homeward voyage!

The arc of Anse des Sévignés separates Cap Fréhel from the equally dramatic, but man-made, site of **Fort la Latte**. The fort has to be reached on foot from the road end car park, the walk passing an impressive menhir known as Gargantua's Finger. When it is reached, the fort is the archetypal castle, a real fairy-tale place. It was begun in the thirteenth century on the dramatic headland of Pointe de la Latte and so sits some 60m (197ft) above the waves. Later, the famous military architect Sébastien Vauban improved and remodelled the castle, producing what we see today. Entrance is across a double drawbridge over natural clefts in the rock. Inside there is an encircling rampart wall and the Échauguette Tower set on a natural mound. The tower can be climbed for an excellent view of the castle, but care is needed as the steps are difficult. Some of the domestic buildings can be visited, as can a curious cannonball oven or foundry. It is not clear whether this was used to make the cannonballs, or was used to heat them before firing. The use of heated cannonballs was a well-known tactic for attacking wooden warships as both the ship's structure and its sails could be ignited.

Fort la Latte sits at the corner of the remarkably square-cut Baie de la Fresnaye, a natural harbour that the castle protected by firing across the bay's entrance. From the castle the road keeps away from the cliff edge at first, but stays closer as lower cliffs are reached. On the other side of the bay is Pointe de St Cast, hooked eastward towards Dinard and so enclosing a small, shallow bay that is backed by the town of St Cast-le-Guildo. The point is another excellent viewpoint, and is topped by the Monument aux Évadés, a memorial to those French citizens who escaped from Nazi captivity during the 1939-45 war.

St Cast-le-Guildo is a very beautiful resort with a good beach. It possesses another memorial, a column set at the end of the aptly named Rue de la Colonne, which commemorates the local victory of the French over the British in 1758. During the Seven Years War the British landed a force of 12,000 men from warships anchored off St Cast and marched on St Malo. The attack on St Malo failed and the army retreated to St Cast to re-embark. In a running fight with troops under the command of the Duke of Aiguillon, the Governor of Brittany, more than 2,000 British troops were killed before their ships got away. The battle has spawned two interesting stories. The first has it that many of the British troops were Welsh and that as they marched on St Malo they sang a Welsh folk song. The Breton defenders, recognising the tune, started up with their own version which, because of the similarities of Breton and Welsh, both derived from an original Celtic language, was almost identical. When they realised this the Welsh and Breton troops ran to each other and hugged like long-lost cousins. The second, more likely, tale has it that the Duke of Aiguillon directed his troops from a mill some distance from the action. The duke was an enemy of La Chalotais, the Rennes Procurator, and when La Chalotais was told that Aiguillon had covered himself with glory noted that he had likely also covered himself with flour. The column that commemorates the action is quite simple, and finished off with a French greyhound trampling the British leopard.

South from St Cast there is a good beach at Pen-Guen, and then the road heads into **Le Guildo**, a picturesque village set on a very pretty part of the thin estuary of the Arguenon river. The village is domi- nated by the ruins of the fifteenth-century castle of Gilles de Bretagne, son of Jean V, Duke of Brittany and a cousin of Henry VI of England. Gilles was a poet and a noted Anglophile having spent his childhood in England. At a time when France was in conflict with England, and Gille's brother François, who had become Duke of Brittany after their father's death, was allied to the French cause, Gilles continued to correspond with his English cousin, passing several letters across the Channel. This was discovered and François had no choice but to arrest his brother. Gilles was taken to Moncontour where he was murdered. It is not clear whether François had any part in the murder, but he was overwhelmed by grief and guilt, and died soon after.

The Arguenon estuary's eastern edge is defined by a finger of land that ends at the Pointe du Chevet a good viewpoint: look for the poles erected in the estuary — these are artificial mussel beds. On this spit of land is **St Jacut-de-la-Mer** noted for being surrounded by eleven fine beaches. Another good viewpoint, and a very interesting one, is offered by the Château d'Eau, a somewhat elaborately named water tower at **Ploubalay**. The tower has a circular viewing terrace over 100m (328ft) high from which, on clear days, Mont St-Michel can be seen. More locally, the Fremur river can be seen, the border between Côtes d'Armor and the neighbouring *département* of Ille-et-Vilaine. The visitor crosses the river and border at **Lancieux**, another village

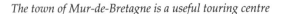

The town of Mur-de-Bretagne is a useful touring centre

with a good beach, one with firm sands and a view of the off-shore Ile Ebihens.

The Inland Département

As the N12 is being used as an arbitrary border between coastal and inland Côtes d'Armor, this tour begins with the exploration of the *argoat* at **Belle-Isle-en-Terre** a town that is now bypassed by the road. Close to the town, an old and pretty place set where two rivers meet, is **Locmaria** where the chapel has a superb sixteenth-century rood screen decorated with painted figures. At the Fête de Locmaria, held on the third Sunday in July (and now held at the larger venue of Belle-Isle-en-Terre) a Breton wrestling championship is held. The wrestlers wear a strange outfit of long shorts and loose shirts and

Exploration inland of the argoat *leads to the discovery of many picturesque places*

after exchanging three loud kisses attempt to put one another on to the mat. To the east, and also just a little way north of the N12, is Ménez-Bré, an isolated peak rising to 302m (991ft), which makes it the highest point in northern Brittany. It is topped by a chapel dedicated to St Hervé, a saint who was born blind because his mother prayed that he should never see the cruelty and deception that was rife in the world. The answer to her prayers seems to be just as cruel, but Hervé used his blindness to his advantage, becoming a poet and monk with an ability to 'see' into people's souls. It is said that he had a wolf on a lead that acted as a guide dog, and became the patron saint of Bretons who were depressed or suffering from irrational fears, a local belief being that such problems were brought about by seeing a werewolf. From the chapel the view is expansive, taking in the Monts d'Arrée, Cornouaille and the river valleys of the Trieux, Jaudy and Léguer.

South of Belle-Isle-en-Terre are the forests of Coat an Noz and Coat an Hay, the Night Wood and the Day Wood. These fine woodlands, which are crossed by pathways, GR341 crosses the woods from east to west, and ideal for picnics, probably have Druidic names. It is known that twins held a special position in Druidic thinking, and woods were equally special as the Druidic rites were carried out in oak groves. The idea of twin woods is likely, therefore, to have been particularly appealing. Quite why they are named for night and day is a mystery. At the western edge of Coat an Noz is **Loc-Envel** a very pretty village whose chapel has another beautifully decorated rood screen, together with some excellent panelling. As another twin, there is an equally pretty village, at the eastern edge of Coat an Hay. **Gurunhuel**'s church is also interesting for its sixteenth-century Calvary. Note, especially, the thieves on the crosses each side of Christ whose souls are depicted as figures leaving their bodies, and being met by angels.

South from Gurunhuel is **Bulat-Pestivien**, a real gem of a village whose church has an impressive spire. A *pardon* is held to the church on the first Sunday after 8 September. There are three sacred fountains in the village, a clear link with the Druidic and early Christian heritage of the area. Two of the fountains can be found beside the road to **Callac**, a village that claims to be the original home of the Breton spaniel, a form of pointer. Today the village is more famous for its racehorse stud farm outside which stands a bronze of one of the stud's more famous horses. To the west, at **Plourac'h** those interested in Breton costume will find a visit to the church interesting as one of several fine statues housed there is a Deposition in which the Virgin Mary is wearing a traditional Breton mourning cloak.

South of Bulat-Pestivien an upthrust of Brittany's rocky backbone forms a wide semi-circular ridge, the northern flank of which is heavily and delightfully wooded. At two points rivers draining down from this ridge have created impressive gorges, one of which is followed by one of the French GR's. To the west is the Gorges du Coronc, reached by a long walk, allow 30 minutes each way, that is superb all the way. The river, a tributary of l'Hyere that flows past Carhaix-Plouguer, flows sometimes under, sometimes over huge piles of boulders, occasionally appearing or disappearing as a spectacular short falls. To add an extra dimension, the gorge is also deeply wooded. Towards the centre of the semi-circle of high ridge, close to the hamlet of Trémargat, is the Gorges du Toul Goulic, through which runs the River Blavet. GR341 follows the gorge and is a fine walk. For about 400m (440yd) the river flows underground, but can be heard crashing along under the moss-covered boulder heaps of the valley floor. Some of the individual boulders are huge, and it is believed that they may have been used as shelters by Stone Age Bretons. South-west of Toul Goulic there is another fine gorge, the Gorges du Daoulas. But before visiting that one we go west to **Kergrist-Moëlou**, set on top the semi-circular ridge, where there is a superb Calvary with around 100 figures in blue granite. Sadly, the figures were damaged during a local outbreak of Revolutionary fervour, and the re-instatement seems to have owed more to enthusiasm than to artistic excellence. Nearby, at **St Nicolas-du-Pélem**, the chapel has a carillon bell which is rung by those who wish to attract the attention of the saints before their prayers. Just to the east of St Nicolas is **Corlay**, famous throughout France for its horse breeding and racing. Within the town there are the the ruins of a twelfth-century castle, and, in the town hall, a Museum of the Horse, with exhibitions on the evolution of the horse and Corlay's races, together with a collection of horse-drawn carriages.

South from Kergrist is **Rostrenen** a beautiful little town set on a hill from the top of which, near the weather station, there is a fine view of the unwooded, southern flank of the semi-circular ridge. The town church is the chapel of a former castle built in the fourteenth century but destroyed by fire in the late sixteenth century. Nearby is another sacred fountain. A little way south of the town is one of the most interesting stretches of the Nantes-Brest canal. Here the canal reaches a high point on its journey, and the towpath can be followed westward for a view of the forty-four locks that took barges down to Carhaix-Plouguer. Considering that the canals and locks were constructed around 1830, that is when all work was by hand, the engineering is monumental.

The N164 bypasses Rostrenen, but is easily reached and can then be followed to **Lac de Guerlédan** and Mur-de-Bretagne. This is one of the finest sections of *argoat* now remaining in central Brittany, the trees set off beautifully by the waters of the lake. The lake is a reservoir created by the construction of the huge *barrage* (dam) at its south-eastern tip. The flooding of the valley has created numerous watery arms among the trees, and a path traces out this sinuous shoreline, crossing into and out of Morbihan, for total of 48km (30 miles). That is too far for a quiet stroll, but a section of it is really worthwhile. The lazier way of seeing the lake is to hop on a boat tour at Beau Rivage near Caurel. The more energetic can hire a canoe in **Mur-de-Bretagne**, a lively little town that is a useful touring centre. Close to Mur are **St Aignon**, to the south, where the twelfth-century church houses a carved wood tree of Jesse, and **St Gilles-Vieux-Marche**. This superb village, alive with flowers in summer, lies at the end of the very picturesque Poulancre Valley.

Lake Guerlédan is fed by the beautiful River Blavet. About 3km (2 miles) upstream of the lake, the Blavet is joined by the Daoulas which has flowed through the **Gorges du Daoulas**, arguably the finest of the three gorges. In the gorge the Daoulas is fast-moving, the rock scenery being ledges and spikey pinnacles rather than boulders, the greenery big shrubs rather than trees. Close to the confluence of the Daoulas and Blavet is the twelfth-century Cistercian abbey of Bon-Repos. As elsewhere, the Cistercians chose a wild, but beautiful, spot for their abbey which was huge.

Guingamp, where it is said gingham cloth first originated, lies close to the N12, a road which not only divides the *département* in two, but very roughly traces the dividing line between the *armor* and the *argoat*. Despite this auspicious position, however, the visitor will find that Guingamp is a modern light-industrial, rather than a medieval, Breton town, although the centre, with its imposing grey buildings is still attractive. Most imposing are the ruins of the old town castle and ramparts, built in the fifteenth century, which can be seen beside Place du Valley, with a section running beside the church, and another section close to Place St Sauveur, to the north. The town hall, in Place de Verdun, is also very solid. It is more properly called the Hôtel-Dieu, and was once the town hospital. When it was built, in the late seventeenth century, it was a Hospitalers monastery, and the cloisters and chapel (in Italian style) and other parts can be visited. The great hall houses a permanent exhibition of work by the Pont-Aven school of painters.

Close to the town hall is the Basilica of Notre-Dame-de-Bon-Secours an excellent, and interesting, fourteenth-century church.

When first constructed the church was in the Gothic style appropriate to its date, but 200 years later, after the south tower had collapsed, demolishing the southern section of the nave but, thankfully, causing no injuries, it was rebuilt in Renaissance style. Inside the church there is a famous Black Virgin. The first Black Virgin is believed to have brought back from the Middle East by returning Crusaders and rapidly became very popular in France. The statues are carved in cedar or other dark woods which age to a dark brown or black. The Guingamp statue has been the object of processions in the town since very early times, and today thousands attend a *pardon* to the church on the first Sunday in July. On the preceding Saturday there is a torch-light procession and the *pardon* is followed by bonfires in the Place du Centre. Later in the year, usually during the second week of July, Guingamp holds the festival of the Danse du Loup (Wolf Dance). It is said that the origins of the dance was a rhythmic stamping that shepherds evolved to keep wolves at bay. From this a music-less, stamping dance evolved. Examples can be seen at the festival, though this has now expanded to include many forms of traditional dance and music.

Close to Guingamp is the little town of **Grâces** whose church was originally a pilgrim chapel. Inside, the wood carvings depict hunting scenes and monsters, and a somewhat comical, but instructive, view of the perils of drink. The church also houses a wooden reliquary containing the remains of Charles de Blois who was killed at the Battle of Auray. Close by, at **Bourbriac**, the town church also contains a reliquary, in this case of the Merovingian St Briac. The reliquary was visited by those suffering from epilepsy.

East of Bourbriac lies delightful country, pretty villages and hamlets set among remnant patches of *argoat* woodland. A fine section of woods, the Bois d'Avaugour stands close to the village of **Avaugour**, whose chapel has some excellent wood carvings. Further east, the Bois Meur is a bigger stretch of wood. South lie the villages of Plasidy, Senven-Lehart, St Gildas and Vieux-Bourg, each of which is worth seeing before the small town of Quintin is reached.

Quintin is quite charming, its houses rising in terraces from the picturesque Gouét river, the whole set off by remnants of the medieval town walls. The best section of the old walls is that which includes the fifteenth-century Porte Neuve. In medieval, and later, times the town was famous for the weaving of linen and the making of veils, chiefly for woman's hats. One of Quintin's best markets for the veils was America. It is said that at the time of the Revolution there were 30,000 workers in the industries, a remarkable number as it is almost ten times the population of Quintin today and, since some of the weavers would have had children, actually implies a population even larger. Perhaps the number of 'outworkers', those who worked in their own homes in local villages, was included. Even if that is assumed, the effect of the industry's crash, which followed the Revolution, can be envisaged. Some of the houses of the linen merchants still remain, the best of them, superb half-timbered, overhung houses, can be seen in Place 1830, Place du Martray and in the roads that lead off from them.

The Château de Quintin is, in fact, two castles on one site, the remnants of a seventeenth-century building standing close to an elegant eighteenth-century house. The newer, complete, building is open to visitors, its room being, in part, a museum with exhibits on the town's history, including a collection of locally made linen, a collection of fans and some chinaware. Those rooms that are not part of the museum are equally interesting for the glimpse they offer of the gentle life in the eighteenth-century Brittany. Note, especially, the kitchen with an unusual granite oven which has holes for the warming of plates.

The town church is a century newer than the castle, but it houses items that are far older and, in one case, priceless. In the thirteenth century Geoffrey, the Lord of Quintin, travelled to the Holy Land as a Crusader, returning with a piece of the Virgin's girdle which he had acquired in Jerusalem. Not surprisingly, the piece has pride of place in the church, and draws childless women from all over Brittany who came to pray in its presence in the hope of being made fertile. The efficiency of the prayers is perhaps reflected in the statue of Our Lady of Safe Delivery, a statue to which expectant mothers pray in the hope of problem-free childbirth.

Close to Quintin are two more interesting castles. To the south is the **Château de Robien**, the third building on the same site and with remnants of the earliest chapel, dating from the fourteenth century, standing close to the present eighteenth century château. The castle is not open to the public, but its parkland can be visited. It offers fine walking and good views. Finally, go north-west to Le Leslay to see the **Château de Beaumanoir,** a still occupied castle that has often been used as a film set, most notable by Roman Polanski in the filming of *Tess*. A guided tour includes the castle interior, where there is a collection modern art, and the outbuildings where the film can be seen in the stables.

South-east from Quintin is **Loudéac**, a market town famous for its animal fairs and for for the racecourse which lies to the south on the Pontivy (D700) road. Race meetings are held at Easter and late May / early June. A few miles south-east of Loudéac is **La Chèze**, a village with the remnants of a thirteenth-century castle and one of Brittany's most impressive craft centres. The Centre Cultural des Métiers de Bretagne specialises in the county crafts of old Brittany with a saddle-maker, blacksmith, slate cutter, clay pipe maker and so on. There are also exhibits that illustrate other aspects of Breton culture.

Moncontour is built on the spur of a high ridge, a naturally defensive position that was fortified from the eleventh century, some of the old ramparts remaining, the last surviving section despite an order from Cardinal Richelieu in 1626 that they were to be destroyed. Within the walls there is a maze of narrow alleys and stepped paths between the houses, most of which are of granite though there are also a few half-timbered buildings. At a high point in the town is the church, to St Mathurin, which has some excellent sixteenth-century stained glass windows. On another high point to the north is the Château des Granges, a medieval castle rebuilt in the early nine-teenth century.

Close to the town are two very interesting places. To the south, near **Trédaniel** is the chapel of Notre-Dame-du-Haut which has painted wood statues of seven Breton healing saints, all posing so as to depict their particular ailment: St Mamert holds his intestines out for approval — he cures colic and other digestive difficulties; St Yvertin holds his head — he cures headaches and migraines; St Leobinus cures rheumatism and eyes problems; Ste Eugenia, the only female saint, also cures headaches, but helps women with the pains of childbirth; St Hubert assists with dog bites; St Méen helps with nervous disorders and St Houarniaule offers help with irra-tional fears.

To visit the second spot, the **Château de la Touche-Trébry**, go east from Moncontour. The castle, which is set among trees beside a small lake, was built in the sixteenth century, but to a much earlier design, looking very medieval with its domed turrets, courtyard and walls. The walls were more decorative than practical, they, and the towers that protect the entrance, being an indication of the importance of the Governor of Moncontour whose castle it was.

Heading north from Moncontour the visitor passes through fine country where, occasionally, huge clumps of mistletoe (a plant sacred to the Druids), can be seen in the poplars at the roadside. The road heads directly for **Lamballe** where the Tourist Information Office is housed in the Maison du Bourreau, the Executioner's House. Previous clients did not, presumably, approach with the same enthusiasm as today's visitor. The house, a fifteenth-century half-timbered building that is extremely attractive, is also home to two museums. The Musée du Vieux Lamballe et du Penthièvre on the ground floor, has prints of old Lamballe, local costumes and arts and some local pottery. The Musée Matherin Méheut, on the first floor has a collection of paintings by Méheut, a local artist who died in 1958, and some items of local Breton culture.

The Executioner's House stands in Place du Martray where there are other equally picturesque houses, some that were standing in 1591 during the Wars of Religion, when Lamballe was the stronghold of the Catholic Duke of Penthièvre, and was besieged by a Protestant force under the command of Captain La Noué. La Noué was known as Bras de Fer because he wore a metal contraption finished off with a hook to replace an arm he had lost in an earlier conflict. During the siege he was wounded and died soon after at Moncontour. King Henry IV, when told of the news was distraught claiming that Bras de Fer was worth an army, and should not have died for so small a castle. Ironically, the castle itself did not survive long, being destroyed on Richelieu's orders just thirty-five years later. Almost exactly 150 years later the son of a later Duke of Penthièvre was giving his father grey hairs with his debauched lifestyle. The duke, anxious to slow the lad down, married him to an attractive Italian princess. This clearly failed to work, the boy, who was only twenty, dying of excess within a matter of weeks. The

In Brittany a variety of quality cheeses can be bought at the fromagerie

young widow was presented at Court a little later, and became a lady-in-waiting to Marie Antoinette. She served loyally until the Revolution when she was brutally beheaded by the Paris mob, her head being displayed on a pole. The Queen she had served so well outlived her by a mere twelve months.

Lamballe is a charming town, and for a good view of it the visitor should climb to the hill-top church of Notre-Dame-de-Grande-Puissance, a fine Gothic building with a southern terrace that over-looks the town and the valley of the River Gouessant. Finally, those interested in horses should visit the French National Stud, one of the country's largest stud farms with around 150 breeding stallions, with Trait Breton draught horses as well as race animals. Guided tours only are allowed, these including visits to the blacksmith's

A shopping street in Lamballe

forge and harness rooms. There is also a riding school that specialises in dressage.

To the east of Lamballe is a fine, large piece of woodland named for the castle that stands at its eastern edge, the **Château de la Hunaudaye**. Though it is ruinous, Hunaudaye is still remarkably impressive. It stands among the last of the trees and is almost completely surrounded by a moat. It was built in the early thirteenth century, partially destroyed in the War of Succession, rebuilt, but partially destroyed again during the Revolution. Thereafter it was used as a handy quarry by the locals until it was bought and stabilised by the French Government. Entry is by fixed bridge, but at the point where the drawbridge once crossed the moat, and a gateway between the keep (to the left) and the chapel tower. Beyond is the courtyard. To the left now are the kitchens, below the Black Tower, and the sixteenth-century manor house built against the curtain wall and with a superb Renaissance stairway. Beyond, the Glacière Tower (which acquired its name because it faces north and so was a little chilly in winter) can be climbed for the best view of the building. The last tower, the Manorial Keep, is the best preserved of the five towers and also offers a fine view of the castle and moat.

To the south of the castle, near the village of **Le St Esprit**, is the Ferme d'Anton de St Esprit-des-Lois, a farm restored in nineteenth-century Breton style. The old farmhouse is authentically furnished and has a fine bread oven, while outside the outbuildings, stables, cart sheds etc, are furnished with period farm implements.

To the east of Hunaudaye is the ribbon lake/reservoir of the Arguenon. To the south another reservoir fills the valleys where the Rosette and Rieule rivers join the Arguenon. This is the Jugon Lake, covering 67 hectares (166 acres), and beside it stands the town of **Jugon-les-Lacs**, a fishing and sailing centre with numerous elegant houses and a fine church. A seventeenth-century fortified mansion anchored firmly on a rock gives the name to Rue de Château, one of the most interesting streets.

To the south-east of Jugon are the last villages of Côtes d'Armor, the visitor soon reaching Ille-et-Vilaine. To the north-east that *département* is reached even sooner, with the 'outpost' around Dinard (which lies to the west of the Rance) lying only a few miles from Corseul. **Corseul** has a long history, as a visit to the town museum, housed on the second floor of the Town Hall, will show. Here there are items, excavated locally, from the Celtic, Gaullish and Roman periods. The town's name derives from a local Celtic tribe. Elsewhere, there are the remains of a Roman villa in Clos Mulon, and an inscribed stele in the church. The inscription is to Silicia, the mother

of a Roman officer, who died in the town. The most interesting
Roman find is the so-called Temple of Mars at Haut-Bécherel a little
way along the D794 towards Dinan. Beyond the temple it is an easy
trip into Dinan.

Dinan is the highlight of a tour of Côtes d'Armor, a beautiful old
town with medieval fortifications, late medieval houses and numerous sites with interesting tales to tell. It is a difficult place to drive and
park in, but the old town, within the medieval walls, is quite compact
and can be comfortable visited in one walk. Most visitors will park
in Place du Guesclin or in the parks beside the Promenade des Petits
Fossés or the Château close by. This tour will therefore start in the
Place du Guesdin.

The Place du Guesdin, together with the adjacent Place du Champ
Clos, is still a market-place as it was in medieval Dinan, but then it
was not a statue of Bertrand du Guesclin, mounted on a horse, but the
real man who would have been seen here, de Guesclin having been
born in Dinan in 1320.

From the Place take Rue Ste-Claire and turn left into Rue de
l'Horloge, named for the Clock Tower that stands at its far end. To the
right here is the granite-pillared Hôtel Kératry (the Tourist Information Office). To the left is the Maison du Gisant (the House of the
Recumbent Figure). When the house was being restored the recumbent figure of the name, dating from the fourteenth century and now
on show outside, was found. Opposite the Maison an alley leads off
to the town church, but before going that way walk along to the Clock
Tower. The clock of the name dates from 1498, the bell being a gift
from the Duchess Anne a few years later. The duchess was fond of
Dinan and often spent time here. The Clock Tower can be climbed,
and offers a splendid view of the old town. It is said that below the
tower the most famous incident in Dinan's history took place.
During the War of Succession Bertrand du Guesclin held Dinan
against an English force under the Duke of Lancaster. After some
time, during which du Guesclin's men were several times routed by
the English when they tried to break out, Bertrand proposed to
Lancaster that there should be a forty day truce. If by its end Dinan
had not been relieved then du Guesclin would surrender it to the
English. Lancaster accepted, and peace descended on the area.
Taking advantage of this Bertrand's brother, Olivier, went out of the
town and was promptly seized by Sir Thomas Canterbury who
demanded a 100 *florin* ransom for his return. Bertrand was appalled
by this unchivalrous act and challenged Canterbury to single combat. The duel took place near the Clock Tower, though a stone in
Place du Champ Clos claims that the duel was fought a little further

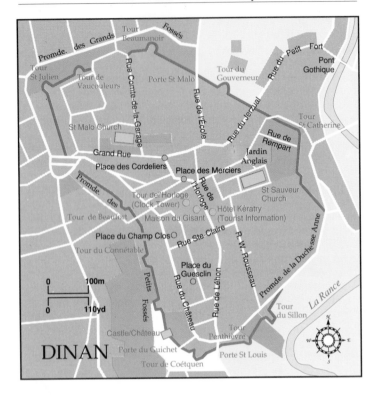

DINAN

to the west. Bertrand beat Canterbury, the Englishmen being ordered, by Lancaster, to hand back Olivier and to pay a 100 *florin* fine to the du Guesclins. Bertrand's chivalry had a second reward, a local girl Tiphaine Raguenel, falling in love with him. By all accounts Bertrand was ugly, Tiphaine beautiful, but despite that the marriage was successful and long lasting.

The basilica of St Sauveur reached from the Clock Tower is in a mix of Romanesque and Gothic styles, its earliest parts dating from the twelfth century. Inside, a fifteenth-century cenotaph holds the heart of Bertrand du Guesclin. After the siege of Dinan Bertrand fought at the Battle of Auray where he was knocked from his horse. An English knight persuaded him to surrender, suggesting that though he had lost the day another would come. It did: Bertrand was ransomed and fought valiantly for the French king rising to the rank of Constable (commander-in-chief) before dying of natural causes while besieg-

ing the English in the Massif Central. Bertrand's dying request was
to be returned to Dinan so a convoy set off for Brittany. It was a slow
convoy, and by the time it reached Le Puy-en-Velay something
needed to be done with the body. It was therefore disembowelled,

Dinan is the main attraction of a tour around the Côtes d'Armor

the innards being buried at Le Puy, and embalmed. The embalming failed however, and by the time Montferrand was reached firm action was needed. The body was boiled and bones were carried on towards Dinan. Next, at Le Mans, a message arrived from the king that Bertrand was to be buried in Paris. The bones were therefore shipped off to the capital while the heart alone was returned to Dinan. As a result of this saga Bertrand now lies in four different places in France.

To the east of the church is the Jardin Anglais, a fine garden on top of an old cemetery. From it, or the nearby St Catherine's Tower on the town ramparts, the views of the town and Rance valley are superb. In view are the Pont Gothique over the Rance and the imposing viaduct. From the garden the visitor can go south along the Promenade de la Duchesse Anne which follows the south-eastern section of the old wall, but the better walk is to follow Rue du Rempart to Rue Haute-Voie. Go right to Rue Michel, then left down steps to reach the Porte du Jerzual which was the most important of the old town's four gates. Turn right along Rue du Petit Fort (away from the gate) to reach the Maison du Gouverneur (Governor's House, at number 24) a superb fifteenth-century house, now a weaving and tapestry centre.

Return to the Porte du Jerzual, going through to Rue du Jerzual, arguably Dinan's finest street. This was once the town's main trading street so it is appropriate that it has been re-colonised by craftsmen. Turn right into Rue de l'École to reach Porte St Malo and the Promenade des Grands Fossés which follows the northern town wall. Do not walk beyond the Tour de Vaucouleurs, turning back into the town to reach the church of St Malo, a fifteenth-century building in Flamboyant Gothic style with a rare English organ (a French national monument) and twentieth-century stained glass windows giving the history of the town. To the east of the church is a fifteenth-century Franciscan monastery, now a school.

Take Grande-Rue from the church to reach Place des Cordeliers. To the left here is Rue de la Lainerie one of several fine streets that is named for an ancient trade. Ahead are Place des Merciers and Rue de l'Apport. Here three quite distinct types of house can be seen: casement houses have large windows built by ship's carpenters — they look like the sterns of sailing ships and could be used as shop fronts; houses *à porche* have the upper storey supported on granite or wooden pillars, the pillars forming arcades over the street; and the overhung houses characteristic of the fifteenth century. The streets that lead off from Place des Merciers are equally good, perhaps the best being Rue de la Cordonnerie which leads to Rue du Château and the western town wall. Beyond the wall is the Promenade des Petits Fossés which can be followed to the castle. The castle took more than two centuries to build, the oldest sections being the Guichet Gate and the keep, the latter being called the dungeon (from *donjon*, French for keep), of Duchess Anne, commemorating her stay here in 1507. The keep, which is tall, but oval rather than circular, now houses the town museum with displays on Dinan's history, local costume, including a collection of *coiffes*, and furnishings.

To the south of Dinan is **Léhon**, a village which can be reached by a walk across fields. Here stand the ruins of a medieval castle and the Prieuré de St Magloire a monastery founded in the nineth century, though the present building dates from the twelfth century, the earlier one having been destroyed by Viking raiders. The abbey church still stands, and houses an effigy of Tiphaine, Bertrand du Guesclin's wife, who is shown in full armour, a costume she is unlikely to have worn when alive. Beside the church are the ruinous, but still magnificent, seventeenth-century cloisters. The abbey's refectory has been carefully restored to its thirteenth-century glory, and nearby a small museum displays the best finds from excavations of the site. Interestingly, the excavations revealed that the abbey was connected to the Rance by a covered canal, and the remains of this can be seen in the abbey's very pretty gardens.

Nearby, at **Le St Esprit**, there is a tall cross, nearly 8m (26ft) high, erected by John of Gaunt during a siege of Dinan. The cross supports statues of God holding Jesus aloft, and the Virgin.

On the north side of Dinan, near **Taden** are the ruins of an old castle, and the far older menhir of La Tiemblaye which is one of the best examples in Brittany of an inscribed stone.

Finally in Côtes d'Armor, cross the Rance, visiting **Lanvallay** from where there is a superb view of Dinan, and **Pleudihen-sur-Rance** where there is a cider museum housed in an old farm. In part, the museum is outdoor, the farm's orchards being planted with the different apple varieties that are mixed to give distinctive tastes. The tour of the site usually ends with a cider tasting.

Additional Information

Places to Visit

Beaumanoir Castle
Open: July, August daily except Tuesday 2-7pm. Guided tours only of interior and outbuildings.
☎ 96 749082

Beauport Abbey
Open: mid-June to mid-September daily 9am-12.30pm, 2-7pm. Mid-September to mid-June by appointment only. Guided tours available.
☎ 96 208159

Bégard
Armoripark
Open: all year Saturday, Sunday, Monday, Tuesday, Thursday 12.30-7pm. Wednesday 2-6pm. Friday 4-7pm.
☎ 96 453636

Binic
Museum
Open: Easter, mid-June to mid-September daily 2.30-6.30pm. At other times by appointment.
☎ 96 737648

Bon Repos Abbey
Undergoing restoration at time of writing. Enquire at abbey for opening times or ask at Tourist Information Office at Mûr-de Bretagne.
☎ 96 285141

Cap Fréhel
Lighthouse
Open: May to October daily, but hours variable because of keepers' duties. Guided tours only.

Boat Trips
These operate between Cap Fréhel and Dinard/St Malo during the summer months. Details from Cie Emeraude, Gare Maritime, St Malo.
☎ 99 404840

Corlay
Museum of the Horse
Open: July, August daily 11am-12.30pm, 3-7pm. September to June by request.
☎ 96 294041

Corseul
Museum
Open: July, August daily 9am-12noon, 2-5.30pm. September to June, Monday to Friday 8.30am-12noon, 2-5pm. Saturday 8.30am-12noon.
☎ 96 279017

Dinan
Clock Tower
Open: July, August daily except Sunday 10.30-11.30am, 3-7pm.
☎ 96 397540

Castle
Open: June to mid-October daily 10am-12noon, 2-6pm. Mid-March to May and mid-October to mid-November daily 1.30-5.30pm. Mid-November to December, February to mid-March daily except Tuesday 1.30-5.30pm. Closed January.
☎ 96 394520

Post Office and Telecommunications
Promenade des Petits Fossés
Market Days: Thursday and Saturday.

Fort la Latte
Open: June to September daily
10.30am-12.30pm, 2.30-6.30pm.
May Saturday, Sunday 10.30am-
12.30pm, 2.30-6.30pm.
At other times by appointment.
☎ 96 414031

Guingamp
Town Hall
Open: all year, daily 10am-12noon,
2-5pm, but can be varied according
to requirements of working day or
town hall officials.
Ask at the Tourist Information
Office (☎ 96 437389)

Hunaudaye Castle
Open: July, August daily 10am-
1pm, 3-7pm. Easter to June,
September Sundays 3-7pm.
☎ 96 341847

Ile de Bréhat
Reached by boat from Pointe de
l'Arcouest in about 10 minutes, and
on longer trips (about 1½ hours)
from Binic, St Quay-Portrieux and
Erquy. All trips are dependent on
the tides, but the following timings
give a good general guide.

Pointe de l'Arcouest
April to September daily every
hour between 8.30am-7.30pm.
Mid-February to March, October
daily every hour between 8.30am-
6.30pm. January to mid-February,
November, December daily every
hour between 8.30am-5.30pm.

Binic, St Quay-Portrieux, Erquy
July, August One trip weekly.
Boat trips from Bréhat to the Trieux
estuary and Château de la Roche-
Jagu, and around the island mid-

June to mid-September daily.
For information on all trips:
☎ 96 200011, 96 200066 or 96 204598

Ile de Grande
Ornithological Centre
Open: July, August daily 10am-
1pm, 2.30-7pm. June, September
daily except Monday 10am-
12noon, 2.30-6.30pm. October to
May Wednesday, Saturday,
Sunday 2.30-6.30pm.
☎ 96 919140

Jugon-les-Lacs
St Esprit-des-Lois Farm
Open: July, August daily 10am-
12noon, 2-7pm. May, June,
September to mid-October Sunday
2-7pm.
☎ 96 341467

Kerfons Chapel
Open: July, August daily 10am-
12noon, 2-6pm.
☎ 96 471551

Kergrist Castle
Castle and Gardens
Open: June Saturday, Sunday 2-6pm.
July to September daily 2-6pm.
Guided tours lasting 30 minutes only.
☎ 96 389144

La Chèze
Craft Centre
Open: July, August daily 10am-
12noon, 2-6pm. June and September daily 2-6pm. October to May by
appointment only.
☎ 96 266316

La Touche-Trébry Castle
Open: July, August daily except
Sunday 2.30-6.30pm.
Guided tours available.
☎ 96 427855

Lac de Guerlédan

Boat Tours
Open: July to mid-September daily.
1½ hour and 3 hour lunch or dinner
cruises available in glass-topped
boats. Information of times from the
Beau Rivage land stage near Caurel.
☎ 96 285264 or 96 285225

Lamballe

Town Museum
Open: July, August daily 9.30am-
12noon, 2.30-6.30pm. Mid to end
June, early September daily 10am-
12noon, 2.30-6pm.
☎ 96 310538

Mathurin Méheut Museum
Open: June to September daily
except Sunday 10am-12noon, 2.30-
6pm. Also open at Christmas and
Easter.
☎ 96 311999

National Stud
Open: all year, daily 9am-5pm.
Note that most of the stallions are
away from the stud between March
and mid-July.
☎ 96 310040

Lanvellec

Rosanbo Castle
Open: July, August daily 10.30am-
6.30pm. April to June and September daily 2-6pm.
☎ 96 351877

Léhon

St Magloire's Priory
Open: July to September daily 3-
6pm. Guided tours available.
☎ 96 851475

Les Sept Iles

Open: mid-March to September
daily, but times according to tides.
Three hour tour which stops only

on Monks' Island. The lighthouse is
open as follows: mid-June to mid-
September 10am-12noon, 3-6pm.
☎ 96 201014

Paimpol

Sea Museum
Open: Easter and July to mid-
September daily 10am-12noon, 3-7pm.
☎ 96 208015

The Mad Atao
Open: June to August daily 2-8pm.

Costume Museum
Open: July, August daily 10am-
12noon, 2-6pm. September to June
by appointment only.
☎ 96 208316

Sea Mill
Open: weeks including Good
Friday and Easter Monday daily
10am-12noon, 2.30-6pm. July to
mid-September Wednesday to
Sunday 10am-12noon, 2.30-6pm.
☎ 96 221408

Pléneuf-Val-André

Bien Assis Castle
Open: mid-June to mid-September
Monday to Saturday 10.30am-
12.30pm, 2-6.30pm. Sunday 2-
6.30pm. April to mid-June, mid to
end September Sunday only 2-
6.30pm.
☎ 96 722203

Pleubian

Seaweed Centre
Open: July, August Tuesday to
Thursday 2-3.30pm.

Pleudihen-sur-Rance

Cider Museum
Open: June to August daily 10am-
12noon, 2-7pm. April, May and
September daily 2-7pm.
☎ 96 832078

Pleumeur-Bodou

CNET TV/Radar Dome
Open: July, August daily 9am-
12noon, 1.45-6pm. September to
mid-October, April to June daily
except Saturday 9-11am, 2-4.45pm.
Guided tours lasting 1 hour only.
☎ 96 484149

Trégor Planetarium
Open: mid-June to mid-September
daily 11am-12.30pm, 2pm-6.30pm.
Shows at 11am, 2.30, 4.15 and 6pm.
Mid-September to mid-June daily
except Monday 10am-12.30pm, 2-
6pm. Shows at 10.30am and 3pm
on Tuesday, Thursday and Friday
and at 3pm and 4.30pm on
Wednesday, Saturday and Sunday.
☎ 96 918378

Ploubalay

Water Tower
Open: April, May, September
Wednesday to Friday 10am-7pm.
Saturday, Sunday 10am-2pm.
June to August daily 10am-dusk.

Pontrieux

Roche-Jagu Castle
Open: Easter to October daily
10am-12noon, 2-6pm (2-7pm in
July). November to Easter by
appointment only.
☎ 96 956235

Quintin

Castle
Open: June to October daily 10am-
7pm. Mid-March to May daily
except Tuesday 10am-12noon, 2-5pm.
☎ 96 749479

Robien

Castle
Open: park only April to August
daily 10am-6pm.

St Brieuc

Museum
Open: all year daily except
Monday 9.30-11.45am, 1.30-5.45pm.
☎ 96 333912

Tonquédoc Castle

Open: July, August daily 10am-
7pm. September to June by
appointment only.
☎ 96 471863

Trégastel-Plage

Sea Aquarium
Open: July, August daily 9am-8pm.
Easter to June, September daily
10am-12noon, 2-5pm. October to
Easter school holidays only 2-5pm.

Trégomeur

Moulin de Richard Zoo
Open: mid-April to September
daily 10am-7pm. October to mid-
April daily 2pm-dusk.
☎ 96 790107

Tréguier

Cathedral Cloisters and Treasury
Cloisters open: July, August daily
9.30am-6.30pm. September to June
daily 9.30-11.30am, 2.30-6.30pm.
Treasury open: June to September
daily 9am-7pm.

Renan Museum
Open: Easter to September daily
10am-12noon, 2-6pm.
☎ 96 924563

Tourist Information Centres

Comité Départemental du
Tourisme des Côtes d'Armor
29 Rue des Promenades
BP 620
22011 St Brieuc
☎ 96 627222

Ile de Bréhat
Le Bourg
22870
☎ 96 200415

Dinan
6 Rue l'Horloge
22100
☎ 96 397540

Guingamp
2 Place Vally
22200
☎ 96 437389

Lamballe
Place Martray
22400
☎ 96 310538

Lannion
Quai d'Aiguillon
22300
☎ 96 370735

Mur-de-Bretagne
Place l'Église
22530
☎ 96 285141

Paimpol
Rue Feutren
22500
☎ 96 208316

Perros-Guirec
21 Place Hôtel-de-Ville
22700
☎ 96 232115

Quintin
Place du Martray
22800
☎ 96 740151

St Brieuc
7 Rue St-Gouéno
22000
☎ 96 333250

Tréguier
Place du Martray
22220
☎ 96 923019

3

MORBIHAN

Morbihan, the only one of the four *départements* of Brittany to have a Breton name, is gentler than the two previous *départements*, the coastline having fewer cliffs and more beaches, the climate being a little warmer, a little sunnier, and less windy. In addition, Morbihan has a remarkable collection of megalithic sites, not only the best collection in Brittany, but the best in Europe. It also has fine castles, with those at Josselin, Elven and Vannes being among the best in the province, not only for their architecture but also for their wealth of historical interest. As well as having a fine castle Vannes also has an array of beautiful houses which makes a walk around it a fascinating tour. Finally, Morbihan has the Gulf for which it is named, a huge, circular saltwater lagoon virtually cut off from the sea. The Gulf is surrounded by places of interest, has safe beaches, offers exciting boat trips, and its collection of shorebirds makes it a must for the birdwatcher.

As with Côtes d'Armor the *département*'s coastline shall be explored before moving inland, using the N165 road as the border between the two areas.

The Atlantic Coast

Crossing the Laïta from Finistère to Morbihan the visitor can follow the coast closely around the Anse du Pouldu and the Pointe du Talut to reach **Larmor-Plage**, an excellent resort with good beaches and fine views across the River Blavet. The church at the resort is of interest for its artwork, especially a fine sixteenth-century stone *Pietà* and an altarpiece of the same date with around forty Calvary figures. At a service in the church on the Sunday closest to 24 June the water between the town and the Ile de Groix, a channel known locally as the Coureaux, is blessed. In another interesting tradition, any warship leaving Lorient fires a salute of three guns when it is abreast of the church, the priest responding by ringing the bells, hoisting a flag, and blessing the ship.

A little way north of Larmor-Plage is **Lorient**, a thriving town, the third biggest fishing port in France (after Boulogne and Concarneau), Brittany's largest commercial port, and an important base for the French navy. For such an important place it has a very short history and the distinction of having been completely rebuilt. In 1666 the Compagnie des Indes (the India Company) was needing a new base after the failure of Le Havre, a failure due almost entirely to English pirates preying on the Company's ships in the channel. The Company decided to build at the point where the Scorff river ran into the Blavet. This gave them a safe anchorage and, equally important, a site that was remote from the Channel pirates. Even then the venture might have failed, as an earlier attempt operating from Port-Louis had done, had it not coincided with the Scotsman John Low being Controller General of the French Treasury. Low is an interesting character. Forced to flee Britain for killing a man in a duel he revolutionised the French economy when he set up a bank in Paris and was offered the job of controlling the Treasury soon after. Sadly Low also had a number of hair-brained schemes in addition to his good ones and finished up dying in Venice in poverty, forced out of France by personal bankruptcy and irate investors.

The India Company's new port was one of Low's better investments and rapidly grew into a very successful town which the Company decided to call, somewhat prosaically, L'Orient — the East. The excellence of its port facilities were immediately obvious to the Germans who occupied the town in 1940. They built submarine pens, and these led to massive aerial bombardments over many years. In 1944 the Germans held on to Lorient long after it had become pointless to do so and the town was further pounded, this time by Patton's land army. It is estimated that when it was finally relieved over 85 per cent of its buildings had been fully or partially destroyed. From that destruction modern Lorient has arisen, a modern commercial centre of limited interest to the tourist.

The interest lies in Notre-Dame-de-Victoire church, a concrete structure with beautiful coloured glass windows that light up the interior; in the Maison de la Mer and the fishing port. The Maison de la Mer occupies the first floor of the Tourist Information Office and has photographs, models and other items on the history of the town from the days of the India Company to the present. The fishing port, Port de Pêche de Keroman, lies at the southern end of the town, close to the French navy's submarine base (which occupies the old German U-boat pens, these having survived the 1939-45 war virtually intact, so strong were they). The port is interesting for its design, which is more intricate than expected, and the fish market which is noisy, smelly and delightful as would be expected. As with Brest, the French navy's submarine base, and the Naval Arsenal at the point where the Scorff reaches the Blavet, are open only to French nationals.

From Lorient boats cross the Coureaux to reach the **Ile de Groix**. The island is 8 x 2½km (5 x 1½ miles) and has a real variety of coasts, from wild and rocky on the north side to sandy beaches on the south. For so remote a spot there is a surprisingly large number of villages. The villages are interesting for the low, slate-roofed houses: Groix, the largest, and the island's capital, has a population of almost 3,000. To help exploration cars, mopeds and bicycles can be hired at Port Tudy where the ferries dock. Apart from the villages the exploration will include some of the many excellent viewpoints on the island: the best are Pen Men, at the western tip, and Pointe des Chats, at the south-eastern tip. Near Pen Men, at Pointe de Bileric, there is a bird sanctuary. This is not open to the public, but the seabirds that nest there can be observed from other points on the cliff edge. The birds can also be observed at the François le Bail Nature Reserve close to Pen Men set up to preserve the unique vegetation of the headland.

At **Port Tudy** an old fish canning factory is now the Ecomusée de l'Isle de Groix, with exhibits on the island's geology and history, and the culture of the island folk. Exhibits include photographs, models of old island fishing boats and the Maison de Kerland, a restored eighteenth-century island house furnished in authentic style.

Across the Blavet estuary from Lorient is **Port-Louis**, a port named for Louis XIII after he had set up a Naval Arsenal here. Before the name change the fishing port that had long stood here was called Blavet after the river. As Blavet the port became famous during the Wars of Religion when a Spanish Catholic army took it. Many of the local girls, fearful of the likely outcome of the port being under the control of an occupying Spanish force, attempted to get away in a boat. The Spaniards pursued them, but rather than be taken prisoner the girls, about forty in total, joined hands, jumped into the sea and drowned. They became known as the 'Virgins of Blavet' and were a source of strength to local Protestants. Following Louis XIII's interest in the port Cardinal Richelieu set up the headquarters of the India Company here (during the reign of Louis XIV) though this was not a success. With the building of Lorient, Port-Louis declined severely, though it did stage a slight recovery when a sardine fleet and canning factory were set up in the port. Today, it still has a small fishing fleet,

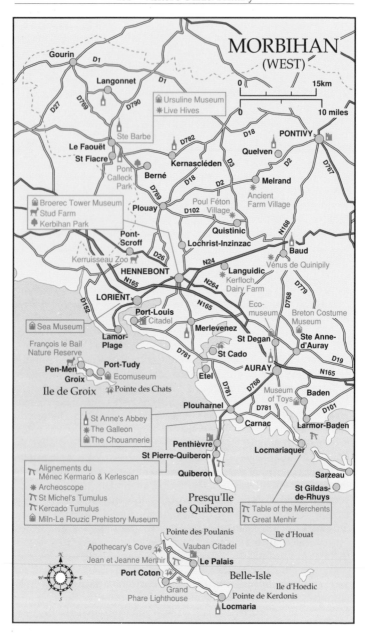

MORBIHAN
(WEST)

Gourin
Langonnet
Ursuline Museum
Live Hives
Ste Barbe
Le Faouët
St Fiacre
Pont Calleck Park
Berné
Kernascléden
Quelven
PONTIVY
Melrand
Ancient Farm Village
Broerec Tower Museum
Stud Farm
Kerbihan Park
Plouay
Poul Féton Village
Quistinic
Pont-Scroff
Lochrist-Inzinzac
Baud
Vénus de Quinipily
Kerruisseau Zoo
HENNEBONT
Languidic
Kerfloch Dairy Farm
LORIENT
Sea Museum
Port-Louis
Citadel
Merlevenez
Eco-museum
Breton Costume Museum
François le Bail Nature Reserve
Lamor-Plage
St Degan
St Cado
Ste Anne-d'Auray
Pen-Men
Groix
Port-Tudy
Ecomuseum
Etel
AURAY
Museum of Toys
Baden
Ile de Groix
Pointe des Chats
Plouharnel
Larmor-Baden
St Anne's Abbey
The Galleon
The Chouannerie
Carnac
Penthièvre
Locmariaquer
St Pierre-Quiberon
Alignements du Ménec Kermario & Kerlescan
Archeoscope
St Michel's Tumulus
Kercado Tumulus
Miln-Le Rouzic Prehistory Museum
Quiberon
Sarzeau
St Gildas-de-Rhuys
Presqu'Ile de Quiberon
Table of the Merchents
Great Menhir
Pointe des Poulanis
Ile d'Houat
Apothecary's Cove
Vauban Citadel
Jean et Jeanne Menhir
Le Palais
Port Coton
Belle-Isle
Grand Phare Lighthouse
Ile d'Hoedic
Pointe de Kerdonis
Locmaria

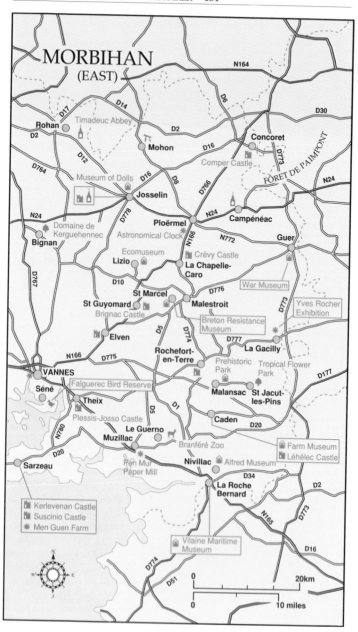

but is also a lively resort town. Within the town there are several fine old houses.

The most obvious building in Port-Louis is La Citadelle, which guards the entrance to the Blavet. The fort was begun in 1591 during the time of the Spanish occupation that led to the drowning of the 'Forty Virgins', though building continued through to the time of Richelieu and the India Company. It is of granite and rectangular with corner bastions. At all times during its history the fort has been a prison, the most significant of its prisoners having been Louis Napoleon who later became the Emperor Napoleon III. The fort's walls can be walked, and inside there are no less then five museums. The Musée des Bateaux has several old fishing boats, but is chiefly concerned with life saving. The main exhibit is the lifeboat *Commandant Philippe de Kerhallet* which dates from the early years of this century and was propelled by twelve oars. The fort's old powder factory (*poudrière*) has a collection of naval munitions, while the old arsenal has a superb collection of model ships and many interesting nautical items. The Musée du Port-Louis tells the story of the port, while the Musée de la Compagnie des Indes, housed in a new building separate from the other museums, tells the story of the Company.

Port-Louis lies at the northern tip of the entrance of the 'sea' of Gâvres, a virtually land-locked saltwater lagoon. Unfortunately this area, and much of the coast from here to Quiberon, forms the Champ de Tir de Gâvres, a military range to which access is restricted. It is better, therefore, to go inland a little and then to cross the extraordinary, spidery inlet of the Etel river to reach Quiberon. At **Merlevenez** there is one of the very few Romanesque churches in Brittany, a lovely little church with modern stained glass windows which show scenes from the life of the Virgin. At **Etel** a road can be followed through a section of the range to reach the Barre d'Etel, a sandbank on to which the sea crashes with impressive fury. Etel itself is a little fishing port close to the mouth of the river of the same name. From there it is more than 30km (19 miles) to Nostang, the point at which the Etel looks more like a river than an inlet of the sea. Dotted through this unusual inlet are a number of small islands which specialise in oyster farming, while on the shores there are several fine viewpoints, one of the best being at **St Cado**, a tiny village on a short finger of land near Belz. At the end of the finger is the chapel of St Cado, another Romanesque building. It is named for St Cado, a Celtic saint whose stone bed can be seen in the chapel, and whose help was sought by the deaf. The view of the Etel from the chapel, a view that takes in a small Calvary and some pretty little houses, is stunning.

The **Presqu'ile de Quiberon** is the most correct of all the peninsulas with that 'nearly island' name, the causeway that links it to the mainland being only 7½m (25ft) wide at one point. It is likely that at once time Quiberon really was an island, but became attached to the mainland by drifting shingle. At the mainland side of the peninsula is **Plouharnel**, where *Le Galion* (set where the causeway narrows) is a replica of an eighteenth-century galleon which houses a series of shell pictures. Less obviously 'touristy' is La Chouannerie, a museum that deals with the Chouan revolt, a local Breton movement against the Revolutionaries. In 1795 a large number of French aristocrats and other Royalists who had escaped to Britain decided to mount an invasion of France. Their idea was to land in Brittany to link up with the Breton Chouans and to march on Paris. Plans were laid and it was anticipated that more than 100,000 soldiers would be ready to move out of Brittany. However, on the day, 27 June, only 10,000 men were on board the British ships that anchored off Quiberon, the remaining Royalists (and all the major aristocrats) thinking it safer to stay in Britain. Worse was to come, for when the men landed near Carnac they found that their plans had been betrayed and General Hoche of the Revolutionary Army was waiting. Hoche attacked and drove the Royalists along the peninsula. Hasty messages caused the British ships to mass off Port-Haliguen, but the weather worsened and the ship's captains could only watch as the landing force was destroyed. Large numbers of Royalists were captured, but Hoche showed no mercy, having many of them shot at Quiberon. The rest were taken to Auray and Vannes where, after interrogation, they, too, were executed. The Plouharnel museum has exhibits from this and other Chouan incidents and, most interestingly, has a number of dioramas explaining the stories. There are also collections of arms, and a guillotine. A little way north of the town the abbey of St Anne can be visited. It is an occupied Benedictine abbey, and so visiting is restricted, but the late nineteenth-century building is wonderfully peaceful.

From Plouharnel the peninsula narrows down to **Penthièvre** where there are two good beaches. Beyond, the causeway narrows to its most meagre width and reaches Penthièvre Fort, an old castle that once protected the approach to Quiberon and which has been restored. Near it a memorial has been erected to fifty-nine members of the French Resistance executed here in 1944. The 'mainland' of Quiberon is distinctly different on its two sides. To the west is the Côte Sauvage, the aptly-named wild coast with rugged cliffs and rocks on to which the sea thuds and thunders. There are beaches here, but they should not be used for swimming as the sea is very

St Cado, an aerial view of the small village

The lighthouse at Port-Haliguen

dangerous. To get the best out of the coast, go to the viewpoints at either end, Pointe de Percho (reached on foot from the road-end car park) near the village of Portivy, and Beg er Goalennec, just west of Quiberon. A fine walk follows the cliffs all the way between the two viewpoints: it takes about 2 hours and a return can be made by bus.

From Penthièvre the peninsula road goes through **St Pierre Quiberon** a resort village with two good beaches and a small menhir alignment—the Alignment St Pierre with twenty-two stones. A turn to the left beyond the village reaches **Beg Rohu** and the École Nationale de Voile, the French National Sailing School.

Finally, the road reaches **Quiberon**, once a small fishing port — boats still land sardines here, but the trade is much reduced — but now a busy resort town. The village has a fine sandy beach, and from its port (Port-Maria) boats leave for Belle-Ile and the smaller island of Houat and Hoedic. From the village the excellent viewpoint of Pointe du Conguel, from where the view extends over all the islands, and across Quiberon Bay to the Morbihan coast, is reached by a road that passes the Quiberon Thalossotherapy Centre. Here seawater is used to alleviate the symptoms of arthritis and rheumatism.

Belle-Ile, reached from Quiberon is an excellent spot to spend time, being one of the most interesting of all Brittany's islands. It is

Sunset over Belle-Ile, the largest of Brittany's islands

also the largest, almost 17km (10½ miles) long and averaging 7½km (5 miles) wide. It is an island of amazing contrasts, its high centre being weatherswept moorland (despite the occasional wheatfield), the valleys (of which there are many) being lush and green, and the coast being rocky and sandy by turns. To complete the picture there are also stands of pine trees, several sea caves and some rock pinnacles. Because of its size it is worth taking a car, or hiring a bicycle from Le Palais, the island's main town.

Belle-Ile (occasionally called Belle-Ile-en-Mer to distinguish it from the land-locked Belle-Ile-en-Terre) has a long and varied history. The Romans certainly settled here, calling it *Vindilis*, and they probably came in the wake of Celtic settlers. Later, Celts from Wales resettled the island, one of the villages still being called Bangor. Saxons and Normans came and went, and the English invaded it often over a period of centuries, holding the island for several long periods. When Britain held it again in the mid-eighteenth century its transfer back to France was written into the Treaty of Paris, Britain receiving Nova Scotia, and the French settlers of that island being re-settled on Belle-Ile. Many of the present inhabitants claim, with pride, a descent from those Canadian settlers. Later, the island became popular with artists, with Monet and Matisse acknowledging a debt to its scenery and peace. Sarah Bernhardt also came, having a house built near Pointe des Poulains. The house was demolished by the Germans who built a gun battery on the site. The battery is now known as Fort Sarah Bernhardt, a name that reflects the lack of sympathy between the actress and the islanders as well as the sense of history.

Belle-Ile's most interesting historical phase was in the mid-seventeenth century when it was held by Nicholas Fouquet, the French Superintendent of Finance. Fouquet fortified the island and had a private navy stationed there. His stated reasons was to be ready to strike against the king if he found him to be defrauding the State, but it is more likely to have been a bolt-hole for when his own frauds were discovered. Fouquet eventually fell foul of Louis XIV by having a private château built (not on Belle-Ile) that was so lavish that the king had him arrested by his Musketeers. (He also had Fouquet's architect and landscape gardener transferred to his own land at Versaille). With Fouquet's departure the island passed to the Crown, and Louis sent Vauban to make it impregnable. It is his work, the Citadelle Vauban, that we see in Le Palais, the port where boats from the mainland arrive.

The citadel, which dominates the northern edge of Le Palais' harbour, was started in the sixteenth century though virtually all that now exists is as a result of Vauban's rebuilding. In has inner and outer defensive walls and huge corner bastions, yet for all its impressive looks it was successfully taken by the British in 1763, the action that led to the transfer of the French Canadians from Nova Scotia. Inside the citadel is a museum, housed in rooms decorated in Louis XIII style, devoted to the history of the island.

From Le Palais the visitor should circle the island. Going clockwise, the island's biggest beach, Les Grands Sables, is reached, it still has the remnants of eighteenth-century fortifications, beyond which is Pointe de Kerdonis and a fine view of the smaller islands to the east. Nearby is the village of **Locmaria** where the church of Notre-Dame-de-Boistord is built on the spot where once a huge elm tree grew. Legend has it that when this tree was felled to make a mast it shrieked loudly, terrifying those who were cutting it. Since then the village has been said to be home to sorcerers, and the church may have been built in an attempt to placate ancient gods.

From Locmaria follow the road to Bangor, a neat little village, then take the road to the *Grand Phare*, the island's lighthouses. The lighthouse can be climbed to a viewing balcony, at 46m (151ft), from where the whole island can be seen. Close to the lighthouse is Port Goulphar where the island's Côte Sauvage starts. This rugged coastline can be viewed from here, but is better seen at Port Coton and Port Donnant further on. Port Coton is named from the sea, which always seems to be a boiling mass here, the mass looking like cotton wool. The view of the sea and the cliffs is excellent, but the eye is drawn to the series of rock towers, known as the Aiguilles (Needles) off-shore. At Port-Donnant the sea cliffs are at their highest. At points like this one the islanders abseil down the cliffs in mid-winter to gather barnacles from the wave-washed ledges. This is hard, dangerous work, and is carried out to supply Spain with *percebes*, a shellfish delicacy.

On the sides of the road to Port Donnant from the main D25 road there are a pair of distinctive menhirs which are known as Jean et Jeanne and are said to be a pair of young lovers who came here for an illicit meeting because they could not wait for their wedding night, and where they turned to stone for their sin. Next along the Côte Sauvage is the bird reserve of Koh-Castell where auks, gulls and petrels can be seen. The reserve is not open during the nesting period, but can be visited when the young birds are leaving the nests. An extension of the reserve's nesting area is the Grotte de l'Apothicairerie (Apothecary's Cove) named for the nesting cormorants who are said to resemble medicine bottles in an old-fashioned chemist's shop. The cleft — it is a cleft rather than a cave — can be reached by stone steps. In rough weather the site is wonderfully impressive, but the steps can be very wet and slippery, so please take care.

The last good viewpoint is the Pointe des Poulains, beyond Fort Sarah Bernhardt. From it return to Le Palais by way of Sauzon a very pretty little port and marina.

Ile d'Houat, the island closest to Quiberon has one town, Houat, with delightful little alleys among the houses: in summer many of the houses have colourful window-boxes. The town church is dedicated to the English monk St Gildas who visited the island before establishing his monastery at St Gildas-de-Rhuys on the mainland. **Ile Hoedic** also has a single town, with some fine granite houses, and the remnants of a couple of old forts. Both of the islands have fine beaches, and are excellent for the visitor who really wants to get away from it all.

Back on the mainland, on the coast to the east of the Quiberon Peninsula and Plouharnel is **Carnac**, the world's premier site for megalithic monuments. The most famous of the Carnac megaliths are the alignments to the north of the village. The biggest, the Alignements du Ménec, beside the D196, starts with an oval of 70 stones, and then has a further 1,099 stones arranged in 11 lines, the lines approximately 10m (33ft) apart and over 1km (almost ¾ mile)

This crêperie *at Carnac is one of many found throughout Brittany*

Carnac is the world's premier site for megalithic monuments

long. The stones vary in height, going from about 4m (13ft) down to about half that, and do not, at first glance, seem to have been chosen so that alternate stones are triangular or upright as might be expected if there was a fertility rite evolved in raising them. Various astronomical theories have been put forward, but the lines are not straight, precisely parallel or exactly spaced, which would not seem to support such suggestions. Gustav Flaubert, the French writer, was scornful of the theorising about the stones, and there has been a great deal more since his time, claiming that there were more pages of rubbish written about them than there were stones, and there were thousands of those! In one sense he is right, but his comment denies the power of such sites. Come here at dawn or dusk when the visitors have gone and a light mist is shrouding the stones and it is difficult to be unmoved. Whatever it was that moved those ancient folk to haul the stones here and erect them it must have been a powerful urge. Just a thought about the labour involved in raising one, let alone thousands, proves that.

The alignment is presently enclosed within a strong mesh fence erected to allow the ground between the stones to recover from the trampling of millions of feet, today's visitor having to content himself with a view through the fence — though a viewing platform, as has been erected at the Alignement de Kermario — will be erected soon. As compensation, there is the Archeoscope, a new centre next to the stones where a film and slide show on the stones and their archaeology is shown. Two shows daily are in English.

Further along the D196 there are two further alignments. That of Kermario has 1,029 stones in 10 rows, and is also about 1km (¾ mile) long and 100m (328ft) wide, while at **Kerlescan** 555 stones form 13 lines. Here, as at Ménec, there is also an oval of stones. The three alignments are separated by a few hundred metres from each other, there being a rather larger separation to that of Petit Ménec, which is also on a different bearing. Finally, close to Erdeven, a village on the D781 north-west of Plouharnel, there is the Alignment de Kerzerho with 1,129 stones in 10 rows.

Close to the alignments there are other examples of monuments from the megalithic cultures. Near **Kériaval**, on the northern side of the D768, is a group of three dolmens. The upright of one of these is inscribed with axes, spirals and other curious designs. Close to the Kermario alignment is the tumulus of Kercado, an earth-covered dolmen surmounted by a tall menhir. Here, too, the dolmen uprights have been inscribed. The finest of all such tumuli is that of St Michel closer to Carnac itself. Here a mound over 120m (394ft) long and almost 12m (39ft) high covers a burial complex with numerous galleries and chambers. The chambers , which are contained in a revetment wall, an astonishing piece of dry-stone engineering, can be visited by way of a dimly lit tunnel, a very atmospheric trip. The mound is topped by an ancient menhir, and the more recent additions of a tiny chapel to St Michael, a Calvary and a panorama dial. The dial helps the visitor to identify the stone alignments and other local megaliths. The items excavated from the burial chambers can be seen in the pre-history museums at Carnac and Vannes.

The Carnac museum that holds some of the excavated items from St Michel's tumulus is the Musée de Prehistoire J-Miln/St le Rouzic, the name of which commemorates the Scot James Miln who began excavating in the Carnac area, and Zacharie Le Rouzic, a Carnac man who supported the work. The museum covers an enormous period of human history, from the Lower Paleolithic (about 450,000 years ago) through to the early medieval period. The exhibits are well displayed, and supported by an audio-visual presentation, and include tools in stone, bone, wood, bronze and iron, jewellery and several fine models and re-constructed scenes, the latter including a burial as might have been found in one of the many dolmen in the Carnac area.

Within the village of Carnac the most interesting spot is the church, dedicated St Cornély, the patron saint of farm animals.

Legend has it that Cornély was one of the early Christians in Rome, and fled from Rome in an ox-cart pursued by a whole army of pagan Romans. Through Italy they chased him, then over the Alps into Gaul, and through Gaul to Brittany. Cornering Cornély by the sea, the army marched in on him but the saint turned and called down the wrath of God on them. The men were promptly turned to stone, maintaining their ordered ranks, and so creating the alignments to the north of Carnac. On the outside of the church, Cornély can be seen together with his oxen. Inside there is some good eighteenth-century wrought ironwork and a reliquary bust to the saint.

Carnac is now almost two villages, the older one, grouped around St Cornély's church, and the newer resort village of Carnac-Plage, a lively place with a superb beach that offers not only safe swimming, but fine views of the Quiberon Peninsula.

To the west of Carnac are two abbeys to which the visitors are allowed access. The abbeys of St Michel-de-Kerganon and Ste Anne-de-Kerganon are both Benedictine, the former for nuns, the latter for monks (despite the gender of the saints of the dedications being the other way around) and were both founded in 1897 as daughter abbeys of Solesmes in the Loire Valley. Of the two, St Michel, the nun's building, is the better, a stout granite structure with fine wooden vaulting. In each of the abbeys the visitor can hear Gregorian chant if a visit coincides with the monastic offices.

To the east of Carnac is the fishing port and resort village of **La Trinité-sur-Mer**. The Crac'h estuary here is one of France's leading yachting marinas with an array of expensive boats riding at moor and anchor. The array is matched only by that of the *crêperies*, boutiques and boating shops. From the resort cross the Kerisper Bridge over the Crac'h and bear right to Locmariaquer and the Pointe de Kerpenhir. From the point, where there is a granite Virgin, Notre-Dame de Kerdro, created to protect local sailors (*kerdro* meaning safe return in Breton), Port Navalo the village on the tip of the other enclosing arm of the Morbihan Gulf, is just a few hundred metres away.

Locmariaquer is a small port, too often overlooked by visitors rushing off to see the Grand Menhir and the Table des Marchand. But it is these two megalithic monuments that command the attention. Until the mid-eighteenth century the Grand Menhir stood upright and, at 20m (65ft) must have been an astonishing sight. It is probable that this 350-ton stone was the largest menhir ever erected, and the effort and skill required to do so can only be marvelled at. It is conjectured that it was erected here so that it could be viewed from Quiberon. Sadly, about 250 years ago the menhir was struck by

The granite statue of Notre-Dame de Kerdro, Locmariaquer

Locmariaquer, like Carnac, has also inherited megalithic monuments (the Mané-Rethual)

lightning and now lies in pieces. Even in pieces it is an impressive sight. Almost as impressive is the Merchant's Table, a huge dolmen in which the capstones are held aloft by seventeen support stones. Some of the supports have clearly been worked to give them a pointed end, and have also been inscribed. The carvings have been disputed: some see crooks and a cooking pot, others ears of corn and the sun, but it is clear that the art is more representational than at, say, the Gavrinis Tumulus further to the east.

Close to the main site there are several other dolmen. That of Mané-Lud has carved stones, while Mané-Rethual is a large *allée couverte*. To the south of the village are Pierres-Plates with beautifully carved stones, while the tumulus of Mané-er-Hroueg has a series of steps to a dry-stone burial complex.

From Lochmariaquer the main road (the D781) can be followed to Auray. **Auray** is a beautiful place, one of the best towns in Brittany, picturesquely set on a bend of the Auray river. Perhaps the prettiest area is Quartier St-Goustan, on the east side of the river. Here there are narrow alleys of fine old houses, some of the alleys stepped, some leading down to Quai Benjamin Franklin. The latter is named for the great American who landed here in 1776 when his ship was forced to abandon the trip to Nantes in wretched weather. Franklin was visiting France to drum up support against the British throne during the American War of Independence, and his stay (at number 8) is commemorated by a plaque. For a good long view of the St Goustan quarter take the Promenade du Loch, a fine, shady walk along the right bank of the Auray (the river is also known as the Loch, hence the name) from where the view is delightful.

The town is famous for two bloody incidents in Breton history. The first occurred to the north of the town in 1364 where the final battle of the War of Succession was fought. On one side were Charles de Blois and his general, Bertrand du Guesclin, on the other, Jean de Montfort, the brother of Charles' wife, who was supported by the English in his bid for the Dukedom of Brittany. Against the advice of du Guesclin, Charles attacked de Montfort's strong position and his army was destroyed. Du Guesclin was captured and ransomed, living to fight on many another day, but Charles de Blois was killed. The story is told that Jean de Monfort, coming upon his brother-in-law's body on the field, knelt down and wept. One of his captain's helped him up, telling him that it could never have been possible for him to win the dukedom and to have Charles remain alive.

The second bloody historical event took place 400 years later when the Breton Chouans rebelled against the Revolutionaries. Following the execution of Louis XVI the Reign of Terror descended upon

Brittany. A guillotine was set up in Rennes and its blade began to fall fervently. The Bretons were appalled: they had little sympathy with the French at the best of times, still feeling like a foreign country, and were not in sympathy with the methods of the Revolutionaries particularly when it inflicted more suffering, as they saw it, on the peasant farmers. The Chouans, who took their name from the French description of the screech of the barn owl, a screech which they used as a signal for night-time rendezvous, were a group opposed to the Revolutionaries, and were led by Georges Cadoudal, a young farmer from Morbihan. Cadoudal saw in the movement a chance to re-establish Breton independence and supported the Quiberon landing in June 1795. But those who landed had no intention of supporting an independent Brittany, seeking only the restoration of both the monarchy and their old importance and affluence. They would have betrayed Cadoudal at a later stage, but as it was both the Royalists and the Chouans were betrayed by others and routed. Many of those captured were taken to the Champ des Martyrs, between Auray and Ste Anne d'Auray, where they were shot. At the same site many others were executed for being Chouans over the next ten years. Cadoudal escaped, and was offered a pardon and the position of general by Napoleon. He declined and in 1804, in a mad bid to capture Napoleon, Cadoudal went to Paris. He was captured, tried and convicted of treason, and executed. The authorities allowed his body to be returned to Morbihan where it was buried on Kerléano Hill on the southern edge of Auray. On the hill top Cadoudal's tomb can still be seen, overlooking the town and his family's farm.

The town below Kerléano Hill, the quarter on the river's right bank, is not as picturesque as St Goustan, but is still a fine place. The church, dedicated to St Gildas, has a good seventeenth-century marble altarpiece and some excellent woodwork, and in the streets close to it there are some appealing houses.

Auray's historical sites can be visited in a short journey northward. Take the D768 to Baud to arrive at the Chartreuse d'Auray. After the battle in 1364 Jean de Monfort (by then Duke Jean IV) built a church on the site. Later this was enlarged, and transformed into a Carthusian monastery or charterhouse. The monks left about 200 years ago, and a serious fire damaged the buildings in 1968, but they have been restored and can be visited. The funeral chapel houses the bones of the Chouans executed at the Champs des Martyrs. The Martyr's Field itself is a little further along the same road and is marked by a chapel.

A little further north, at **St Degan**, there is an Ecomuseum, a restored farm. The house is granite with a thatched roof, and is furnished in the local style (known as Bas-Vannetais after this area of Morbihan). The outbuildings are complete with nineteenth-century implements.

To complete this fine tour continue to **Ste Anne d'Auray.** An old Breton legend tells that Ste Anne was born and married in Brittany, but after being widowed travelled to Palestine and re-married. She had a daughter, Mary, who was the mother of Christ. The legend also tells that when Mary reached adulthood Ste Anne returned to Brittany to live out the rest of her years and was visited here by her grandson Jesus. This legend was being told in Brittany before 1623, but in that year a farmer from his tiny village north of Auray, Yves Nicolazic, was visited by Ste Anne as he was ploughing one day. Ste Anne told him he must build a chapel in her honour, and that she would show him where. Two years later as he was ploughing again, he unearthed a statue of the saint. Taking this as a sign, Yves started to build a church. By the time of its completion the church was the foremost pilgrimage site in Brittany, and is still the centre for one its most important *pardons*, on 26 July each year.

The church that now stands in Yves' field replaced the earlier chapel in the mid-nineteenth century. It has a statue of Ste Anne, but not the original one which was almost destroyed in a fire. A section of the face of the original is set into the base of the present statue. The church's treasury holds a gold and silver reliquary to the saint given to the church by Anne of Austria in thanks for the safe delivery of the baby who was to become Louis XIV. There are also some further sections from the old statue. The church stands in the pilgrimage Close where there is also a fountain, claimed to have healing powers, and a war memorial which was raised to the 250,000 Bretons who died in the 1914-18 war, but has now become a memorial to all those who have died in conflicts this century.

To the right of the war memorial is a most interesting museum, the Musée du Costume Breton, in which the costumes are displayed on dolls. Close by is the Historial de Ste Anne, a wax figure diorama of how the pilgrims to the church might have look in medieval times. It is hoped that the house of Yves Nicolazic will also soon be opened to visitors. Ask at the tourist office for details.

Morbihan is the only one of Brittany's *départements* that has a Breton name, *mor bihan* meaning 'little sea', and referring to the huge lagoon of the Gulf des Morbihan which is enclosed by the pincer-arms of Locmariaquer which we have already visited, and the Presqu'ile de Rhuys. Geologically, the Gulf is remarkably recent. It was formed when the land surface of a complex of estuaries and sea inlets between Auray and Vannes dropped allowing the sea to claim

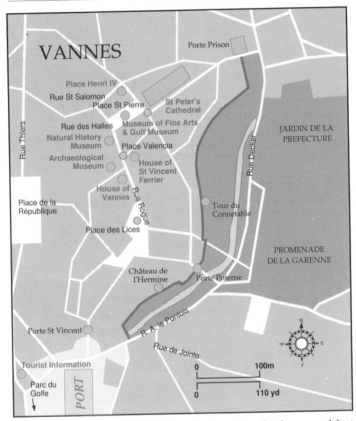

VANNES

Porte Prison

Place Henri IV
Rue St Salomon
Place St Pierre
St Peter's Cathedral

Rue Thiers

Rue des Halles
Natural History Museum
Museum of Fine Arts & Gulf Museum
Place Valencia
Archaeological Museum
House of St Vincent Ferrier

JARDIN DE LA PREFECTURE

Rue Decker

House of Vannes

Rue Roque

Tour du Connétable

Place de la République

Place des Lices

PROMENADE DE LA GARENNE

Château de l'Hermine

Porte Poterne

R. A. le Pontois

Porte St Vincent

Rue de Jointo

Tourist Information

Parc du Golfe

PORT

0   100m

0   110 yd

the low-lying land. It is not absolutely clear when this happened, but it must have been after the construction of the twin stone circles on the island of Er Lanic, one of the circles now being partially underwater. As an aside, the visitor who is an experienced sub-aqua diver will find a swim around this circle at high tide fascinating. Some authorities place the creation of the Gulf about 4,000 years ago, but others claim it might well have been formed as recently as 2,000 years ago. Strangely for such a land-locked sea the tidal range is impressive, the good beaches along its edges being left high and dry as the sea retreats across the flat-bottomed Gulf. When the tide is in a boat trip around the Gulf offers a splendid trip. Boats shuttle around on a route that starts at Auray, visits several points along the way, including Port-Navalo and some of the Gulf's islands, and ends at Vannes.

From Auray the first point of note on the Gulf is **Baden**, a village
a short distance inland, but worth visiting for the Reflets du Passé, a
museum of old toys, games and automatons (some of them musical)
housed in a beautiful little cottage. There is also a collection of dolls'
houses.

Beyond Baden is **Larmor-Baden**, a delightful little port with a
good beach, backed by an excellent campsite. From the port a boat
makes the short (15 minutes) crossing to the Ile de Gavrinis. On the
island is a late Neolithic, or early Bronze Age, burial chamber that is
often claimed to be the most interesting in Brittany, and which has
also been claimed to be one of the wonders of the world. The burial
is a circular tumulus of stones about 50m (164ft) in diameter and
some 6m (20ft) high covering a gallery and single burial chamber.
The gallery is 15m (49ft) long and is made up of 9 large slabs held aloft

St Peter's Cathedral,
Vannes

on 23 supports. The burial chamber is similar in construction, its roof comprising a single huge slab of granite. So far the tomb appears to be normal, if large and elaborate. The difference is in the decoration of the stones which, with their spirals and swirls, are breathtaking.

Other interesting islands with the gulf are Er Lanic, as already mentioned, which lies south of Gavrinis, Ile d'Arz, which also has several megalithic monuments, and **Ile aux Moines**. Moines is the largest island. Bicycles can be hired for an exploration of the island whose scenic virtues, which include beautiful woods, palm and orange trees and numerous mimosas, have been extolled by generations of Breton poets (who also made a point of noting the beauty of the island girls). The town, with its tight alleyways and unexpected Gulf views, is also interesting.

From Larmor-Baden a drive around the Gulf goes though **Arradon**, another port/resort. From the nearby Pointe d'Arradon there is one of the best views of the gulf. Next is **Vannes**.

The story is told that when Julius Caesar invaded this north-western tip of Gaul he faced stout resistance from the Veneti tribe. The tribe were a fishing folk whose navy threatened to cut off the Roman legions from their supply lines. Caesar therefore had galleys built, and with these the Romans, under Brutus, attacked the Veneti fleet near Port-Navalo. Whether the battle was in the Gulf or on the sea depends upon which authority is believed, but wherever it was fought the Romans won, their oared galleys getting the better of the Veneti sailing ships when the wind failed. Caesar took terrible revenge on the tribe, but their name is commemorated in the name of Vannes, Morbihan's major city.

Vannes is built at the head of an inlet of the Gulf and with its beautiful old houses, parkland and curios is the ideal place for those seeking a few hours change from the sun and sand of the Gulf's beaches. Beyond the unique centre is the modern city, an industrial and urban complex that is unlikely to detain the visitor long.

Vannes had probably existed for centuries before Nominoé, a Breton from a lowly family, was befriended by Charlemagne and made Count of Vannes. A short time later, in AD826, Nominoé became Duke of Brittany after he had defeated the other Breton counts. Not content with this, Nominoé next turned on the Franks who had supported him, defeating Charles the Bold, who had succeeded Charlemagne, and setting up a Breton state which was to remain intact for centuries. Vannes was Nominoé's capital, and later, in 1522, it was at Vannes that the Breton council met to confirm the Act of Union with France.

Of the old town walls three gates remain, even though there is now little left of the ramparts. The Porte St Vincent lies close to the squared-off inlet of the gulf, a port where the masts of pleasure craft have replaced those of trading ships. Just a couple of hundred metres to the east is Porte Poterne (follow the line of the wall) from where a bridge takes you away from the old town to the Promenade de la Garenne, once the park surrounding the now-destroyed castle. Within the park the Allée des Frères-Jolivel, a short walk, offers a superb view of the old wall. Note especially the Constable Tower, rising above the water and the sixteenth-century half-timbered wash-house. This communal wash-house, its users protected by a remarkable low slung roof supported on stone columns, is still used, the occasional lines of washing adding a curious touch. Continue along the Allée and Rue Decker to reach the Porte Prison, the last of the three remaining medieval gates.

Ahead now is Vannes cathedral. St Peter's Cathedral is a curious building, the 600 years it took to complete it, from the thirteenth century through to the 1850s, meaning that it comprises bits of virtually all architectural styles from that long period, including a rotunda chapel in Italian Renaissance style, one of very few examples of that style in Brittany. The chapel houses the tomb of St Vincent Ferrier, a Spanish monk who died in Vannes in 1419. An early seventeenth-century tapestry details several of the miraculous cures associated with the saint and there is also a painting of him. The cathedral's treasury is housed in the old chapterhouse and includes a beautiful twelfth-century painted chest and several fine crosses, one in ivory. The chapterhouse itself has some excellent wood panelling.

Across Place St Pierre from the cathedral is La Cohue, the twelfth-century town market hall. *Cohue* means crowd, or crush, and either must have been entirely appropriate when the medieval markets and fairs took place here. La Cohue is a little more tranquil today. Indeed, it is a delightful spot, fully restored and with a collection of shops, chiefly food and craft, on the ground floor and a pair of interesting museums on the first floor. In what was once the Vannes courtroom is the Musée des Beaux-Arts with a collection of works by nineteenth- and twentieth-century local artists. There is also a collection of older folk art. The Musée du Golfe et de la Mer deals with the Gulf of Morbihan, its geology and history, and the history of the local fishing industry.

Heading north between the cathedral and La Cohue (that is, going away from the town walls) Place Henri IV, with its beautiful sixteenth-century houses, is reached. Rue St Salomon leaves Place Henri: take this and turn left into Rue des Halles to reach the far side of La Cohue and, to the right, the Musée de Histoire Naturelles. Here, in a fine seventeenth-century townhouse are collections of local birds, butterflies and fossils. Further on, Rue des Halles widens. To the left here, in Place Valencia, is the house in which St Vincent died in 1419. The house, named for the saint, was remodelled in the sixteenth century, but remains a superb building, half stone, half timbered. Ahead, on the corner of Rue Rogue, is the House of Vannes, a famous old house with two external carved figureheads. The pair are known as Vannes and his Wife, for no reason other the affection the townsfolk have for the amiable pair. To the right is the Musée de la Préhistorie (Archaeological Museum) an excellent museum that occupies the first floor of the fifteenth-century Château Gaillard, once the Breton parliament house. The museum deals with the archaeology of the Morbihan area and includes items from Carnac and Locmariaquer. Now follow Rue Rogue, going past the House of Vannes, to Place des Lices, where tournaments were held in medieval times, and continue on to reach the town walls again.

Elsewhere, Vannes has other worthwhile sites: the Town Hall, north-west of Place Henri IV, follow Rue Burgault, is in Renaissance style, and in front of it stands a mounted statue of the Constable de Richemont who, together with Jean of Arc, commanded the French army that defeated the English to end the Hundred Years War. The

Château de Suscinio, near Sarzeau, was once surrounded by a sea-filled moat

constable become Duke of Brittany in 1457. Next, go to the Parc du Golfe, Vannes' pleasure boat harbour, to see the Aquarium Oceanographique et Tropical, where thousands of fish from all over the world are held in more than fifty tanks in a huge building. Here there are sharks, electric eels, piranhas, giant American catfish, and many more. Opposite the Aquarium is the Palais des Automates, an excellent collection of puppets and automatons, together with exhibitions on construction methods. Finally, close to those two sites is the Serre des Papillons Tropicaux, with an interesting collection of exotic butterflies. The various 'greenhouses' allow the visitor to follow the butterflies' evolution from caterpillar through pupa to adult insect.

South of Vannes the land and the sea of the Gulf merge gradually, the one giving way to the other among a series of saltmarshes. Set among these are **Conleau** a small fishing port from where boats leave for the Ile d'Arz, and **Séné** another fishing port where a specific form of fishing boat, known as the *sinagot*, was developed. Close to Séné is the Falguerec Bird Reserve, a saltmarsh area that is home to egrets, stilts, avocets and other waders, together with herons, ducks, and cormorants. The 'dry-land' birds include bluethroats, and the re-

A view of the River Vilaine and bridge as seen from The Cannon House, La Roche Bernard

serve is also used by many migrating species.

To continue around the Gulf the visitor leaves Vannes on the N165, bearing south on the D780 before the village of Thiex is reached. **Thiex** is a pleasant little place from where the Château du Plessis-Josso can be reached. The castle, more of a fortified mansion than a real war engine, is a delightful place set in parkland beside a small lake. It was built in three phases beginning with an early fourteenth-century fortified mansion to which wings were added in the fifteenth and seventeenth centuries, the latter a pavilion in Louis XIII style. Inside, the various parts are furnished in authentic style.

The visitor on the D780 soon reaches the Presqu'ile de Rhuys as the southern pincer enclosing the Gulf is known. The first place of note on the peninsula is the Château de Kerlevenan, an eighteenth-century castle with a classical façade. The castle and its surrounding park can be visited, but only on request. The first peninsula town is **Sarzeau** an attractive place close to several fine beaches. The bust in the market square is of Alain-René Lesage, one of France's best known eighteenth-century satirists who was born in the town. South of Sarzeau is the Château de Suscinio, surrounded by a moat that was once filled each high tide. The sea has retreated a little now, though the moat remains and must be crossed to gain access to the castle's courtyard. Suscinio was built in the thirteenth century and became the summer residence of the Dukes of Brittany. It changed hands several times during the War of Succession and was partially dismantled during the Revolution. Restoration began in 1966 and has continued since then, five of the original eight towers now having been completely renovated. The visitor can admire the new work and the old design by walking along the outer wall and climbing the north tower (from where the view of the sea is also splendid). The castle also contains a museum of Breton history. In the domestic buildings of the castle Henry Tudor, who was later to be Henry VII, was held captive by the Breton Duke François II over a fourteen-year period until 1485. At that time, Henry escaped to sail to Milford Haven from where he continued to Bosworth Field and the Crown. François seems to have had mixed feelings about Henry, ignoring several offers, from English kings, of money in exchange for his prisoner, and allowing Henry some freedom, certainly enough to allow him to father a son by a local Breton girl. The son, Roland de Velville, became the constable of Beaumaris Castle (Anglesey Castle) when Henry became king.

Also close to Sarzeau is Men Guen Farm which specialises in ancient breeds of farm animals, including Breton cows and Ouessant sheep, and showing a range of ancient farm implements.

From Sarzeau the main peninsula road continues to Arzon and Port Navalo, passing, to the right, the Tumulus de Tumiac, a Neolithic burial mound from which, legend has it, Julius Caesar watched the sea battle between the Romans and the local Veneti Gauls. **Arzon** is a small port whose church has stained-glass windows that record a vow made by the local sailors in 1673 that if they were spared in the war with Holland they would join the *pardon* to Ste Anne d'Auray each year. They were, and today the local sailors still take part. **Port Navalo** is another small port, though it is now more of a resort, taking advantage of its position at the very tip of the Rhuys Peninsula.

The village of **St Gildas-de-Rhuys** is named for the peninsula and St Gildas, a sixth-century British monk who is one of the principal sources for Celtic and Saxon history at the time of Arthur. In later life Gildas, who was born in Cornwall, came to Brittany and founded a church here on the Rhuys Peninsula. Later an abbey was built on the site of the church. In the twelfth century the abbot was Peter Abelard one of the most famous of all early medieval monks. Abelard was born near Nantes in 1079 and was a theology teacher in Paris when he fell in love with Heloise, a girl twenty years his junior. Heloise had a son and the pair married, but recognising that Abelard's work was not compatible with married life Heloise decided to become a nun. Her relatives had Abelard castrated and he become a monk. In 1126 he reluctantly agreed to become abbot here at St Gildas-de-Rhuys. He found it as unbearable as he had feared, disliking the 'wild country' and the 'strange and horrible' language of the Bretons whom he saw as 'savages'. The monks of the abbey were also unfriendly: indeed, their hatred of their new abbot, not only a foreigner, but an infamous one, was such that they tried to murder him, Abelard escaping only by using a secret underground passage. He returned to Paris and teaching, but continued to exchange letters with Heloise, for whom he had managed to secure the position of Abbess of a convent at Troyes. The letters tell the remarkable story of a love that endured countless difficulties and separation. Peter Abelard died in 1142, Heloise in 1162. They now lie together in a single sarcophagus in Peré-Lechaise cemetery in Paris. The village church is the old abbey church and houses most of the remains of St Gildas in a tomb behind the altar. The treasury of the church has fifteenth-century reliquaries holding the limbs of the saint and his embroidered mitre.

From the peninsula return to the N165 and go east to reach **Muzillac** a pleasant town with a paper mill that still uses the old techniques to make high quality paper from rags. The mill can be ❋

visited. To the north-east is **Le Guerno** an old pilgrimage centre whose church has one hollow column into which pilgrims dropped their offerings. Nearby is the Parc Zoologique de Branféré, a zoo set in 50 hectares (124 acres) of beautiful, lake-studded parkland surrounding an old castle. The zoo has 2,000 animals representing over 200 species, and a collection of birds. The animals are held in semi-wild conditions.

Eastward now is the Vilaine river and the *département's* border. Sat on the river is **La Roche Bernard**, the last Morbihan town. In the past La Roche was an important port, the Vilaine being one of the area's major navigable rivers. The town was also a boat-building centre, a plaque commemorating the launch of the French Navy's first warship, *La Couronne*, here in 1634. Today the river traffic is mainly pleasure craft, passage on the river being easier now that the building of the Arzal dam, downriver, has virtually eliminated tides. One of the highlights of a visit to La Roche is a trip on the Vilaine, going downriver to view the dam, or upriver to Redon. Because of its position, sat on the border between Brittany and France, the town has had an eventful history. The most significant event took place during the Revolution when the town took the Revolutionaries' side and held out, with only 150 men, against 6,000 Chouans. Eventually the Chouans took the town, and ordered the Major to shout 'Long him the King'. He shouted 'Long live the Revolution' and was shot dead.

Within the town there is a series of narrow streets with delightful houses woven around Place Bouffay. During the Revolution the Place would have seemed a less friendly square, because it was here that the Revolutionaries who held the town erected a guillotine. One of the houses in the square is the 'The Cannon House' named for the cannon which was retrieved from an English warship that sought shelter in the Vilaine, in 1759 after a battle off Le Croisic to the south.

The Château des Basses-Fosses, built in the sixteenth century on a spur above the Vilaine, now houses a museum (the Musée de la Vilaine Maritime) which deals, in part with the history of the town, but is chiefly concerned with the history of the Vilaine as a seaway.

Finally on this tour of the Morbihan coast, go north of La Roche Bernard to **Nivillac** where the Musée d'Alfred has an interesting collection of old cars dating from 1905, together with collections of toy pedal cars (from the same period), farm tools, old planes and much more.

The Inland Département

As its north-western corner Morbihan's border with Finistère runs along the ridge of the Montagnes Noires. Nestling below this high ridge is **Gourin**, a small town whose prosperity is based on quarrying the mountains. The sixteenth-century church houses a beautiful painted wood *Pietà* that dates from the same period. Heading south from the town along the D769 the visitor soon comes to a turn off, to the left, for **Langonnet**, a pretty village famous for the abbey that is named for it but actually stands several miles to the west. The abbey was founded in the twelfth century, though it has been massively reconstructed, only the chapterhouse being of an early date (thirteenth century). Today, this old Benedictine house is a retreat for priests of St Esprit. Visitors can take in the fine architecture and see a collection of African memorabila brought back by missionaries whose work is still supported by the residents. There is also an interesting collection of Breton butterflies and beetles.

South of Langonnet, but back on the D769, is **Le Faouët**, a gorgeous little place with a superb market hall. The hall has a slate roof held aloft by stout granite columns and an array of marvellous woodwork. Today the town market spills over into the square in front of the hall, a square with a monument to a local, Corentin Carré, who enlisted as a pilot in 1915 when he was only fifteen years old, and was killed in 1918 by which time he was a veteran flier and had been promoted several times. A fine museum in the town, the Musée des Ursulines, houses work, from the first half of the twentieth century, by non-Breton artists who were inspired by the landscapes and farmers of Brittany. None of the artists are household names, but their work is interesting for the way it depicts the peasant farmers, sometimes heroic, sometimes amusing.

Nearby is L'Abeille Vivante, a prize-winning presentation of the life of the honey bee with glass sphere hives that allow observation of the activity at the very heart of a swarm. This fascinating exhibition has, quite rightly, won several prizes since its inception just a few years ago.

Close to Le Faouët are three excellent chapels, each of which is worth a visit. Closest is Ste Barbe, a little way to the north. The Chapelle Ste Barbe stands in a beautiful site on a rocky outcrop about 100m (328ft) above the Ellé Valley. Legend has it that in medieval times a local knight was out hunting in the valley when a sudden storm dislodged a huge rock that hurtled towards him. The knight fell to his knees and prayed to Ste Barbe for salvation and the rock miraculously stopped. The next day the knight started work on a chapel to the saint at the site on which the miracle occured. At a later stage the stairway to the chapel, the oratory to St Michel and the bell enclosure were added. The bell is rung by pilgrims, who still visit the site, as it is said to call down Heaven's blessings on the ringer. The chapel is in flamboyant Gothic and is lit by Renaissance stained glass. *Pardons* are held to the chapel twice annually, on the last Sunday in June and on 4 December. Close to the chapel is a fountain where, legend has it, a floated hairpin will tell a girl if she will marry within a year. If the hairpin sinks, she will not.

East of Ste Barbe is the chapel of St Nicolas with a superb Renaissance style carved wood rood screen above which the story of St Nicolas is depicted in a series of panels. There is a *pardon* here, too, on the second Sunday in July. The St Nicolas screen should be seen before that in the chapel of **St Fiacre** in the hamlet of the same name a little way south of Le Faouët, which is acknowledged as a masterpiece of Breton art. The screen was completed around 1480 and is an exuberant mix of intricate carving, some of it painted, and figures. The latter are intriguing for their portrayal, on the chancel side, of vices. Theft is illustrated by a man picking fruit, laziness by a man playing bagpipes, and most strikingly drunkeness by a man vomiting a dog. Elsewhere in the chapel, the sixteenth-century stained glass windows are also very good.

To the west of St Fiacre, beyond the picturesque woodland of the Forêt de Pontcallec, there is another beautiful chapel at **Kernascléden**. Legend has it that this chapel and that at St Fiacre were built by the same workmen, who were ferried between the sites by angels so that building would not be held up. The chapel has an excellent collection of fifteenth-century frescoes, one of the best in France. The frescoes represent incidents in the life of the Virgin and Christ, together with a Dance of Death and a vision of Hell that suggest an artist with a real gift for imagining tortures. Sadly for the legend it is known that Kernascléden was completed thirty years before St Fiacre.

Close to Kernascléden, at **Berné**, is the Parc de Pont Calleck, a beautiful area of parkland that surrounds a château built in the late nineteenth century and now an orphanage. The castle cannot be visited, but the parkland, with its trees and lake can, and offers superb walks and opportunities for picnics. There is a chapel in the grounds which is open to visitors if services are not being held.

East of Kernascléden is the valley of the River Scorff, one of the most beautiful of Morbihan's rivers. By common consent the section between **Guéméne-sur-Scorff,** which has some fine medieval houses and the ruins of an old castle, and **Plouay**, a pretty little town, is the finest. Following the Scorff southward from Guéméne many delightful villages are passed: **Persquen** has an interesting parish close, **Lignol** is beautifully set in a heavily wooded portion of the valley. Close to **Pont-Scorff**, by which time the river has grown in stature, there is a zoo which makes use of the valley of a tributary of the river to present animals in semi-wild conditions. The Parc Zoologique de Kerruisseau, at the hamlet of the same name, is remarkable for the sheer number of species it houses in this way, with lions, tigers, leopards, black and brown bears, bison, yaks, llamas and many more. There is also a collection of reptiles.

East of Pont-Scorff and the zoo is **Hennebont**, a fine town on the banks of the Blavet, another contender for Morbihan's finest river. The town was the scene of one of the most remarkable incidents of the War of Succession. After the French had taken Jean de Montfort (who was supported by the English) prisoner, his wife Jeanne held out in Hennebont Castle. The French battered it for weeks and eventually breached the walls. The garrison wanted to surrender but Jeanne, a resolute lady, wanted to continue to fight. Eventually she was forced to negotiate and agreed that if relief did not arrive within three days the castle would surrender. Two days later an English fleet sailed up the Blavet to relieve the siege. The town itself was spared during the siege, which took place in 1342, but was less lucky during the 1939-45 war when it was badly damaged. Little of medieval Hennebont now remains, though the Porte Broerec and part of the thirteenth-century town wall has been restored. The walls can be walked for a splendid view of the river. The Tours Broerec houses a museum that deals with the history of the town, and has a collection of local costumes.

Elsewhere in the town the church, completed by a large tower itself topped by a 65m (213ft) steeple, has some good stained glass, while horse-lovers will want to visit the Haras, the stud farm. Here there are about 150 stallions, both race horses and working animals. A tour includes the stables and saddle room, and can be extended to visit the ruins of the thirteenth-century Cistercian abbey of La Joie. Also nearby, and worth a visit, is Parc de Kerbihan, a well-laid out park with shrub and tree species from each of the five continents.

Going north along the Blavet Valley the visitor soon reaches a turn to the left for **Lochrist-Inzinzac** and the Ecomusée Industriel based on on the site of the Hennebont Ironworks, one of Brittany's most important industrial sites for over a century until its closure in 1966. The open-air site includes a museum, in the old site laboratory, to the history of both the ironworks and its workers, and a second museum to the history of the River Blavet as an industrial thoroughfare.

Leaving the valley, briefly, by going east, **Languidic** is reached, a pleasant little town grateful for having been bypassed by the N24. Close to the town is the Ferme Latière de Korfloch, a working dairy farm where visitors can see all aspects of milk and butter production as well as assisting with the cows, calves and horses. Continuing upriver the visitor reaches **Quistinic** and the Village de Poul Féton, a very picturesque restored sixteenth-century Breton village with numerous thatched cottages. The village is the centre for numerous exhibitions, many by Breton craftsmen.

Beyond Quistinic, turn right out of the valley to reach **Baud**, a pleasant village whose La Clarté chapel contains a revered statue of the Virgin that is the subject of a *pardon* on the first Sunday in July. A more unusual, and much more controversial, statue can be found by following the Hennebont road from Baud, to reach the hamlet of Coët Vin. Go left there and park in the car park about 500m further on. Go through the gate and take the steep path to reach the *Venus de Quinipily*, a statue positioned above a fountain in the park of the restored Château de Quinipily. The origins of the statue are uncertain. It has been ascribed to the ancient Egyptians, the Celts and the Romans, but also dismissed as a worthless fake. Folk memory claims that the 2m (7ft) semi-naked statue was dug up near Castennec to the north, and it is certainly true that it was at one time set up there and was the centre of a Pagan cult. Some Bretons called the Venus *Ar Gurreg Houarn* (Iron Woman), and found strength in her presence, women seeking her assistance to find husbands and to ease the pains of childbirth. Other locals called her *Groac'h en Couard*, the Witch of Couard, and feared her. Eventually the church took a hand, hurling the statue into the Blavet. It was retrieved, thrown in again, and retrieved yet again. After several more disposals the local lord of the manor had the statue copied as the original had become battered. The original is now lost, the copy remaining as an enigma.

North of Baud the Blavet flows through fine country, less wooded than the valley of the Scorff, but no less beautiful. A succession of pretty villages is passed to reach the Site de Castennec where the *Venus de Quinipily* once stood. Here the river makes a tight 180° turn, the view from the site taking in the whole of the turn and several picturesque villages, the best of which is **St Nicolas-des-Faux** with its thatched cottages. To the west of the Site is **Melrand**, a lovely little Breton town with granite houses and a Calvary and, nearby, the Ferme Archéologique de Melrand, a reconstructed farm in the excavated ninth-century village of Lann Gouh.

North of Melrand is **Quelven** where the chapel houses an extraordinary statue of the Virgin, seated and holding the Infant Jesus. The statue opens to reveal twelve panels depicting the life of Christ. Back in the Blavet Valley the visitor next reaches Pontivy.

Pontivy is actually two towns, an older, medieval town having been extended during the earlier years of the Republic. The name derives from the first bridge over the Blavet, built by a Welsh saint called Ivy. The town grew prosperous in the period after the construction, in the fifteenth century, of the castle by the powerful de Rohan family whose main castle, at Josselin, will be visited later. The castle still remains, its outer walls, all of 20m (66ft) high, still dominating the old town. The surrounding 'moat' was always dry and must still be crossed to visit the main building, built in the eighteenth century. The walk around the walls offers fine views of old Pontivy. The best of the houses in the old town, half-timbered, overhung houses that date from the sixteenth and seventeenth centuries, are in Rue du Fil, Rue du Dr-Guépin and Rue du Pont, streets that radiate from the picturesque Place du Martray. Nearby is the church of Notre-Dame-de-la-Joie, built in the sixteenth century and housing a statue of the Virgin of Joy, to whom prayers were offered, and answered, when plague struck the town in 1696.

The new town at Pontivy, begun in the last years of the eighteenth century, owes its existence to the old town's position, roughly halfway along the Nantes-Brest canal, and to its enthusiasm for the Republican cause. So enthusiastic was the town that Napoleon made it the capital of Brittany and built a barracks and several new buildings. Later, when the British fleet threatened the southern coast

A roofscape view of Château de Josselin on the bank of the Nantes-Brest canal

of Brittany and, more importantly, the French naval bases of Brest, Lorient and Nantes and ships sailing between them, Napoleon had the Nantes-Brest canal dug, a canal that used the Blavet for part of its route. Pontivy was about half-way between the terminal ports and became a strategic town. A new town sprang up, and Pontivy changed its name to Napoleonville. The Empire fell and the name changed back. There was a reversion to Napoleonville during the Second Empire, but that too was short-lived.

North-west from Pontivy the beautiful Forêt de Quénécan can be reached, a forest in which wild boar can still be seen. At the forest's edge is the southern (Morbihan) shore of Lac de Guerlédan. **Les Forge des Salles**, close to the lake is Morbihan's most delightful spot in this area, a village that was once a centre for charcoal production, but which now nestles sleepily below its ruined castle. Heading east from Pontivy the visitor reaches **Rohan**, a pretty town beside the canal, but one which now offers no trace of the family who gave it its name. Close by is the Cistercian abbey of Notre-Dame-de-Timadeuc, built only in the mid-nineteenth century, despite its Gothic appearance, and in beautiful and peaceful woodland position. The abbey can be visited and has an audio-visual show on its history. There is also a range of craftwork produced by the monks.

After visiting Pontivy and Rohan, the visitor is drawn, inevitably, along the line of the Nantes-Brest canal to **Josselin**, another of the highlights of a tour of Morbihan, a pretty town and a wonderfully picturesque castle. The first castle built here was erected by Guthenoc de Porhort, a local count, in about 1050. Porhort's son, Josselin, added the first village, naming it for himself. The castle was destroyed and rebuilt in battles with the English and, in 1351, became the scene of one of the most famous of all Breton battles. At that time, during the War of Succession, Josselin was held for Charles de Blois by Jean de Beaumanoir, but besieged by an English army under Richard Bemborough. Worn out by the siege and inconclusive skirmishes the two commanders decided to settle the matter with one fight between hand-picked bands of thirty soldiers. These two bands, lead by Beaumanoir and Bemborough, met on 27 March 1351 to fight Le Combat des Trentes, the Battle of the Thirties. The men were formidably armed and fought all day stopping only when they were exhausted. Incredibly only nine men, Emborough and eight others, were killed on the losing (English) side.

In 1370 the castle passed to Olivier de Clisson when he married Beaumanoir's widow, a de Rohan. Clisson was a brute of a man, though it is not hard to see why. His father, who held Nantes castle, was beheaded during the War of Succession after having been falsely accused of betraying the French cause. His widow, Clisson's mother, nailed his severed head to the castle door and made her son swear vengeance. She then led a small army that ravaged the area killing every follower of Charles de Blois she could find, and even when driven back to the coast continued her campaign at sea. Clisson cleverly changed sides at the time of the Hundred Years War, eventually succeeding de Guesclin as Constable (commander-in-chief) of the French army. Eventually Clisson fell from grace and retreated to Josselin Castle, strengthening its walls and giving it a total of nine towers. On his death the castle passed to the de Rohans who added sumptuous living quarters. Henri de Rohan was a Protestant leader during the Wars of Religion and, as a result, Richelieu attacked the castle, knocking down five of the towers. It is said that Richelieu then sent de Rohan a message that he had thrown a ball amongst his skittles. During the Revolution the castle was a prison, but was returned to the de Rohans who restored it and live in it still.

The castle is best viewed from Pont Ste Croix over the Oust river from where it is both elegant and imposing, and the towers, with their Rhine-like pepperpot roofs, are seen to good advantage. But though that is the best view, the façade that faces the courtyard is also splendid, especially for the intricate sculptures which are all in granite, a very hard stone to work with such delicacy. Visitors are allowed access only to the castle's ground floor rooms. One of these, the drawing room, is richly furnished and hung with portraits of the de Rohan family.

In the castle's old stable block is the Musée de Poupées in which more than 500 dolls of the Rohan collection are exhibited. The dolls are from all over the world, some dating back to the seventeenth century.

Close to the castle is the basilica of Notre-Dame-du-Roncier, Our Lady of the Brambles. Legend has it that in the ninth century a peasant, returning home from the fields one evening, found a statue of the Virgin in a bramble bush. He took it home, but the next morning it had vanished. He found it in the bush again and after the same thing had happened several times realised it was a sign to build a church. The original statue was burned during the Revolution, only a few fragments now remaining. These were central to a *pardon* held on the second Sunday of September, though since 1728 the emphasis has shifted to the fountain beside the church. In that year it became the Pardon des Aboyeuses (Barker's Pardon) because three town children were cured of epilepsy after drinking from the fountain (barking being an ancient term for epilepsy). However another

Equestrian leisure-time around Lizio

The octagonal tower of Tours d'Elven

version of the story claims that the name derives from an incident when the Virgin appeared in the town disguised as a beggar. The townswomen set their dogs on Her and as a penance their voices changed to dog-like barks until they had attended the *pardon*.

The basilica itself is an interesting building with the mausoleum of Olivier de Clisson and his wife in the south chapel. The tower can be climbed for a view of the castle's façade and the old town. The best of the old houses are in Rue des Vierges, Rue des Trentes and Place Notre-Dame close to the church.

Rue des Trentes can be followed to reach the N24 for Ploërmel. A dual carriageway section of this road some 3km (2 miles) east of Josselin has a carriageway on either side of a stone obelisk that marks the spot where the Battle of the Thirties was fought. Before visiting Ploërmel there are two other interesting sites near Josselin. To the north, near **Mohon**, is Le Camp des Rouets, an example of the use, in medieval Breton, of earth fortresses which had changed little since Celtic times. Of more visual appeal is the Domaine de Kerguehennec, near the village of **Bignan**, to the south of the Josselin to Locminé road. The estate comprises a huge (170 hectares, 440 acre) arboretum around an early eighteenth-century château. In addition to its trees, the arboretum also has a number of large outdoor sculptures by

A display of traditional village craft at Lizio

contemporary artists. The elegantly symmetrical château, set before a lake, is furnished in an equally elegant manner in nineteenth-century style.

It was from **Ploërmel** that Richard Bemborough and his men marched to the Battle of the Thirties, the battle having been fought mid-way between Josselin and the English base. Then as now, the town was at the heart of a rich farming area, an area that brought great prosperity in sixteenth and seventeenth centuries when Ploërmel was the major local market town. Rue Beaumanoir, named for the victor of the Battle of the Thirties, and Rue des Frones-Bourgeois have the best of the houses from this period. By common consent the best example is Maison de Marmousets with its beautiful woodcarvings. The two streets converge on the church of St Armel, named for the Celtic saint who founded the town. The saint was another who made his area safe by disposing of a dragon, an episode depicted in the superb stained glass windows. These are reached through a doorway with some irreverent carvings. Look out for the shoemaker sewing up his wife's mouth!

Across Rue Charles de Gaulle from the church is the abbey of the Frères de Ploërmel in the courtyard of which is an astronomical clock built in the 1850s by one of the brotherhood as a teaching tool for local teachers. The clock is adorned with a picture of the brother, Bernadin Morin.

Taking the D766 northwards from Ploërmel, the visitor will pass the Étang du Duc (Duke's Pool) a natural lake with an artificial beach that has become popular as a water sports centre. North again the border with Ille-et-Vilaine is reached close to the Forêt de Paimpont. The forest lies almost entirely outside Morbihan, but one site, close to the border of the two *départements* is both within Morbihan and within the forest. The site is the Château de Comper near the village of **Concoret**. The castle is linked with several of the forest legends, and is said to have been the birthplace of Viviane, the fairy who entranced and captured Merlin. Little remains of the fourteenth-century castle, though it is a very romantic site, but a later addition has been restored and houses an exhibition to the forest's Arthurian legends.

Closer to Ploërmel, at **Campénéac**, is the modern Cistercian abbey of La Joie Notre-Dame. Visitors are welcomed, and can see the monks making cheese, cakes and chocolate, all of which can be bought.

Heading south on the N166 from Ploërmel the visitor soon reaches **La Chapelle-Caro** and the Château de Crévy which houses one of the best costume museums in Brittany, with examples from the eighteenth century through to the present day. Many of the costumes are

displayed in tableaux complete with furnishings that evoke historical periods. On the other side of the N166 from the castle is a museum
of a very different kind close to the village of **Lizio**. This Ecomusée
de la Ferme et des Vieux Métiers displays more than 10,000 old farm
and craft implements representing over 50 different country crafts,
together with displays on old village life.

South again the road crosses the Landes de Lanvaux. This stretch
of high land stretches from Baud to Pleucadeuc and, until the
nineteenth century, was a narrow ridge of barren moor and heath, a
very ancient landscape dotted with menhirs and steeped in legend.
Now, however, much of that original heath has been lost to farming
and forestry so that the ridge is largely indistinguishable from the
surrounding land. At the foot of the Landes, at **St Guyomard**, the
Château de Brignac dominates the Claye Valley. The castle was built
in the fifteenth century and can be visited, but only by groups who
book in advance. A more visitor friendly castle can be seen on the far
side of the Landes near **Elven**. The Fortresse de Largoët is usually
called the Tours d'Elven (Towers of Elven), and is a marvellous ruin.
The castle was built in the fourteenth century, but was owned by the
Marshall de Rieux when France reached the spot during their
invasion of 1488. The marshall strongly supported the Breton cause,
and his castle was burned, only two ivy-encrusted towers and some
ruined walls remaining. The octagonal tower, itself turetted, is
almost 50m (164ft) high and has walls almost 9m (30ft) thick. With its
lake and the beautiful surrounding woodland the castle is an en-
chanting place.

East of Elven is **Questembert**, a pleasant little market town with a
superb covered market hall and a monument, in the appropriately
named Place du Monument, to the victory of Alain-le-Grand over
invading Norsemen in AD888. Legend has it that of 15,000 Viking
raiders only 400 survived. To the east of the town are a small
collection of worthwhile places for the visitor. At **Caden** the Musée
Agricole retells the life of the Breton farmer at the turn of this century,
while a little way south is the Château de Léhélc, a red schist and
granite manor house dating from the seventeenth century. The three
courtyards set it off in fine style. Inside the furnishings cover the
range from the sixteenth to the nineteenth century.

At **Malansac**, north of Caden the Parc de Préhistoire is an outdoor
museum where the Palaeolithic and Neolithic Ages are brought to
life in a series of tableaux, with life-size people and animals.
Malansac is close to Rochefort-en-Terre, but before visiting the town
go east on the D153 to **St Jacut-les-Pins** to see the Tropical Floral Parc
and the Ferme Conservatoire du Petit Moulin. The former, as the

name implies, is a park specialising in tropical plants. Within the hothouses there are bananas, cacti and a superb collection of orchids. The Petit Moulin is a working Breton farm using traditional methods. Here the visitor can see Ouessant sheep being worked and see some of the conservation methods that have been introduced. Visits are by appointment only, and a knowledge of French is essential.

Rochefort-en-Terre is a picture-postcard town with pretty houses, almost all decorated with colourful window boxes, or covered with climbing plants, in neat streets adorned with flower-filled stone troughs, the whole set on a ridge above wooded valleys. To see the best of the houses, find Rue des Halles and the Place du Puits, or just follow the camera-hung tourists. The castle is equally as picturesque, though little of it is original. After its destruction in 1793 it remained ruinous until the 1900s when the American artists Alfred and Trafford Klots bought it and built a new mansion that incorporated the older remains. In part the Klots used stone from other derelict castles in the area to complete their transformation. The castle is open to visitors who can admire the building, the paintings of the brothers Klots, some early Flemish tapestry and a collection of medieval Quimper porcelain Virgins. A museum in the gardens has a collection of old tools and kitchen utensils, another of Morbihan *coiffes* and a display on the history of the area.

The town church, Notre-Dame-de-la-Tronchaye, houses the statue of the same name that a local story tells was found in a hollow tree in the twelfth century. It is conjectured that the statue may indeed have been hidden to protect it from Norse invaders as it is clearly very old. It is now the object of a *pardon* on the first Sunday after 15 August.

North-east of Rochefort the Nantes-Brest canal is crossed again amid some beautiful country. On the border of Morbihan and Ille-et-Vilaine is **La Gacilly**, a town that is alive with craftsmen and has a small industry producing flower-based beauty products, an apt idea in view of the number of window boxes. The use of flowers is illustrated in the Espace Yves Rocher which combines a botanical garden with hundreds of plants that go into the processes, and an exhibition on the processes themselves and the end-products.

Malestroit lies to the north of Rochefort, sandwiched between sections of the Landes de Lanvaux. It is a picturesque little town with an array of fine houses, that grew prosperous when the Nantes-Brest canal was cut. The best of the houses can be seen in Rue des Ponts and Rue au Froment, though one of the most interesting is in Place du Bouffay, a house with a façade enriched by irreverent carvings. All these spots are close to the church of St Gilles where the statues of two of the four Gospel writers on the buttresses close to the south door create a curiosity in mid-afternoon. Then, the shadows of St Luke's ox and St John's eagle are said to create a likeness of the profile of Voltaire. Close to Malestroit is **St Marcel** and the Musée de la Résistance Bretonne. This huge and impressive museum spreads over 6 hectares (about 15 acres) and includes films on Brittany's part in the 1939-45 war, reconstructions of part of the Atlantic wall, a reconstructed wartime Breton street and a collection of army vehicles and weapons. Close by is a monument erected to commemorate a battle fought on 18 June 1944 between the German army and members of the Breton Resistance.

Finally, and maintaining the military theme, there is the Musée du Souvenirs des Écoles Militaires at **Guer**, to the north-east of St Marcel, and on Morbihan's border with Ille-et-Vilaine. The museum houses mementoes of France's war heroes and its military campaigns.

Additional Information

Places to Visit

Auray
Charterhouse
Open: all year Monday to Saturday 10-11.45am, 2-5.30pm, Sunday 10-11.45am, 2-5.15pm. Guided tours available.
☎ 97 242702

Baden
Museum of Old Toys
Open: all year, on request.
☎ 97 570242

Beg Rohu
National Sailing School
Open: February to November. Times according to courses.
☎ 97 502702

Belle-Ile
Vauban Citadel
Easter to September daily 9am-7pm. October to Easter daily 9am-12noon, 2-6pm.
☎ 97 318417

Grand Phare Lighthouse
Open: July to mid-September daily 10.30-11am, 2-5pm. Guided tours available.

Koh-Castell Bird Reserve
Open: July, August daily except Monday. Guided tours only (allow 2 hours). For information on times
☎ 97 409295

Boat Trips
Boat trips to Belle-Ile, Ile d'Houat and Ile Hoedic depart from Port-Maria in Quiberon. The trip takes 45 minutes to Belle-Ile. A single boat visits the two smaller islands, taking 1¼ hours to reach Ile d'Houat and a further 30 minutes to reach Ile Hoedic. Times are dependent on tides and passenger numbers. For information contact Campagnie Morbihannaise et Nantaise de Navigation in Lorient, Quiberon or Le Palais
☎ 97 230397 (Lorient)
☎ 97 500690 (Quiberon)
☎ 97 318001 (Le Palais)

Berné
Pont Calleck Park
Open: all year except for the first
two weeks of August daily 10am-
dusk.
☎ 97 516117

Bignan
Domaine de Kerguehennec
Open: April to October daily 10am-
7pm.
☎ 97 605778 or 97 602112

Caden
Farm Museum
Open: June to September Saturday,
Sunday 9am-12noon, 2-6pm.
☎ 97 678044

Léhélec Castle
Open: July, August daily except
Tuesday 2-7pm.

Campénéac
La Joie Notre-Dame Abbey
Open: all year daily 10am-dusk.
☎ 97 934207

Carnac
Archeoscope, Alignements du Ménec
Open: March to mid-November
daily 10am-7pm. English shows at
10.30am and 2pm.
☎ 97 520749

Kercado Tumulus
Open: all year daily 10am-12noon,
2-6pm.
☎ 97 521352

St Michel's Tumulus
Open: July, August daily 9.30am-
7.30pm. Mid- to end June, 1 to mid-
September daily 10am-6pm. Easter
to mid-June and mid- to end
September daily 10am-12noon, 3-
6pm. Guided tours only.
For information:
☎ 97 521352

Miln-Le Rouzic Prehistory Museum
Open: July, August daily 10am-
12noon, 2-6.30pm. September to
June daily except Tuesday 10am-
12noon, 2-5pm.
☎ 97 522204

*St Michel-de-Kerganon Abbey
    and Ste Anne-de-Kerganon Abbey*
Open: all year Monday to Saturday
offices at 10am and 5pm Sunday
offices at 10am and 4pm.

Concoret
Comper Castle
Open: June to August daily except
Tuesday 10am-7pm. May, September daily except Tuesday and Friday
10am-7pm. October to April by request.
☎ 97 227996

Elven Towers
Open: February to November daily
8am-8pm.
☎ 97 533596

Guer
War Museum
Open: all year, daily except
Monday 9am-12noon, 2-6pm.
☎ 97 757575

Gulf of Morbihan
Boat Trips
There are several companies which
sail the route around the Gulf. There
are individual route differences,
but in general the boats ply from
Auray to Vannes calling at several
intermediate ports, chiefly Locmariaquer and Port-Navalo, and some of
the islands. Ile de Gavrinis is reached
by a short boat ride from Larmor-
Baden. For information on the boat
services contact the tourist information offices in Auray or Vannes.
☎ 97 240975 (Auray)
☎ 97 472434 (Vannes)

Hennebont
Broerec Tower Museum
Rue Maurice Thorez
Open: mid-June to mid-September
daily 10.30-11.30am, 2-7pm.
☎ 97 362918

Stud Farm
Rue Victor Hugo
Open: mid-June to August Monday
to Saturday. Tours at 10am,11am,
2.15pm, 3.15pm and 4.15pm.
September Monday to Saturday
tours at 2.15pm, 3.15pm, 4.15pm.
October to February Monday to
Saturday tours at 3.15pm.
☎ 97 362027

Kerbihan Park
Rue Léo-Lagrange
Open: all year daily, any reasonable time.
☎ 97 363441 for information on the
plants.

Ile de Gavrinis
Tumulus
Boats from Larmor-Baden take
about 15 minutes to cross to the
island and leave at 30 minute
intervals. Open: June to September
daily 10am-12noon, 2-6pm. March
to May Monday to Friday 2-6pm.
Saturday, Sunday 10am-12noon, 2-
6pm. October daily 2-6pm.
☎ 97 570863

Ile de Groix
Boats cross from Lorient throughout the year on Mondays to
Saturdays. Times are variable with
tides and number of passengers.
For details contact Société Co-
opérative de Vedettes at Locmiquélic
☎ 97 334055.
To explore the Ile de Groix cars,
mopeds and bicycles can be hired
at Port Tudy.

François le Bail Nature Reserve
Open: July, August daily 10am-
dusk. September to June by request.
☎ 97 865597 or 98 490718

Ecomuseum
Open: May to mid-September daily
9.30am-12.30pm, 3-7pm. Mid-
September to April daily except
Monday 10am-12.30pm, 2-5pm.
☎ 97 210397

Josselin
Castle
Open: Easter to May Wednesday
and Sunday 2-6pm. June, September daily 2-6pm. July, August daily
10am-12noon, 2-6pm.
☎ 97 223650

Museum of Dolls
Open: June to September daily
10am-12noon, 2-6pm. April, May
and October Wednesday, Saturday,
Sunday 2-6pm.
☎ 97 223645

Notre-Dame-du-Roncier Tower
Open: July, August daily 11am-
12.30pm, 3-6.30pm. June, September Thursday to Tuesday 11am-
12.30pm, 3-6.30pm.

La Chapelle-Caro
Crévy Castle and Costume Museum
Open: April, May Wednesday,
Saturday, Sunday 2-6pm. June
daily 2-6pm. July to mid-Septem-
ber daily 10am-12noon, 2-6pm.
Mid-September to mid-November
Wednesday, Saturday, Sunday 2-
6pm.
☎ 97 749195

Le Faouët
Ursuline Museum
Open: mid-June to mid-September
daily 10am-12.30pm, 2-6.30pm.
☎ 97 232323

Live Hives
Kercadaret
Open: April to October daily 10am-12noon, 2-7pm.
☎ 97 230805

La Gacilly
Yves Rocher Exhibition
Garden and Video open: July to mid-September Monday to Friday 8am-12noon, 2-5pm. Saturday, Sunday 2-5pm. Mid-September to June Monday to Friday 8am-12noon, 2-5pm. Exhibition open: mid-June to mid-September daily 8am-12noon, 2-5pm. Mid-September to mid-June Saturday, Sunday 2-5pm.
☎ 99 085811

La Roche Bernard
River Trips
July, August daily 2-5pm.
Trips leave at hourly intervals and take about 1½ hours to reach the Arzal dam or Redon. Meals available on board. For information contact the tourist information office, Place du Pilori.
☎ 99 906798

Vilaine Maritime Museum (Château des Basses-Fosses)
Open: July, August daily 10am-7pm. June, September daily 10am-12.30pm, 2.30-7pm. October to May Saturday 2-6pm. Sunday 10am-12noon, 2-6pm.
☎ 99 908347

Langonnet
Notre-Dame Abbey
Open: all year Monday, Wednesday to Saturday 9.30-11.30am, 3-5pm. Sunday 3-5pm.
☎ 97 239308

Languidic
Kerfloch Dairy Farm
Open: April to mid-October daily 2-7pm. Mid-October to March by request.
☎ M. Guehennec 97 658248

Le Guerno
Branféré Zoo
Open: June to September daily 9am-6.30pm. October to May daily 9am-12noon, 2-6.30pm.
☎ 97 429466

Lizio
Ecomuseum
Open: all year daily 10am-12noon, 2-7pm.
☎ 97 749301

Lochrist-Inzinzac
Industrial Museum
Open: July, August daily 10am-12noon, 2-6pm. September to June Monday to Friday 10am-12noon, 2-6pm, Sunday 2-6pm.
☎ 97 369821

Locmariaquer
Table of the Merchants and Great Menhir
Open: April to October daily 10am-7pm.
☎ 97 426344

Lorient
Sea Museum
Open: all year Monday, Wednesday to Saturday 9am-12noon, 2-6pm, Sundays 2-6pm.
☎ 97 848737

Malansac
Prehistoric Park
Open: April to mid-October daily 10am-7pm. Mid-October to November Sunday 2-6pm.

Melrand
Ancient Farm and Village
Open: July, August daily 9am-8pm.
September to June daily 10am-5pm.
☎ 97 395789

Muzillac
Pen-Mur Paper Mill
Open: all year daily 10am-12.30pm,
2-7pm. Guided tours available.
☎ 97 414379

Nivillac
Alfred Museum
Open: all year daily 10am-12noon,
2-7pm.
☎ 99 907979

Ploërmel
Astronomical Clock
Open: Easter to All Saints Day
9.30am-11.45pm, 2.30-5.30pm.
☎ 97 740667

Plouharnel
The Galleon
Open: Easter, May daily 10am-
12noon 2-6pm. June to September
daily 9.30am-12noon, 2-7pm.
☎ 97 523956

The Chouannerie
Open: mid-March to September
daily 10am-12noon, 2-6.30pm.
☎ 97 523131

St Anne's Abbey
Open: all year, daily 9-11.15am, 2-
5.45pm. The monks' offices, with
Gregorian Chant, take place daily
at 11.30am and 6pm, and can be
viewed.

Pont-Scorff
Kerruisseau Zoo
Open: Easter to October daily 9am-
7.30pm. November to Easter
Monday, Wednesday, Saturday,
Sunday 10.30am-dusk. Closed in
heavy rain.
☎ 97 326086

Pontivy
Castle
Open: June to September daily
10am-6.30pm. October to May
Wednesday to Sunday 10am-
12noon, 2-6pm.
☎ 97 251293

Port-Louis
The Citadel
April to September daily except
Tuesday 10am-7pm. October to
March daily except Tuesday 1.30-
6pm. Note that the last admission
is 45 minutes before closing time.
☎ 97 211401

Quistinic
Poul Féton Village
Open: April to October daily 10am-
12noon, 2-7pm. Craft exhibitions:
mid-June to mid-September daily
10am-12noon, 2-7pm. Other
exhibitions: mid-June to October
daily 11am-12noon, 2-7pm.
☎ 97 397282

Rochefort-en-Terre
Castle
Open: April to May, October
Saturday, Sunday 10.30am-12noon,
2-6.30pm. Weekdays by request.
June to September daily 10.30am-
12noon, 2-6.30pm.
☎ 97 433505

Rohan
Timadeuc Abbey
Open: all year daily 8am-8pm.
☎ 97 515029

Sarzeau

Kerlevenan Castle
Open: July to mid-September
Wednesday only 2-6pm and only
on request, either by telephone or
in writing.
☎ 97 264110 or 97 264816
Write to M. de Gouvello
Château de Kerlevenan
56370 Sarzeau

Suscinio Castle
Open: April to September daily
(except Wednesday am) 9.30am-
12noon, 2-7pm. October to March
Tuesday, Saturday, Sunday
9.30am-12noon, 2-5pm (also open
Monday afternoons in periods
October to mid-November, mid-
February to March). The museum
of Breton history is open the same
time as the castle.
☎ 97 419191

Men Guen Farm
Open: June to September daily
10am-7pm.
☎ 97 419896

Séné

Falguerec Bird Reserve
Open: July, August daily 10am-
1pm, 2-7pm. April to June
Saturday, Sunday 2-7pm.
☎ 97 427679, or the tourist office in
Vannes (97 472434).

St Degan

Ecomusuem
Open: June to September daily 2-
6pm. At other times by request.
Guided tours available.
☎ 97 576205

St Gildas-de-Rhuys

Church Treasury
Open: July, August Monday to
Saturday 10.30am-12noon, 2-5pm.

St Guyomard

Brignac Castle
Open: by prior appointment only.
☎ 97 759627

St Jacut-les-Pins

Tropical Flower Park
Open: March to November daily
9am-12noon, 2-7pm. December to
February daily except Monday
9am-12noon, 2-7pm.
☎ 99 719198

Petit Moulin Farm
Open: by appointment only.
☎ M. Lesteven, 99 913226

St Marcel

Breton Resistance Museum
Open: mid-June to mid-September
daily 10am-7pm. Mid-September to
mid-June daily except Tuesday
10am-12noon, 2-6pm.
☎ 97 751690

Ste Anne d'Auray

Pilgrimage Close
Treasury open: mid-March to mid-
October daily 10am-12noon, 2-
6pm. Mid-October to mid-March
Sunday 2-6pm, but at other times
by request.
☎ 97 576880
Diorama open: March to November daily 9am-8pm. December to
February by appointment only.
☎ 97 523618

Breton Costume Museum
Open: mid-March to mid-October
daily 10am-12noon, 2-6pm. Mid-
October to mid-March Sunday 2-
6pm, but at others times by
request.
☎ 97 576880

Thiex
Plessis-Josso Castle
Open: July, August daily 2-7pm.
May, June, September, October by
request only.
☎ 97 431616

Vannes
Treasury of St Peter's Cathedral
Open: mid-June to mid-September
Monday to Saturday 10am-12noon,
2-5pm.

*La Cohue (Museum of Fine Art and
    the Gulf Museum)*
Open: mid-June to mid-September
daily 10am-12noon, 2-6pm. Mid-
September to mid-June Monday,
Wednesday to Saturday 10am-
12noon, 2-6pm.
☎ 97 473586

Natural History Museum
Rue des Halles
Open: mid-June to August Monday
to Saturday 9.30am-12noon, 2-6pm.
September to mid-June by request
only.
☎ 97 425980

Archaeological Museum
Rue des Halles
Open: April to August Monday to
Saturday 9.30am-12noon, 2-6pm.
September to March Monday to
Friday 2-6pm.
☎ 97 425980

Aquarium
Parc du Golfe
Open: June to August daily 9am-
7pm. September to May daily 9am-
12noon, 1.30-6.30pm.
☎ 97 406740

Puppet Palace
Parc du Golfe
Open: July, August daily 10am-
6.30pm. Mid-February to July and
August to mid-November daily
10am-12noon, 2-6pm.
☎ 97 404039

Butterfly House
Parc du Golfe
Open: May to October daily 10am-
7pm.
☎ 97 460102

Post Office and Telecommunications
Place de la République
Market Days: Wednesday and
Saturday.
Car Hire: Europcar
46 Avenue Victor Hugo
☎ 97 424343

Tourist Information Centres

**Comité Départemental du
    Tourisme du Morbihan**
Hôtel du Département
BP 400
56009 Vannes
☎ 97 540656

Auray
Place de la République
56640
☎ 97 240975

Belle-Ile-en-Mer
Quai Bonnelle
BP30 (Le Palais)
56360
☎ 97 318193

Carnac
74 Avenue des Druides
56340
☎ 97 521352

Josselin
Place de la Congregation
56120
☎ 97 223643 (June to September).
97 222417 (October to May).

Le Faouët
Rue de Quimper (June to September).
7 Rue du Soleil (October to May).
56320
☎ 97 232323 (June to September).
97 230837 (October to May).

Locmariaquer
Place de la Mairie
56740
☎ 97 573305

Lorient
Maison de la Mer
Quai de Rohan
56100
☎ 97 210784

Ploërmel
Rue du Val
BP 106
56800
☎ 97 740270

Pontivy
61 Rue du Général de Gaulle
56300
☎ 97 250410

Quiberon
7 Rue de Verdun
56170
☎ 97 500784

Rochefort-en-Terre
Place des Halles
56220
☎ 97 433357

Sarzeau
Rue du Général de Gaulle
56370 Sarzeau
☎ 97 418237

Vannes
1 Rue Thiers
56000
☎ 97 472434

4

ILLE-ET-VILAINE

The last of Brittany's four *départements* is the borderland with France. I-et-V, as the name is commonly given, is more obviously French than the *départements* to the west, yet still maintains its Breton identity. This Breton 'feel' is reflected in the scenery: as with the inland countryside to the west the land of I-et-V is one of small fields and remnant woods. To the east, in Normandy, beyond the line of formidable castles that once protected the Duchy's border with France, the country is more open.

The border castles are one of the most prominent of the *département's* features, Fougères and Vitré being among the most impressive castles in the province. Rennes, once the capital of the Duchy, is Brittany's largest city, if Nantes is relegated to the Loire, and has a fine old quarter, all that remains of the medieval town after a disastrous fire. Finally, to prove the link to the ancient Brittany, the land of the Celts, there is the Forest of Paimpont, the Brocéliande of the legends, a superb area of woodland with many features that are linked to the legends of Arthur and Merlin.

This chapter starts in the north of the *département*, on the Atlantic Coast, before moving south to Rennes and the country from there to the border of Loire-Atlantique.

The first point reached on the curious piece of Ille-et-Vilaine that lies to the west of the Rance is **St Briac-sur-Mer**, a resort with good beaches, but more famous for its Fêtes des Mouettes, the festival of seagulls, an annual celebration of Breton culture held on the second Sunday in August. Close to St Briac there is a final viewpoint before the Emerald Coast ends at the Rance estuary. Point du Décolle, near St Lunaire, is very picturesque, its tip joined to the mainland by a natural rock arch over a chasm known as the Cat's Leap. The grotto below the arch is known as the Sirens' Cave. **St Lunaire**, the village close to the point, has two good beaches and an interesting old church standing among trees. The church has a fourteenth-century carved stone effigy lying on a sarcophagus which dates from the Roman occupation of Gaul.

Dinard has been called the 'Pearl of the Emerald Coast' and even the 'Nice of the North' though these titles were more appropriate during Dinard's 'Belle Epoque', the years around the turn of this century. Until the 1850s Dinard was a simple, if pretty, fishing port. Then, an American built a mock château in the village and others began to take an interest. Soon it had become popular with the British leisure class and was being transformed into a typical British resort, with a casino, gardens and a promenade, fine hotels and croquet on the sand. It maintained its position far into this century though of late the opening of the Rance dam, with its roadway, has put Dinard very close to St Malo, with a resultant increase in visitors, an increase in popular appeal and a decline in its exclusive image. Despite this it is still a fine place with many of the gardens, villas and promenades still in place.

The village has three fine beaches, Plage de St Énogat, Plage de l'Écluse and Plage du Prieuré. The first two are separated by the headland of Pointe des Étêtes — backed by the fine terraced garden of Port-Riou — the last two by Pointe du Moulinet, a superb viewpoint, and the Promenade du Clair de Lune, a pedestrian-only walk edged by fine flower beds. Plage de l'Écluse is also known as Grande Plage, and is backed by the deluxe hotels, the casino and the Palais des Congrès, a conference centre. On the Promenade du Clair de Lune stands Dinard's Musée de la Mer, an aquarium with tanks containing Breton fish and crustaceans and a Sea Museum which has exhibits from the Arctic expeditions of Cdr. Charcot, a local man. At the far end of the promenade is the Musée du Pays de Dinard, the town's history museum, housed in a villa named for Napoleon II's wife, Eugenie. Especially good is the section on the Victorian resort of Dinard.

At the end of the Promenade is the Plage du Prieuré whose eastern edge is defined by the mass of La Vicomté. A fine walk here visits Pointe de la Vicomté for a view of the Rance estuary. Dinard is a starting point for boat trips on the Rance, and from it St Malo can also be reached by boat. Another trip visits the Normandy islands of Chausey.

From Dinard, St Malo is reached by crossing the Rance on the road built on the dam system of the tidal power station. The use of the tides to power mills is an ancient one, but the Rance system, which uses the tides to generate electricity is novel. Indeed, when the station was opened is 1967 it was the world's first tidal power station. Set in the 750m (2,460ft) dam wall are 24 power generators that work on both ebb and flow tides, each generator producing 10 megawatts of power. The station can be visited, the less technically minded visitor perhaps settling for a walk along the dam and a view of the tidal sluice gates.

St Malo is named for a sixth-century Welsh saint who converted the inhabitants of the fishing village of Aleth (now St Serven) to Christianity and became their bishop. Later, when Norse raiders became troublesome, the villagers moved to the more easily pro-tected island in the bay. In time the island's natural defences were made stronger, the new city of St Malo becoming a walled fortress whose folk developed an air of independence that helped them become great explorers, but also occasionally put them at odds with the rest of Brittany and France. Two famous sayings arose to reflect this. The earliest was *Ni Français, ni Breton, Malouin suis* — not French, not Breton, but Malouin, a view modified later to *Malouin d'abord, Breton peut-être, Français s'il en reste* — Malouin first, Breton perhaps, French if there is anything left.

One of those who was a Malouin before all else was Jacques Cartier who sailed from here in 1534 and discovered the St Lawrence river. Cartier though he was in Asia, but that did not stop him from claiming the new land for France. Asking a Huron Indian what the land was called he was told 'Canada', and so that was the name he gave it, not realising that the Huron was merely giving him the name of his village. The village itself Cartier renamed *Mont Royale*, a name that has come down to us as Montreal. Cartier is buried in St Malo cathedral beneath a black slab marked only with his name, a most effective memorial.

Other great seafarers followed in the wake of Cartier, the most unlucky being Porcon de la Bardinais who was given a small fleet to defend local ships operating off Africa's Barbary coast. Ironically, Bardinais was defending corsairs from predation by Barbary pirates. When he was captured by the Dey of Algiers the Dey, instead of killing him or making him a galley slave, sent him back to St Malo with a deal involving the cessation of hostilities. The Dey made Bardinais promise he would return even if the offer was turned down. It was, and Bardinais, being an honourable man, duly re-turned. The Dey showed his regard for this chivalrous act by having him bound across the muzzle of a cannon and blown apart.

The St Malo corsairs were a curious breed. Nominally they were not pirates as they were licensed by the king to prey on certain ships, usually those of an enemy or potential enemy, and were required to

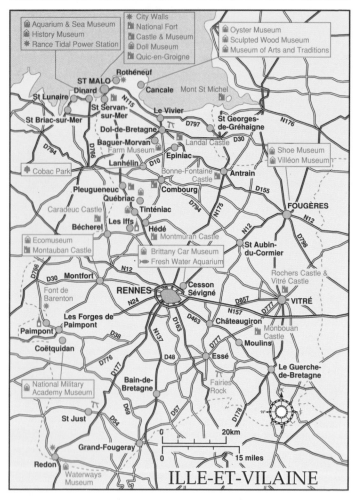

bring all captured ships back to port, complete with their crews. The captured ship's cargo was then sold, 10 per cent going to the King, 67 per cent to the corsair ship's owner, the *armateur*, with the rest being divided up between the corsairs themselves. Not surprisingly many of the captured ships never saw St Malo, being looted at sea and then disposed of, along with the crew. Some were brought back, however, so that the corsairs could maintain their licences and ships and so that they would not fall foul of the law and be branded pirates. On the proceeds the *armateurs* grew rich, building fine houses and further strengthening the city's defences. Two of St Malo's corsairs are remembered in statues on the city walls. René Duguay-Trouin captured 85 English ships and 94 from other countries in a career lasting 17 years, and when he was eventually captured by the English he managed to escape from Plymouth in a longboat (with a sail). One of his final acts as a corsair was to capture Rio de Janeiro from the Portugeuse. He died in St Malo in 1736. Robert Surcouf was a corsair in the Indian Ocean and was so successful that he returned to the town to become an *armateur* when he was only 36. He died in 1827, a very rich man indeed. The third statue on the walls is of Jacques Cartier.

In 1944 St Malo was almost completely destroyed in a battle that lasted throughout the first two weeks of August. After the war it was decided to restore it to its former glory and so successful was the work that many visitors do not realise that the old city, *Intra Muros* as it is often called, is really quite modern. For the best view of the 'old' city, and of the sea, take a walk around the walls, allowing about 30 minutes for the trip. The richest area of old St Malo, where the *armateurs*, lived was that between the Bastions of St Louis and St Philippe. From Bastion St Philippe and the wall section to Tour Bidouone there is a view of the eastern end of the Emerald Coast, while from the tower there is a fine view of the Fort National. The fort was built by Vauban in 1689 and can be reached at low tides. The view of the walls from the fort is also superb, and from it there also good views of the coast. Though the Fort was primarily defensive it also acted as a prison, the old dungeons giving some idea of the

Enjoying the sun on Plage de l'Écluse, Dinard

misery involved in being a seventeenth-century prisoner of war.

At the north-western tip of the walls, near Porte St Vincent, is St Malo Castle. This was begun as part of the city walls in the late fourteenth century though the Great Keep, which dominates it, was added later, and the corner towers later still. The seventeenth-century barracks is now the town hall. The Great Keep houses the city museum (Musée de la Ville) with exhibits on its history and famous sons. The keep can be climbed for an exceptional view of the city, the walls and the sea.

Within the walls, St Malo is a delight, its somewhat sombre, granite-housed, streets being enlivened by the tourist throng with the accompanying noises, smells and visual delights such crowds bring. At its heart is St Vincent's Cathedral with its superb modern stained glass windows and Cartier's tomb. In Rue de Toulouse is the Musée de la Poupée (Doll Museum), with a collection of over 300 dolls and a section devoted to teddy bears.

Close to the castle is the city aquarium, built into the walls to form a gallery over 100m (328ft) long that is lined with around 100 tanks containing, chiefly, fish from French sea and fresh waters, but also some more exotic species. Across the road is an 'Exotarium' with crocodiles, snakes and other reptiles. Nearby is Quic-en-Groigne, a tower which links the walls to the castle. It houses a series of waxwork tableaux illustrating episodes in the history of the city, and waxwork figures of leading Malouins. The name of the tower derives from a reply the Duchess Anne made to St Malo's bishop when he objected to her proposed marriage to Charles VIII. She said '*Qui qu'en groigne, ainsi sera, car tel est mon bon plaisir*'— 'Complain as you may, it will be thus because that is my wish'. To drive the message home the Duchess then had Quic-en-Groigne carved on the tower.

Close to the Bastion de Hollande a slipway leads down to the beach, giving access to the causeway that links St Malo to the Ile du Grande Bé at low tide. The view from the island to the next fortified island and to the Emerald Coast beyond is excellent, but for most the walk is a literary pilgrimage. They come to see the unnamed grave marked by a granite cross. Here lies François-René de Chateaubriand. Although Chateaubriand's parents were from a noble Breton family his father had fallen on hard times, not least because René was the youngest of ten children. However, during a time spent in America René's father earned enough to set up as an *armateur* in St Malo, soon earning enough to buy Combourg Castle. Here René lived almost as a recluse, escaping only when he enrolled at a college in Dinan. After his studying René had a strange career, spending time in America, fighting against the Revolution, spending time in

London, Greece and Egypt. Eventually he became French Ambassador in London and was even a contender for prime minister. All of this time he was writing. When he died in 1848 he had long been recognised as the greatest writer of his era. At his own request he was buried here on the Grande Bé. In the old city his birthplace, near Quic-en-Groigne, is marked with a plaque.

Chateaubriand is not the only famous writer produced by St Malo, Félicité Robert de Lamennais, the philosopher also having been born here in 1782. The economist Gournay, born in 1712, was also a Malouin. His writings are now largely forgotten, but his most famous economic theory, shortened to *laissez faire* (let it be), has passed into popular usage.

St Malo Extra Muros, the city outside the walls, is very modern and unlikely to detain the tourist unless he is seeking a boat trip to Cap Fréhel, the Rance estuary or the Channel Islands. The latter trip can be onboard a sleek and superbly elegant hydrofoil, one of which also crosses to Weymouth.

South of the port, which is also the arrival point for the Brittany Ferries boat from Portsmouth, is **St Servan-sur-Mer**, now a resort suburb of St Malo, but once a little port in its own right. The triangular headland that thrusts out into the sea is very interesting, and is rounded by a walk, the Corniche d'Aleth, which offers fine sea views. On the headland stands the Fort de la Cité, built in 1759 to reinforce the local defences. It was further reinforced by the Germans during their occupation and badly damaged in 1944. The other fort on the headland is the Tour Solidor, a tall (27m, 89ft) tower that comprises three overlapping towers. Solidor is the older of the two forts, having been built in 1382 by Duke Jean III of Brittany during a siege of St Malo. The tower offers fine views from its top, and houses the Musée International du Long Cours Cap-Hornier, a history of those who rounded Cape Horn from the first time, in the sixteenth-century, through to the twentieth century. The museum has many exhibits on the techniques of tall mast sailing and includes a model of the *Victoria*, the first ship to sail around the world, on Magellan's transit of 1519-22.

South of St Servan is the Château du Bos, a granite built *malouinière* as the houses of the *armateurs* were known. The mansion is set in a huge park overlooking the Rance estuary. Going north, rather than south, from St Malo the visitor reaches **Rothéneuf**, a sheltered resort with two good beaches. Here stands the Manoir de Jacques Cartier, a fifteenth-century house that Cartier lived in after his return from Canada. The house is furnished in period style, and an audio-visual show details Cartier's voyage to Canada. Close to the town is the

Sunset over St Malo

(Opposite)
Mont St Michel

Beach life at St Malo

aquarium marina, a saltwater aquarium with Channel fish species. Nearby are the Rochers Sculptés, a series of sculptures made in the late nineteenth century by a local priest, the Abbé Fouré, who worked the cliffs themselves into sea monsters, pirates and other gargoyle-like shapes. Over the years the elements have eaten away at the works so a visit now could save disappointment in a few years time when all trace of the work will have vanished.

East from Rothéneuf the **Pointe du Meinga** offers a fine walk. As no roads go close to the pointe, the walker is usually alone with the view. By contrast Pointe du Grouin is easily reached, though that does not detract from the excellence of the view, which includes the whole of Mont St Michel Bay and the Chausey Islands. The Iles des Landes, just off-shore, are a bird reserve and a blockhouse at the point has details on the birds which might be seen. Between the points is the chapel of Notre-Dame du Verger which contains a collection of model ships. The chapel is a favourite with the fisherman of Cancale who walk in procession to it on the 15 August each year.

Cancale is south of the Pointe du Grouin. It is a picturesque oyster port. Indeed, so much is this the case that it is difficult to avoid oysters: they are in every shop and restaurant, in the harbour and they also dominate the view of Mont St Michel Bay. In the circumstances it is almost sacrilegious not to try some, but beware: the price is dependent upon where you are when you ask, and can be quite radically different in the restaurants from that at the quay.

Oysters have been the mainstay of Cancale for centuries, sales reaching a high point of around 50 million annually during the first empire. In the 1920s disease all but destroyed the bay stock, and young, resistant shellfish, called spat, had to be brought for Auray to maintain the industry, a worthwhile venture as it not only saved Cancale from disaster, but saved the gastronome from a life without the distinctively flavoured bay oyster. The quay, Port de la Houle, backed by a pretty old fisherman's quarter, is the centre of oyster activity and a walk along the jetty (especially Jétée de la Fenêtre, the eastern jetty) is worthwhile. For a better view of the Parc à Huîtres, the oyster 'park', take the Sentier des Douaniers, the custom-officer's path, to the Ponte du Hock. Alternatively, the town's oyster museum can be visited. The museum is within an oyster 'factory' and includes a video, a visit to the museum and the factory, and an oyster tasting.

From Pointe du Hock the path can be followed all the way to Pointe du Grouin — about 7km (4 miles), allow 2 hours for the one-way walk. The pointe can also be reached along Rue du Hock which starts at the church of St Méen, the tower of which can be climbed for a good

view of the town and bay. Close to the church is the Musée des Bois
Sculptés, a remarkable series of detailed wood carvings by Abbot
Quémerais who was born in Cancale in 1879. At the other end of Rue
Duquesne from the church is the Musée des Arts et Traditions du
Pays housed in the old town church, now deconsecrated. The museum deals with the story of Cancale's fishing and oyster industries
and has a collection of local costumes. There are also exhibitions on
the life of Jeanne Jugan, and on the local sailing school which is over
100 years old.

Jeanne Jugan, whose story is told in the museum, was born in
Cancale in 1792, one of seven children of a fisherman who was
drowned while she was in her teens. Jeanne became a maidservant
to an old woman in St Servan-sur-Mer, near St Malo, using her spare
time to help the old and the poor of the town. With money left to her
by her mistress she started an old folks' home, funding the venture
by working and begging. In 1840, with three helpers and the blessing
of the local priest Jeanne found the Little Sisters of Mercy, a quasi-
religious society dedicated to aiding the poor. The society now has
thousands of workers world-wide. The house in which Jeanne, who
died in 1879, was born can be visited on request.

From Cancale the D76 heads south, soon reaching a junction
where the D797 bears left (east) to follow the edge of Mont St-Michel
Bay. Off-shore here are rows of poles (*bouchots*) on which mussels are
cultivated, with around 10,000 tons of shellfish produced annually,
a crop to rival Cancale's oysters. The road continues to hug the shore
beyond **Le Vivier-sur-Mer**, but at that village a journey begins
whose final destination is in Normandy. Journey's end is Mont St
Michel, one of the wonders of France, and few who travel this far east
in Brittany will forego the opportunity to visit. For that reason, and
because the best journey to the mount begins in Brittany, it is
included here.

From Le Vivier-sur-Mer the mount is reached by the Sirène de la
Baie, an amphibious vehicle that runs across the mudflats of the bay,
and also through the shallow waters of high tide. The vehicle gives
a good view of the mussel *bouchots*, and also a spectacular view of
Mont St Michel rising like a fairytale castle out of the bay. In its last
stages the Sirène's journey is parallel to GR34, a footpath that edges
along the margin between land and sea. The land here is the
saltmarsh of the Polders on area famous for the raising of *pré salé*
(salt-meadow) sheep, the lambs of which are another local delicacy.
The walking route is an equally spectacular way of reaching the
mount.

Mont St Michel is an almost perfect cone of rock standing some ✳

78m (256ft) above the bottom of the bay named for it. At the beginning of the eighth century the cone stood at the edge of the Forest of Scissy, an extensive forest that grew around the mouth of the Couesnon river, the ancient border between Brittany and France. In AD708 Bishop Aubert of Avranches had a dream in which the Archangel Michael told him to build a chapel on the rock. The bishop did as he was commanded, the first chapel being extended later: by the tenth century it could hold about one hundred worshippers and was being visited by pilgrims from all over the France. At that time the sea level in the bay rose slightly, the water cutting off the rock and engulfing the Forest of Scissy. The Normans reclaimed the rock by building a causeway, and rebuilt the church in Romanesque style, incorporating the Carolingian church as a crypt. This building work, which took over one hundred years, and the Gothic abbey that was built a century later, and which took 300 years in total to build, were remarkable feats of engineering, comparable in many ways to the construction of the Pyramids. The granite blocks of the abbey were cut on the Chausey Islands, brought to the mainland by sea and transported on rollers, the final haul up the steep-sided rock cone being both epic and dangerous.

In the seventeenth century discipline among the monks broke down and the upkeep of the abbey's fabric stopped. Decay set in, a decay hastened by the abbey's use as a prison from 1811. Only in 1874 when the French Government took it over was the decay halted and the abbey returned to its original splendour.

A tour of the abbey itself starts with a climb of the steps of the Grand Degré, steps that could once be sealed by a swing door, and the abbey steps, the latter spanned by a fortified bridge. At the top is a platform with a fine view of the Bay, the abbey church and La Merveille. The church is excellent, but La Merveille (the Marvel) is the masterpiece of the Mount, a soaring Gothic structure that housed the abbey's domestic and guest quarters. Within La Merveille are the cloisters, another masterpiece with its arcade carvings and different coloured stones. On the bay side of La Merveille are the abbey gardens which offer impressive views of the building's north wall and the Bay. The other buildings that form the abbey complex include the Guest's Hall — which numbered several French kings amongst its occupants — and the Knight's Hall, a vast room over 25m (82ft) long and 18m (59ft) wide. Here the monks illuminated manuscripts.

Below the abbey complex is a small medieval village that once sold food and souvenirs to pilgrims and now does much the same to tourists. The village and abbey are defended by stout walls through which there was, and is, only one gate. In Grande Rue, a very picturesque street, stands the Musée de la Mer with displays on the history of the abbey (including a film presentation) and the geology of the bay. There is also a collection of model ships. Further along Grande Rue is the Archéoscope, which, as at Carnac, uses computer-generated graphics, in conjunction with slides, to cover the history of the Mount, its geological history and the construction of the abbey. Opposite the exhibition is the church of St Peter the apse of which is built over a street. Next to the church is the Logis Tiphaine, the house built by Bertrand de Guesclin for his wife, Tiphaine Raguenel, when he was Captain of the Mount. The fourteenth-century house is furnished in period style though with some later additions, and includes several wax figures in period costume. Behind the church are the arched Maison de la Truie-qui-file, literally the house of the spinning sow, once the mount's inn. Beside it a single building houses the Musée Historique and Musée Grévin, the former with some memorabilia of the mount, including items crafted by both monks and prisoners, the latter with a series of waxwork tableaux that represent various scenes in the mount's history, both as abbey and prison.

South from Mont St Michel the valley of the Couesnon, which forms the border between Brittany and Normandy between Ponteron to Antrain, is formed, on its western side, by the edge of a plateau which overlooks St Michael's Bay. Close to the base of this is **St Georges-de-Gréhaigne**, where the beauties of Mont St Michel, together with those of many other sites in Ille-et-Vilaine, can be explored by way of models at a scale of 1 to 50. Besides the models there is an excellent children's playground.

At the western end of the plateau is **Dol-de-Bretagne**. Until the tenth century the town stood at a cliff edge, the sea of the bay having now retreated. Dol is an old bishopric, very proud of its ecclesiastical heritage. Some idea of its former importance can be gained by a visit to the large cathedral of St Samson, a Welsh saint, which has an excellent fourteenth-century porch and an impressively spacious interior. Here there are many fine works including a carved bishop's throne, from the sixteenth century, and a magnificent window in the chancel. The window is thirteenth century, though restored, and dates from the cathedral's reconstruction by King John of England who was stricken with remorse for having damaged its predecessor. The cathedral has never been completely finished, the northern tower being stub-ended and giving the cathedral a curious lop-sided look. Close to the cathedral is the Musée de la Trésorerie, housed in the cathedral treasury and with a collection of early painted wooden statues and waxwork dioramas on the history of Dol. The history of the town, and the local area, is also explored in the town's history museum. The museum also has a collection of old arms and some medieval statues.

Also close to the cathedral are the best of the houses in old Dol: a triangular walk takes in Rue Ceinte, turning right into Rue Le-Jamptel and Grande-Rue des Stuarts, then right again into Rue des Écoles. Grande Rue des Stuarts, named for James II who sent several years exiled in Dol, is especially good. The walk has to be extended — go left along Rue Le-Jamptel and turn left at Place Châteaubriand — to reach the Promenade des Douves, a garden walkway that has been created along the line of the *douve* (moat) in front of the last surviving piece of town wall.

North of Dol is Mont Dol, an outlier of the plateau that would once have been a granite island in St Michael's Bay. Legend has it that on the island St Michael fought with the Devil, hurling him to the ground before retreating to Mont St Michel. Close to the chapel at the rock's summit are a depression and claw marks where Satan fell, and a footprint left when the saint jumped back across the bay. The marks leave a great deal to the imagination. The view from the rock does not, with Mont St Michel and the Normandy coast visible to the east, Pointe du Grouin to the north-west and Dol-de-Bretagne to the south. To the north are the saltmarshes at the edge of the bay, and the mussel beds beyond. The rock is reached by a lane that runs uphill from a church in which there are fine early medieval frescoes.

Also close to Dol-de-Bretagne is the Menhir de Champ-Dolent, (Field of Grief). The standing stone is enormous, 9½m (31ft) high and was hauled at least 5 km (3 miles) before erection. The name of the spot is said to derive from an ancient battle fought between armies controlled by two brothers, though there is another legend that the stone fell to earth from heaven and is gradually sinking into the ground. When it has disappeared the world will come to an end.

South-east from the menhir, is the village of **Épiniac**, a neat little place, but not one in which to approach small, flickering lights at night. Legend has it that the local women were so lazy that they were forced to do their washing at night, by candlelight. Their ghosts still do, and if the visitor approaches one of the lights the ghost of an old women may force him to wring the washing by hand. If he does he will spend the rest of eternity wringing.

South-east again is the Château de Landal, a very striking castle built close to a lake in a substantial and beautiful park. Only the castle courtyard can be visited, but the park offers an excellent walk. Also close to the Champ-Dolent menhir is **Baguer-Morvan**, another fine

village where the Musée de la Paysanniere will be of interest to
visitors wishing to know a little more about the life of the Breton
farmers of a century ago. Here a farm has been restored and is used
to house a collection of old farm implements and Breton furniture.
There is also a collection of old photographs.

South of Dol-de-Bretagne is **Combourg**, a town beside a lake that
mirrors its sombre houses, with their grey slate roofs, and the huge
pepper pot turrets of the castle. The castle was built in the eleventh
century, and owned by du Guesclin before coming into the hands of
the Châteaubriand family. Here the count, an odd, reclusive man,
lived with his wife and two of their children after he had returned
from St Malo. The youngest child was François-René, the writer who
was buried on Grand Bé off St Malo. Combourg made a lasting
impression on the young boy, laying the foundation for his restless
life and melancholic writing. His father was given to walking up and
down in the drawing room at night with no one daring to interrupt
his silence. The children's mother was ill, and there were never any
visitors. At night François-René would retire alone to his room at the
top of the lonely Tour de Chat (Cat's Tower) where he would lie
awake listening to the sounds of the night, or waiting fearfully for the
ghost to appear: a previous owner's wooden leg haunted the tower
stumping up and down the stairs pursued by a ghostly black cat. It
seems remarkable that the boy stayed sane. His bedroom can be
visited: it is much as he left it, bare and a little forbidding. Elsewhere
there are other mementoes of the writer's life and the castle has been
furnished in period style.

Close to Combourg there are several other interesting châteaux.
To the west is the Château de Bourbansais, near **Pleugueneuc**. The
castle is sixteenth century, though enlarged in the eighteenth, and is
furnished in eighteenth-century style. There is also a collection of
seventeenth-century tapestries. The castle stands in a large and
beautiful park which is now a wildlife park featuring animals from
all five continents. Bourbansais can be reached from Combourg by a
direct route along the D794 (then left along the N137 to Pleugueneuc
or by a prettier drive along the D73 to **Lanhélin**, then left across
country close to the Étang du Rouvre. This route goes close to the
Parc de Loisirs de Cobac, a large country park which is ideal for
children. There are ponies and donkeys to ride, goats and rabbits to
pet. There are also miniature trains and boats, a small adventure
playground, and an exhibition room with stuffed specimens of all
Brittany's animals.

To discover more castles head east from Combourg on the D794,
then turn off right for the Château de Lanrigan, a Renaissance castle

which is, sadly, not open to the visitor, though its gardens are. From Lanrigan continue east to reach the valley of the Couesnon and follow the N175 north through it. The valley is a rich farming area, its main town, **Antrain**, showing evidence of the local prosperity in its fine sixteenth-century houses. Close to the town is the Château de Bonne-Fontaine, an elegant manor-house that was built in the sixteenth century but remodelled in the last century. The little pepper pot towers are delightful when viewed across the beautiful parkland in which the castle is set. It is said that within this park Duchess Anne once dispensed justice while sitting in the shade of a large oak tree. Continuing east the fine Château du Rocher-Portail can be reached from St Briac-en-Cogles. It is not open to visitors, but is a fine sight with its pool, moat and chestnut-tree drive.

Finally the visitor arrives at **Fougères**, and a castle that vies with Fort La Lotte as the finest in Brittany. It is likely that the defensive potential of the site occupied by the castle, a ridge of rock around which the Nanson river formed a tight loop, attracted attention from earliest times though surviving work dates only from the twelfth century. At that time a tall keep was protected by an outer wall, the whole then being protected by a moat formed in part by the river, and in part by a ditch filled by redirecting the river at the southern end

The castle at Combourg

of the site. Later alterations in the river's course mean that the moat is no longer complete. In 1166 when Henry II of England forced the Breton Duke Conan IV (Conan the Little) to accept English dominion, Raoul, the baron who held Fougères, refused to submit. Henry besieged and took Fougères, destroying the castle. However, Raoul immediately rebuilt it, though not the tall keep, enhancing the defences. Over the years that followed the castle was besieged, taken and retaken many times, its position on the border between Brittany and France, and close to the Norman heartland of 'English' France making it a valuable place.

The castle that now dominates the ridge and town is largely thirteenth century, though there were additions through to the fifteenth century. Entrance is over the moat and through a square

Fougères Castle is one of the finest in Brittany

tower which leads to a courtyard cut off from the main castle by a second diversion of the river which formed the inner moat. Attackers therefore had to storm the outer wall and then withstand withering fire from the positions above the courtyard merely to reach the inner defences. Inside it can be seen that the castle is roughly triangular, following the contours of the ridge rather than the accepted circular shape of medieval fortress architecture. The walls themselves are defended by towers, these showing the development of castle design. The Cadron Tower, as with most of the towers named for a former governor, is thirteenth century. Though it is semi-ruinous its basic form can be seen. It was built to be defended by archers against archers and the odd siege engine, being solid, but not massive. The next stage of development is represented by the fourteenth-century towers of Mélusine and Gobelin at the north-western corner. The development of artillery meant that towers of this period had to be thicker and taller. The Mélusine Tower is 31m (102ft) high and has walls 3½m (11ft) thick, wall thickness contributing over half of the tower's diameter. The final stage of development is represented by the Raoul and Surriene towers built in the fifteenth century. Here the walls are even thicker, 7m (23ft), to withstand the improved artillery, and the tower are U-shaped, the floors and top serving as platforms for gun batteries.

The Raoul Tower is named for the baron who defied Henry II, and houses a small museum to Fougères' shoe industry. In early medieval times the town was a centre for the production of wool and sailcloth. The latter industry developed as the French merchant and navy fleets increased and brought great prosperity, Fougères virtually having a monopoly in sailcloth manufacturing. When steam replaced sail the town became a centre for shoe production, and still has a modest shoe industry. The museum deals with the history of shoe-making in the town. The Mélusine Tower, the castle's most impressive tower, is named not for a former governor but for a fairy mentioned in the Arthurian legends. The castle was once held by the Lusignan family who claimed descent from her, and her ghost is said to haunt the tower even now.

In medieval times the castle was attached to the town walls, a section of the walls still reaching it at Porte Notre-Dame. Close to the gate is the fifteenth-century church of St Sulpice a slim, elegant building. Inside there is the statue of Notre-Dame des Marais, the Nursing Virgin, which is credited with having promoted miraculous healings. The statue is older than the church and had to be restored after retrieval from the castle moat where it had been hurled by English soldiers. Close to the church is the best remaining section of old Fougères, the Quartier du Marchix, a picturesque area of mainly sixteenth-century houses in streets close to the Place du Marchix.

Fougères has a second, and equally interesting church, St Léonard's, in the town gardens on the other side of the Nanson. The church is a curious barn-like building with a pagoda-like tower, but has some fine stained glass windows, some from the sixteenth century, some modern. The terraced gardens in which the church stands are very pretty and offer a good view of the castle. Close to St Léonard's is the Musée de la Villéon a gallery of the work of Emmanuel de la Villéon, an Impressionist painter born in the town, housed in a fine sixteenth-century house. Beyond the museum is Rue Nationale, to the left of which is the town's fourteenth-century bell tower.

From Fougères to the Normandy border there is more fine country dotted with pretty villages and, to the north-east, a superb section of ancient woodland, the Forêt Domaniale de Fougères, where the visitor can wander at will through the beech trees. After a visit the visitor can drive directly to Rennes along the N12, or go southwards first to visit Vitré. On the N12 **St Aubin-du-Cormier** is passed, a small town with the ruins of a thirteenth-century castle. In 1488 the battle that ended Brittany's full independence from France was fought here. The French under the Duke de la Trémoille defeated the Bretons under Duke François II, the beaten duke being forced to sign the Treaty of Verger. François died the following year and was succeeded by his daughter Anne whose marriage, in 1491 to Charles VIII, united France and Brittany in a less hostile manner.

When approached from Fougères the view of **Vitré** from the hill into the town is superb, though to be fair, it is matched by that from the Tertres Noirs, a hill beside the road to Rennes. Vitré is often said to be the best preserved medieval town in Brittany, a claim that was more valid before the mainline railway demolished much of interest and beauty, but one that still has its supporters. The prosperity that built the houses was based on the manufacture of wool and cotton, and the cloths made from them, especially cotton stockings. One Vitré tailor, Pierre Landais, became wardrobe master to Duke François II. Landais was an astute man and soon rose to become the duke's treasurer, a rise which infuriated the nobility who had no interest in Breton commoners bettering themselves. They accused him of embezzling money from the duke, had him seized, taken to Nantes Castle and tortured. He 'confessed' to his crimes and was hanged at the castle, to the duke's great sorrow.

Landais' Vitré was dominated by the castle, which is still much as he would have known it. It is a delightful building, triangular in

Vitré Château dominates the medieval town

shape and reached across a drawbridge. It dates from the eleventh century, though has been remodelled several times. Today the castle houses the Town Hall, beside which the Montafilant tower can be climbed for an excellent view of castle, town and the Vilaine Valley. The Argenterie Tower has a collection illustrating Breton wildlife, while the St Lawrence Tower houses a collection of medieval bits and pieces, sculpture, items from Vitré's older houses, tapestries and some interesting engravings of old Vitré.

Almost any walk around the town is worthwhile, but there are a few spots that should not be missed. Rue Beaudrairie, a street that derives its name from the leather-workers who once lived there, is the most picturesque with its cobbles and its stone and half-timbered houses, though Rue d'Embass and Rue Poterie are almost as good. The remains of the old town walls, a section from the Place de la Republique, where the Bridolle Tower (once part of the walls) stands, towards the castle, is followed by a fine walk on its outer edge. Close to the western end of the wall section is the church of Notre-Dame, most noticeable for its southern side with its gables and outside pulpit. During the Wars of Religion Vitré was owned by the Huguenot Coligny family, some of whose staunchest followers lived in Rue Notre-Dame, across from the church. The Catholic priest of the church, appalled by the effect these folk were having on his flock,

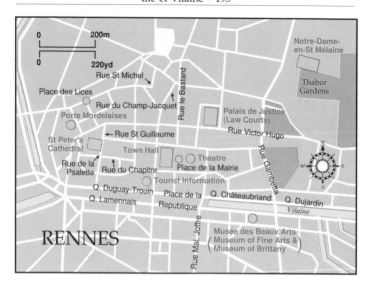

RENNES

*Écomusée de la Bintinais, near Rennes, shows past and present day
farming life*

knocked a hole in the southern wall of the church and harangued the houses opposite. Later a pulpit was built (presumably to stop the rain getting into the church) and the priest took to preaching to the townsfolk in the street as well as carrying on his theological argument with the Colignys.

Medieval Vitré lies on the southern side of the Vilaine. On the northern side of the river the Fauborg du Rachapt is also worth visiting. When the castle was besieged by the English during the Hundred Years War the English soldiers were billeted in this part of the town. The siege dragged on for several years and eventually the towns people, fed up with the English presence, offered to buy back the area if the soldiers agreed to go away. A deal was struck, and from then until now the suburb has been known as the Rachapt, or repurchased. The fifteenth-century Chapelle de St Nicolas in the area is an annex of the castle museum.

Close to Vitré is the Château des Rochers, famous as the home of the Marquise de Sévigné whose *Letters* are one of the joys of French literature for their witty and intelligent observations of life in the Sun King's Court. Ultimately the Marquise had to leave court, her husband having been killed in a duel, but not before he and their son had all but spent the family fortune. At the castle she continued to write, observing both local peasant family life and the goings-on at the Breton parliament (the États) which was held at Vitré. She also busied herself in her gardens and parks, a quite unusual interest for a noble lady at the time (the last half of the seventeenth century). The park, which can be visited, has numerous avenues that the Marquise named — Infinity, My Daughter's Whim — while the garden has a semi-circular wall famous for its whispered echo. All these features appear in her writings. Of the castle itself, a fifteenth-century building with later 'restorations' only the chapel and two rooms may be visited. The rooms are stocked with furnishings and memorabilia of the Marquise.

From Vitré the visitor can take the D857 and N157 to Rennes. **Rennes** takes its name from the Redonnes, the local tribe of Gauls who had set up their town at the confluence of the Ille and Vilaine rivers. The Romans also used the site, three of their major roads joining here, though little now remains from either of those early towns. In medieval times Rennes replaced Nantes as the capital of Brittany, its position, due west of Paris, making it a more central point for government, and it was here, in 1489, that Anne, daughter of Duke François II, was crowned Duchess of Brittany. The following year she ignored the wishes of her advisers and accepted a proxy marriage to Maximilian, the future Emperor of Austria. On hearing this the sister of Charles VII of France brought an army to Rennes and besieged it, the excuse being that the proxy marriage was in breach of the Treaty of Verger that François II had been forced to sign after his defeat by the French at St Aubin-du-Cormier. The treaty gave the French monarch the power of assent, or not, over any proposed marriage. The French told Anne that Charles wished her to marry her, realising that the effect of such a marriage would be to unite Brittany and France as no battle could. Anne refused, but as the siege noose tightened the starving folk of Rennes pleaded with her to accept. She did, marrying Charles and his successor Louis XII when Charles died suddenly. Her shrewdness was such that not only were the marriages successful, but they gave Brittany a degree of independence far in excess of that of other French regions.

Following the final unification of Brittany and France Rennes was a prosperous place, but disaster struck at Christmas 1720 when a drunken carpenter overturned a lamp in his workroom and set fire to a pile of wood shavings. The blaze spread rapidly, all the local houses being stacked with fuel for the winter. Troops were sent in, but they looted the houses of their Christmas food and wine and become drunk. With little or no action to stop it the fire destroyed almost a 1,000 houses, being put out only when heavy rain fell. Louis XV acted quickly to rebuild the city and Jacques Gabriel, one of the foremost French architects, produced a regular grid of granite houses in classical style. This building has resulted in the odd mix of styles in the centre of Rennes, with open squares and tall, elegant buildings leading to tight alleys of half-timbered houses, a mix that gives Rennes real charm.

Today Rennes is home to the Citroen car works and many modern industries (electronics, telecommunications etc), two universities and a medical school, and is very much a French city, though as a tour of the old quarters show, it still retains its Breton heart.

A tour of Rennes should start at the Place des Lices with its appealing mixture of medieval buildings and nineteenth-century market halls. The square is named for the *lices* (jousts), held here in medieval times. At one of these Bertrand du Guesclin was reconciled with his family. When du Guesclin was a boy he was rejected by his parents who were appalled by his ugliness, his rough ways and his love of soldiering. Eventually they sent him away to an uncle in the country. There Bertrand learned to fight and at seventeen returned to Rennes on the day of an important tournament. The youth, fighting with his visor down and refusing to give his name, defeated one knight after another until his father challenged him. He then lifted his visor revealing his identity. His father immediately apologised, welcomed him back to the family and accepted that his son would be a soldier. A house called the Maison du Guesclin, reputedly once lived in by Bertrand, stands at No 3 Rue St-Guillaume, close to Rennes Cathedral. Other fine houses can be seen in Rue de la Psalette, also close to the cathedral, Rue St-Michel, which leads north-east from Place des Lices, and Rue du Champ-Jacquet as well as in several other streets of Vieux Rennes. Look too for the Porte Mordelaises, once the old town's main gate and all that now remains of the town wall.

St Peter's Cathedral, which stands in old Rennes, is the third building on the same site, the first, built in the sixth century, having been replaced by a medieval building which escaped the fire of 1720 only to fall down in 1762. Inside the present cathedral the main interest is a sixteenth-century Flemish altarpiece. The piece, in

The canal village of Tinténiac

carved and gilded wood and representing scenes from the life of the Virgin Mary, is regarded as one of the finest examples of its type.

To the east of the cathedral is the Place de la Mairie, a masterpiece by Gabriel with its classical lines and use of space. The Town Hall is now considered to be the architect's greatest achievement. It finishes with a tower and clock known, affectionately, as Le Gros by Rennes folk. They were a good deal less affectionate about the statuary that once adorned the building. A statue of Louis XV was hauled down during the Revolution, while one symbolising the union of Brittany and France, with Brittany kneeling before France, was blown up by Breton separatists. The Town Hall can be visited if no official functions are being held, visits including the Panthéon set up to the memory of famous Bretons from du Guesclin to René Laénnec, a Quimper doctor who invented the stethoscope. North of the Place is the Palais de Justice, once the home of the Breton parliament. The building pre-dates the great fire and was designed by Salomon de Brosse who also built the Luxembourg Palace in Paris. As Law Courts the building was used for the second trial of Alfred Dreyfus in 1899. The building can be visited, a worthwhile trip to see the Grande Chambre, the original parliamentary chamber, which is huge and richly decorated with carved woodwork and tapestries.

Continuing northward from the Law Courts the visitor should bear right (east) to reach the Thabor Gardens, an oasis of colour and calm. Here, in the sixteenth century, stood a Benedictine abbey

Dolls in local costume are among some of the excellent exhibits at the Ecomuseum in Montfort

named for the Biblical Mount Taber. All that now remains of the abbey are the church of Notre-Dame-en-St Mélaine and the gardens. The church is very grand, and equally spacious inside, but the gardens are the real joy with their collection of trees, shrubs and flowers, the duck pond, formal ponds and aviary. Among the more exotic species here are several sequoia (Californian Redwoods). Exhibitions are occasionally held in the pavilion.

Finally go south of the Vilaine to reach a building housing the Musée des Beaux-Arts, Brittany's most important collection of art, and the Musée de Bretagne, devoted to its history. The art collection has work from the fourteenth century to the present, and includes paintings by Rubens, de la Tour, Gauguin, Sisley and Picasso as well as by Breton artists. The history museum has a variety of objects and models that follow the development of the region from prehistoric to modern times, together with items on the history of Rennes and an audio-visual show on Brittany today.

To the east of Rennes centre, close to the suburb-village of Cesson-Sévigné is the Musée de l'Automobile de Bretagne, a collection of about eighty vehicles, cars, motorcycles, bicycles, even horse-drawn trucks, which are all maintained in working order. Of particular interest is a Dion-Bouton of 1899 in which the passengers sat one to each side of the driver! The village also has an aquarium solely for freshwater fish, with about fifty species in seventeen tanks, together with exhibitions on fishing, fish farming and river pollution. There is also a cinema for a film of the life of a freshwater system.

Equally close to Rennes centre, but to the the south, is the Écomusée de la Bintinais, set up in a large, old farm, which has been restored and equipped to show the development of farming techniques from the sixteenth century to the present day, particularly the affect on farms of the expansion of urban areas. The farm's land is still cultivated, the crops and methods used indicating the same development.

The journey to Rennes was from Vitré, to the east. Equally interesting is the journey southwards to Rennes from Combourg. At Hédé, a delightful village set on a hill between the Ille-et-Rance canal and a large lake, the visitor can admire the houses and the castle ruins or visit the canal itself where a towpath allows a close view of the eleven locks that allow boats to negotiate a 27m (89ft) drop. Close to the village is the Château de Montmuran, entered by drawbridge over a moat. The castle was first built in the twelfth century and has towers from that period, though the main building was much later. In the chapel of the fourteenth-century entrance Bertrand du Guesclin was knighted in 1354. The view of the area around Hédé from the top of the towers is tremendous. Close to the castle, is the village of **Les Iffs** where the church has excellent sixteenth-century stained glass.

To the west is another castle, the Château of Caradeuc, near **Bécherel**. The castle was once the home of the Marquis de Caradeuc de la Chatolais, a man who is claimed to have written the only best-seller ever to have come from the pen of a politician, a work of his demanding the dissolution of the Jesuits in 1762 selling thousands of copies. The reason was straightforward, there being a power strug-gle in Rennes, where La Chatolais was Public Prosecutor, between the Jesuits and the Breton Parliament. With the help of the pamphlet the parliament enacted the dissolution. The king sided with the Jesuits, had La Chatolais arrested and ordered the Breton Parliament to reverse its ruling. The parliament refused and La Chatolais was released. It was the first time the king had ever been defeated, and is now accepted as having been the event which planted the seed that was to grow into Revolution. The castle is not open to the public, but the beautiful park that surrounds it is. With its trees, ponds and statues it is a fine place, and the view northward from the terrace in front of the castle is magnificent.

North of Hédé is **Tinténiac** another canal village, with two inter-esting museums. The Musée de l'Outil et des Métiers is housed in an old wooden grain store near the canal and has a fascinating collection of tools from the old trades of the blacksmith, cartwright, cooper, clay pipe maker and so on. The Musée International de la Faune, at **Québriac** on the D20 just north of the village, is a collection of stuffed animals.

Travelling west from Rennes the visitor reaches the vast and mysterious Forêt de Paimpont, although before reaching it a slight detour northward to Montfort is worthwhile.

Montfort, a very pleasant red stone town named for a castle built on the hill in the eleventh century, is home to the Ecomusée du Pays de Montfort, a collection of items on local history and folklore housed in the Papegaut Tower. The Ecomuseum has a collection of dolls in local costume, another of *coiffes*, and some other really fascinating items. Look out for the *pied de cochon*, a clever stone sling made from a split stick. The tower that houses the museum is fourteenth century, and is all that now remains of the town's castle. The name derives from a medieval game. Within Montfort, the birthplace of the missionary St Louis-Marie Grignion can also be visited.

A little way north-west of Montfort is the Château de Montauban, a castle named for the Duchess Anne's Chancellor who had it built for himself in the last years of the fifteenth century. The castle is pleasantly sited beside a pool, and houses a collection of items that depict its history.

The Forêt de Paimpont is the ancient Forest of Brocéliande, an area steeped in Arthurian legends. Today the forest covers just over 7,000 hectares (some 25sq miles) but at one time stretched for nearly 150 km (93 miles) east to west and was at least 40km (25 miles) north-south. One legend has it that it was to Brocéliande, not Glastonbury, that Joseph of Arimathea brought the Holy Grail and that the ghosts of Lancelot and Guinevere still haunt the woods. Near the village of **Tréhorenteuc**, a pretty little village that is actually in Morbihan, is the Val Sans Retour (Valley of No Return) where Merlin, Arthur's magician, was held captive in a magic circle by the fairy Viviane, also known as Morgan le Fay. Another legend has it that the Rocher des Faux Amants, the Rock of False Lovers, is where Viviane lured young lads to their doom. In the village church mosaics and paintings illustrate this legend and that of the Barenton Fountain further north. The stained glass windows illustrate the search for the Holy Grail, and there is a painting of the knights of the Round Table in the chancel.

The Fountain of Barenton lies deep in the forest. Water from the fountain was said to cure nervous disorders and if sprinkled on the Perron de Merlin, a flat stone at the fountain's edge, could summon up thunder. Close to the village of **Les Forges de Paimpont,** a very pretty village named for the iron forges that operated in the sixteenth century, utilising local deposits of iron ore and charcoal from the forest, is the Fontaine de Jouvence, a magic fountain that rejuvenated those who drank from it, and the Tombeau de Merlin, a pair of flat slabs that reputedly cover the grave of Merlin. North of the village is **Paimpont**. Here, at the very heart of the forest, a monastery was built in the seventh century. In the twelfth century an abbey replaced the original building, and though this was dissolved at the time of the Revolution, the abbey church still remains, a fine building the treasury of which houses some excellent woodwork and statues. Look, too, for a fifteenth-century silver reliquary that holds an arm of St Judicaél and a fine eighteenth-century ivory Crucifix. To the west of the town is the Étang du Pas-du-Houx, an enormous, but picturesque, pool on the shore of which are the ruins of the Château de Brocéliande. From here, and from elsewhere, walks of almost any length can be made into the forest, but be cautious: periodically the French Druids pull out forest walk and site markers to maintain the forest's 'purity'. The signs you are following could, therefore, suddenly disappear. The southern part of the forest has now been taken over by the Coëtquidan military camp which includes the National

Military academy. The Academy has a small museum to its own history.

Taking the D177 south-west from Rennes the visitor drives between the airport and the huge Citroen factory before crossing fine farmland to reach the border of Brittany and the Loire *départements* at Redon. **St Just**, a pleasant town just off this main road, is at the centre of an area which is second only to Carnac in terms of the density of its megalithic sites. The sites are not well signed, and are very poorly documented, but the local *curé* is very willing to share his knowledge of the monuments with the visitor.

Redon stands at the junction of three *départements*, and at the point where the Nantes-Brest canal meets the Vilaine. It is a small industrial town, with a prosperous history based on the trade the waterways brought. That history is explored in the Musée de la Batellerie de l'Ouest, though, as the name implies, the museum also deals with waterways throughout western France. However, the town's agricultural past as reflected in a large market held on Mondays and in the Teillouse Fair on the fourth Saturday in October. The fair originally celebrated the chestnut harvest, but is now a funfair, craft fair and general good time. The older part of the town is grouped around the church, extending down to the flower be-decked bridge over the canal. The best of the houses are in Grande Rue and the streets that leave it, and in the old port area, especially Quai Duguay-Trouin which runs along the Vilaine. Look, too, for Rue du Jeu-de-Paume, close to the quai, where the old customs house has an interesting exterior fresco of pigherders and fishmongers in traditional costume. The church of St Saveur, at the town's centre, was an abbey church in medieval times, and a centre for pilgrimages. The odd separation of the church from its bell towers was caused by a fire in 1780. The new church tower is a superb structure in a mixture of sandstone and granite.

Heading south from Rennes on the N137 the visitor soon reaches the Loire-Atlantique border. The road bypasses **Bain-de-Bretagne**, a charming little town with one of the better local camp sites, situated beside a big lake, and **Grand-Fougeray**, an equally charming town with an old keep, all that remains of a medieval castle. The castle was taken by du Guesclin during the War of Succession, he and his men disguising themselves as woodcutters when they discovered that wood was to be delivered. They were allowed in, threw down their wood bundles, pulled out swords and slaughtered the castle's garrison.

To the south-east of Rennes the visitor can follow the D463 or the D163. The D463 soon reaches **Châteaugiron** an old sailcloth making town with a fine castle ruin and some equally attractive half-timbered houses. The castle is thirteenth century and defended by a moat, though only the keep, clock tower and some of the domestic buildings, restored in the eleventh century, remain. Continuing along the road the visitor can turn off left at **Moulins** to visit the Château de Monbouan, a late eighteenth-century building built close to a lake and defended by a moat. The castle is in a beautiful setting, and is furnished in period style. Further on again is **La Guerche-de-Bretagne**, separated from Loire-Atlantique by the dense Guerche forest. A market has been held in the centre of La Guerche on every Tuesday since 1121, the prosperity this brought the town being reflected in the fine half-timbered houses in the streets close to the church.

Finally in Ille-et-Vilaine go between the two roads, the D463 and D163, to visit what is, arguably, the most beautiful megalithic site in the whole province. Close to the village of **Esse** is the Roche-aux-Fées, the Fairies Rock. The Roche consists of forty-two slabs of purple schist, at least half-a-dozen of them weighing around 45 tons, erected to form an entrance porch, passageway and high chamber, the whole roofed by flat slabs. The chamber is divided into four by tall pillars. It was long assumed that the Roche was a tomb, but experts are now undecided about the structure's function, considering that it could have had a religious usage with rituals being carried out in the divided chamber. Such was the power of the site on the imagination of the locals that legends grew up around it. One story has it that if a betrothed couple walk in opposite directions around it counting the stones then their marriage will be a successful one if their tallies agree or differ by one or two. If the tallies differ by more than two then they should seek other partners. One version of the story has it that if the tallies agree the marriage will be blessed by the fairies though whether the site's name pre- or post-dates the legend is unclear.

Additional Information

Places to Visit

Antrain
Bonne-Fontaine Castle
Open: Easter to November daily
10am-6pm.
☎ 99 315813

Baguer-Morvan
Farm Life Museum
Open: May to September daily
9.30am-12.30pm, 2-7pm.
☎ 99 480404

Bintinais Ecomuseum
Near Rennes
Open: April to mid-October daily
except Tuesday 2-7pm. Mid-
October to March daily except
Tuesday 2-6pm.
☎ 99 513815

Bécherel
Caradeuc Castle
Park open: April to October daily
9.30am-12.30pm, 1.30pm-8pm.
November to March Saturday,
Sunday 2-6pm.
☎ 99 667776

Cancale
St Méen's Church Tower
Open: July, August daily 9am-7pm.
September to June Tuesday to
Saturday 9-11.15am, 2-5.15pm.
If the church is locked ask for the
key at the tourist information office
in Rue du Port.
☎ 99 896372

Sculpted Wood Museum
Open: mid-July to August daily
except Sunday afternoon 10am-
12noon 2.30-6.30pm.
☎ 99 896372

Museum of Arts and Traditions
Open: July, August daily except
Monday morning 10am-12noon,
2.30-6.30pm.
☎ 99 897932

Oyster Museum
Open: all year Monday to Friday
9am-12noon, 2-5pm.
☎ 99 896999

Jeanne Jugan's House
Open: by appointment only.
☎ 99 896273

Cesson-Sévigné
Brittany Car Museum
Route de Fougères
Open: all year daily 9am-12noon,
2-7pm.
☎ 99 620017

Freshwater Aquarium
43 Boulevard de Dézerseul
Open: mid-May to mid-September
Monday to Friday 10am-7pm.
Saturday, Sunday 2-7pm. Mid-
September to mid-May Saturday,
Sunday, Wednesday 2-6pm.
☎ 99 831111

Coëtquidan
National Military Academy Museum
Open: all year daily 9am-12noon,
2-6pm.

Combourg
Lanrigan Castle
Open: June to September Wednes-
day to Friday 9am-12noon, 2-7pm.

Combourg Castle
Exterior open: April to October
daily 9am-12noon, 2-5.30pm.
Interior open: April to October
daily 2-5.30pm. March, November

by appointment only.
☎ 99 732295

Dinard
Aquarium and Sea Museum
Open: Whitsun to mid-September
Monday to Saturday 10am-12noon,
2-6pm. Sunday 10am-12noon, 2-7pm.
☎ 99 461390

History Museum
Open: Easter to mid-November
daily 2-6pm.
☎ 99 468105

Boat trips
Ask at the tourist information
office, at the northern end of
Boulevard Féart, for details.
☎ 99 469412

Rance Tidal Power Station
Open: all year daily 8.30am-8pm.

Dol-de-Bretagne
Treasury Museum
Open: Easter to mid-September
daily except Monday 10am-6pm.
☎ 99 480484

History Museum
Open: May to September daily,
except Monday 10am-5pm.
October to April Tuesday to Friday
10am-5pm.
☎ 99 480938

Épiniac
Landal Castle
Open: park and castle exterior and
courtyard only. All year daily
10am-12noon, 2-6pm.

Fougères
Castle Shoe Museum
Open: mid-June to mid-September
daily 9am-7pm. April to mid-June
daily 2-5pm. Mid- to end September daily 9.30am-12noon, 2-5pm.

October to December, February,
March daily 10am-12noon, 2-
4.30pm.
☎ 99 997959

Villéon Museum
Open: mid-June to mid-September
daily 10.30am-12.30pm, 2.30-
5.30pm. Easter to mid-June
Saturday, Sunday 11.30am -12.30pm,
2.40-5pm. At other times on request.
☎ 99 991898

Hédé
Montmuran Castle
Open: Easter to October daily 2-7pm.
November to Easter Saturday,
Sunday 2-6pm.
☎ 99 458888 or 99 458362

Lanhélin
Cobac Park
Open: mid-March to mid-September daily 10am-7pm. Mid-
September to November Wednesday, Saturday, Sunday 11am-7pm.
☎ 99 738016

Le Vivier-sur-Mer
Sirène de la Baie
Open: April to September. The two
hour trip leaves several times daily.
For details of actual departure times.
☎ 99 489230

Mont St Michel
Abbey
Open: mid-May to mid-September
daily 9.30am-6pm. Mid-September
to mid-November daily 9.30-
11.45am, 1.45-5pm. Mid-November
to mid-February daily 9.30-11.45am,
1.45-4.15pm. Mid-February to mid-
May daily 9.30-11.45am, 1.45-5pm.
Guided tours available.
☎ 33 601414

Sea Museum
Open: April to mid-November daily
9am-6pm. Mid-November to March
daily except Monday 9am-6pm.
☎ 33 602390

Archeoscope
Open: March to mid-November
daily 9am-6pm.
☎ 33 480937

History and Grévin Museums
Open: March to December daily
8.30am-6pm. January, February
daily 9am-5.30pm.
☎ 33 602390
A combined ticket covering the Sea
Museum, the Archeoscope and the
History and Grévin Museums can
be purchased.

Tiphaine's House
Open: Easter to mid-November
daily 9am-6pm.

Montfort
Ecomuseum
Open: June to September Tuesday
to Saturday 10am-12noon, 2-6pm.
Sunday 2-6pm. October to May Tuesday to Friday 10am-12noon, 3-6pm.
☎ 99 093181

Birthplace of St Louis-Marie Grignion
Open: all year Monday to Saturday
10am-12noon, 3-6pm. Sunday 3-6pm.
☎ 99 091535

Montauban Castle
Open: mid-June to mid-September
daily 2-6pm.
☎ 99 064021

Moulins
Monbouan Castle
Open: mid-July to August daily
9am-12noon, 2-6pm. Guided tours
available.
☎ 99 690151

Paimpont
Abbey Church Treasury
Open: all year Monday to Saturday
9.30am-12noon, 3-7pm.
☎ 99 078137

Pleugeueneuc
Bourbansais Castle and Zoo
Castle open for guided tours only.
June to August daily hourly from
11am-6pm. April, May, September
Monday to Saturday at 3.30pm.
Sunday at 3pm and 4pm. October
to March Sunday only at 3 and 4pm.
Zoo/Park open: June to August
daily 10am-6.30pm. April, May,
September daily 10am-12noon, 2-6pm.
October to March daily 2-5.30pm.

Québriac
International Museum of Fauna
Open: Easter to November daily
2.30-6.30pm. December to Easter
Sunday 2.30-6.30pm.
☎ 99 681022

Redon
Waterways Museum
Open: May to September daily
10am-12noon, 2-5pm.
☎ 99 723095

Rennes
Town Hall
Open: all year Monday to Friday
9am-12noon, 2-5pm.
☎ 99 7901 98

Law Courts
Open: all year. Guided tours only
at 10am, 11am, 3pm and 4pm on
Monday and Wednesday to
Saturday and 10am, 11am, 3pm
and 4.45pm on Sunday.
☎ 99 790198

Thabor Gardens
Open: all year daily 10am-dusk.

Museum of Brittany
Open: all year daily except
Tuesday 10am-12noon, 2-6pm.
☎ 99 285584

Museum of Fine Arts
Open: all year daily except
Tuesday 10am-12,noon 2-6pm.
☎ 99 255585

Post Office and Telecommunications
Boulevard du Colombier

Market Day: daily in Les Valles
Saturday in Place des Lices.
On other days in other areas of the
city: ask at the tourist office for
details.

Car Hire: Budget
11 Rue de la Santé
☎ 99 651321

Europcar
56 Avenue du Mail
☎ 99 595050

Hertz
10 Avenue du Mail
☎ 99 542652

Rothéneuf
Jacques Cartier's House
Open: June to September Wednesday
to Sunday 10am-12noon, 2-5.45pm.
☎ 99 409773

Sea Aquarium and Sculpted Rocks
Open: Easter to October daily 9am-
7pm.
☎ 99 569764

St Georges-de-Gréhaigne
Miniature Mont St Michel
Open: Easter to mid-November
daily 9am-8pm.

St Malo
National Fort
Open: Easter, Whitsun, June to
September daily 9am-7pm, but
dependent on tides. The fort
cannot be reached for two hours
either side of high tide.
☎ 99 469125

St Malo Castle/City Museum
Open: May to September daily
9.30am-12noon, 2-5.30pm. April,
October daily 10am-12noon, 2-6pm.
November to March daily 10am-
12noon, 2-5pm.
☎ 99 407157

Dolls Museum
Open: one week each side of
Easter, daily 10am-12noon, 2-7pm.
July and August daily 10am-
12noon, 2-7pm.
☎ 99 816434

Quic-en-Groigne
Open: April to September daily
9am-12noon, 2-6pm.
☎ 99 408026

Boat trips
For information on all the trips ask
at the tourist information office
near Port St Vincent.
☎ 99 566448

St Servan-sur-Mer
*International Museum of Cape Horn
Trips*
Open: June to September daily
10am-12noon, 2-6pm. April, May,
October daily except Tuesday
10am-12noon, 2-6pm. November to
March daily except Tuesday 10am-
12noon, 2-5.30pm.
☎ 99 407111

Château du Bos
Open: July, August daily 3.30-5pm.
Guided tours only.
☎ 99 814011

Tinténiac
Museum of Old Tools and Trades
Open: July to September Monday
to Saturday 10.30am-12noon, 2.30-
6.30pm. Sunday 2.30-6.30pm. All
others times by request.
☎ 99 680203

Vitré
*Castle Museums Montafiliant Tower
and Chapel of St Nicholas*
Open: July to September daily
10am-12.30pm, 2-6.15pm. April to
June daily except Monday morning
and Tuesday 10am-12noon, 2-5.30pm.
☎ 99 750454

Rochers Castle
Open: July to September daily
10am-12.30pm, 2-6.15pm. April to
June daily except Monday morning
and Tuesday 10am-12noon, 2-5.30pm.
☎ 99 967651

Tourist Information Centres

Comité Départemental du Tourisme des Ille-et-Vilaine
1 Rue Martenot
35000 Rennes
☎ 99 029743

Cancale
Rue du Port
35260
☎ 99 896372

Combourg
Maison de la Lanterne
35270
☎ 99 730018

Dinard
2 Boulevard Féart
35800
☎ 99 469412

Dol-de-Bretagne
3 Grande-Rue des Stuarts
35120
☎ 99 481537

Fougères
Place Briand
35300
☎ 99 941220

Redon
Place Parliament
35600
☎ 99 710604

Rennes
Pont de Nemours
35000
☎ 99 790198

St Malo
Esplanade St-Vincent
35400
☎ 99 566448

Vitré
Place St Yves
35500
☎ 99 750446

5

LOIRE-ATLANTIQUE

A t first sight it seems inappropriate to include a parcel of land which lies outside the borders of Brittany in a book on the region. But as every Breton will tell you, Brittany is not defined by some arbitrary line drawn by an official pen in Paris. Rather, it is defined by history and geography, and by its people. On that basis Brittany ends at the Loire, enclosing that section of the Pays de Loire *département* of Loire-Atlantique that lies between the river and the Ille-et-Vilaine border. That area has been defined as Breton by history, most particularly by the fact that Nantes was once the capital of the Duchy. It can be similarly defined by its geography, the country here being a continuation of the pastoral simplicity of Ille-et-Vilaine, rather than the elegance of the château country to the south. Finally, the division can be seen in the rural housing, especially in the roofs: north of the Loire they are Breton, being of slate, while to the south of the river they are clay tile, a practice that historically spread north through France from Spain, but did not manage to cross the border of Brittany until modern times.

Crossing from Morbihan into Loire-Atlantique the visitor arrives at the edge of the Brière Regional Nature Park, on a stretch of coastline that is as sophisticated as any in Brittany. The coastline starts with a deep incut from **Pen-Bé**, a hamlet set on a headland from which there are views of the local mussel breeding poles. Beyond the incut is a land of saltmarshes and beaches. The saltmarshes were created when the land between the Ile de Batz and Guérande was raised, bringing it just above sea level. Today the settling pans of the marshes are watered by high tides, the sea entering through a series of channels and the salt formed by evaporation being 'harvested' every fifteen days or so by men using *lasses*, long handled flat rakes. Table salt is collected from the top of the pan, with coarser 'road salt'

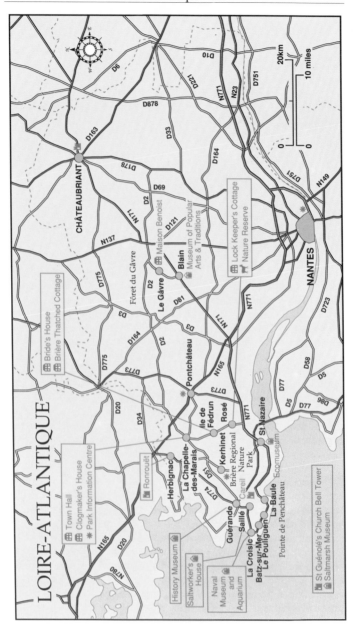

LOIRE-ATLANTIQUE

CHÂTEAUBRIANT

NANTES

Lock Keeper's Cottage

Nature Reserve

Maison Benoist

Museum of Popular
Arts & Traditions

Blain

Le Gâvre

Fôret du Gâvre

Pontchâteau

Bride's House

Brière Thatched Cottage

Ile de
Fédrun

Rosé

St Nazaire

Town Hall

Clogmaker's House

Park Information Centre

Ronrouët

Herbignac

La Chapelle-
des-Marais

Kerhinet

Careil

Brière Regional
Nature Park

Ecomuseum

Guérande

Saillé

La Baule

Pointe de Penchâteau

History Museum

Saltworker's
House

La Croisic

Batz-sur-Mer

Le Pouliguen

Naval
Museum
and
Aquarium

St Guénolé's Church Bell Tower

Saltmarsh Museum

20km

10 miles

0

being extracted from the pan bases. The salt pans, each one covering about 70sq m (about 750 sq ft), yield about 5kg (11 lb) of table salt and 60kg (132 lb) of coarse salt each day, with a working season that lasts from June until September. During the winter months the pan is cleaned and repaired, the channels dredged and prepared for the next season. In medieval times the saltmarshes were a great source of wealth, but production has reduced since the Revolution and now only about 8,000 *oeillets* (pans) are worked, producing a salt that is high in sodium chloride and low in magnesium salts. Those interested in knowing more about the industry and the way of life of the early salt workers can visit the Maison des Paludiers, the salt workers house, in **Saillé**, south of Guérande, where a former chapel houses a collection of tools of the trade, together with the furnishings of a traditional house and the clothing of the workers.

Guérande is a large town whose centre is still enclosed within medieval walls. The walls can be walked, the continuous route passing six towers and crossing four fortified gates. On the northern and western sides the moat on the outside of the wall still exists, on the other two sides it was filled in the eighteenth century, some 300 years after the defences had been constructed, and is now followed by a path and road. Here, on the first Saturdays in July and August competitions and exhibitions of Breton folk dancing are held. The gatehouse of Porte St Michel, sometimes called the Port du Châteaux, which was once the town governor's house, is now a museum of local history. Two rooms are decorated in the style of a local peasant farmer and a saltworker from the last century, while elsewhere there are collections of porcelain and other items of local crafts from the nineteenth century. Elsewhere it is best to wander at will, though do try to see the Merovingian sarcophagus, dated to the sixth century, in the crypt of St Aubin's Church.

To reach Guérande by going along the coastline from Morbihan the visitor must pass the Pointe du Castelli, a headland reached by a short walk from the road end car park, which offers a fine view southward to the Pointe du Croisic. From Guérande the coast can be regained by driving south to **Careil**, where there is an inhabited fourteenth-century castle. Later additions have made the castle a delightful place, the Renaissance wing being especially good. Visitors are allowed into several rooms and up a spiral stairway to what was once the garrison's quarters. South of Careil is La Baule.

La Baule is a remarkable place, a Riviera resort transplanted to the Atlantic Coast. The name is simply a corruption of *la belle* (the beautiful) and there are many who claim it has the finest beach in France. Certainly it is an elegant place with 7km (4 miles) of promenade which has, to one side, a glorious sandy beach complete with beach huts, windsurfer schools, children's playgrounds and restaurants, while on the other is a seemingly continuous line of high-price hotels, restaurants and *crêperies*. At the eastern end of the beach is **La-Baule-les-Pins**, though the name is slightly at odds with history for it was towards the western end that the huge plantations of maritime pines were first planted, in the last half of the nineteenth century, in order to stabilise the dunes and so protect the developing resort from both wind and sand. At La-Baule-les-Pins is the Parc des Dryades, an excellent park planted with numerous species of tree and a large number of different flowers, their colours competing with the swimsuits and windsurfer sails on the beach.

From La Baule the visitor travels through the village of **Le Pouliguen**, reaching it by bridging an inlet of the sea. Today, the village is a resort though there are still a few fishing boats in the harbour, almost lost among the yachts. From the village take the road to Pointe de Penchâteau, an excellent viewpoint, continuing along the Côte Sauvage, not as wild as the name implies unless a storm is forcing the sea against the odd-shaped rocks. At **Batz-sur-Mer** the visitor can ascend the 60m (197ft) tall bell tower of St Guénolé's Church for an excellent view of the local coast, Belle-Isle and the southern edge of the Morbihan Gulf. A closer look can be obtained from the Sentier du Douaniers, the customs officers' path, which starts near St Michel Plage and then follows the cliff edge. The church below the bell tower is a fine building with a roof shaped like a boat's keel, but there is a more interesting church in the town. Notre-Dame-du-Mûrier is now ruined, but is associated with a local legend. This tells of Jean de Rieux who was lost on the sea in a terrible storm some time in the fifteenth century but was guided to shore by a flickering light which he sighted through the gloom. When he landed, exhausted, he found the light came from a burning mulberry bush. Realising that his survival had been the result of a miracle he built the church, naming it for the *mûrier*, the mulberry bush.

Another interesting place in the town is the Musée des Mirais Saluts, devoted to the workers of the salt marshes — known locally as *Marais Saluts*. There is a reproduction of a nineteenth-century Batz saltworkers' house, and exhibitions that explain the production and gathering of the salt.

From Batz the visitor can drive directly to Le Croisic, or arrive there by way of Pointe du Croisic. Though **Le Croisic** is now a thriving resort, it maintains a small fishing fleet which gives added interest to a visit to the port, a picturesque spot when the langoustine boats lie below the quayside's pretty houses. The *criée*, the fish

(Opposite and above) At Batz-sur-Mer the sea fills the marshes where the salt is later 'harvested'

La Baule has one of the finest beaches in France

market, is a fine place: go there around 5am to see the langoustine boats arrive.

Alternatively, go to the aquarium to see the local marine wild-life as nature intended. The aquarium also has tropical fish, including sharks, penguins and a collection of shells and coral. There is also a mounted coelacanth. Elsewhere, there are fine half-timbered houses in the old part of the town — look particular in Rue St Christophe and Rue de l'Église — and the Musée Naval. The museum has a collection of model ships and old naval instruments, and an exhibition on the local salt marshes. There are also a number of objects from French ships lost in a battle between the English and French fleets off Le Croisic in November 1759. The battle, which took place during the Seven Years War, was won by the English under Admiral Hawke.

Heading east from La Baule the visitor reaches **Pornichet**, the village at the eastern end of La Baule's beach, a resort village traversed by the Boulevard des Océanides en route for St Nazaire. But before visiting that town head north of Guérande to visit the Brière Regional Nature Park.

Until about 10,000 years ago the land that is now the Regional Park, extending to about 40,000 hectares (almost 100,000 acres), was a low-lying forest. At that time there was a rise in the local sea level and the area was flooded. The trees died, laying down what is now a rich peat deposit. When the sea level fell again the peat was overlaid with silt from the Loire and this eventually formed the freshwater marshland that makes the Brière so interesting. From medieval times the area's inhabitants drained the more easily worked areas of the marsh, using the other parts to fish for eels and to hunt for ducks using flat-bottomed punts call *chalands* or *blins* to move around. They cut reeds for thatching and basket making, and cut peat for fuel. In 1461 the government recognised the unique nature of the area and granted the people of twenty-one communities perpetual rights to their hunting, fishing and harvesting, rights that are still jealously guarded by the ancestors of those first commoners. Today the old ways are declining, with many of the villages of the Grande Brière being dormitories for workers in St Nazaire, but tourism has helped: a *chaland* will now take the tourist out on to the marsh to see the yellow irises (mid-May to mid-June) and water lilies (mid-June to July) where once it travelled solely to let the punter tend his wicker-work fish pots. These trips are superb, even when apparently taken out of season or time. In autumn and winter the colours of the reed beds are fabulous, at sunset the whole marsh is golden.

For the visitor who wishes to see the marshland, but does not want to take a punt trip the **Ile de Fédrun**, reached from **St Joachim** offers a close look, while the tower of the church at **St Lyphard** offers a more panoramic view. The Ile is a spit of land extending into the marsh and, therefore, surrounded by it, while St Lyphard is a pretty village on the western edge of the marsh.

On the Ile there are several interesting sites. The Maison de la Mariée (Bride's House) is furnished in typical Brière style with a collection of bridal head-dresses decorated with wax orange blossoms. These wax flowers were made at workshops in St Joachim during the late nineteenth and early twentieth centuries and employed many Brière women. The museum also includes a display on the technique of making the flowers which were traditionally used to decorate bridal wear. Nearby, the Chaumiere Brièronne (Brière Thatched Cottage) is a typical local reed-thatched cottage restored and furnished in mid-nineteenth-century style. The decorations include a number of ducks' feet, a collectors' item for local hunters! The position of the cottage, beside a *curée* (canal) on which the owners punt would have been moored, and close to the bank on which vegetables were grown is also typical. An audio-visual display on the life of Brière folk — hunting, fishing, peat cutting and local wedding — is shown in the cottage. Also on the Ile is the Park Administrative Services Office, with a duplication of the information at the main tourist centre in La Chapelle-des-Marais. Note that no information will be provided from here if the La Chapelle office is open.

The main information centre for the park is the Park Information Centre at **La-Chapelle-des-Marais**. Here the visitor will find details on punt trips out into the park's marshes. The village's Hôtel de Ville (Town Hall) should be visited to see the superb 7m (23ft) *morta*, or fossilised tree trunk from the forest which grew where the marsh now lies. Also within the village is the Maison du Sabotier (Clogmaker's House), the last house of a Brière clogmaker, with a display of his and others', tools and of the clogs themselves.

Elsewhere, most of the villages of the park have tourist offices and several have very interesting sites for the visitors. The Maison de l'Éclusier (Lock Keeper's Cottage) at Rosé, a little way south of the Ile de Fedrun, was once lived in by the man who regulated the water level in the marsh by operating the gates in the Rosé canal. Within the house are a collection of (stuffed) wildlife and (preserved) flowers native to the marsh. There is also an aquarium of the types of marsh fish and a display on the evolution of the marsh. Close to Rosé is the Parc Animalier, a nature reserve where visitors can follow a 1km (½ mile) walk which has been created through the marshland. At various observation points there are display panels of the wildlife

Restored thatched cottages, Brière

*A Brière cottage,
adorned with flowers*

the lucky, or patient, visitor might see. Binoculars can be hired from
the reserve's reception centre.

Towards the south-west corner of the park is the hamlet of
Kerhinet, a group of delightful thatched cottages, which has been
restored as a pedestrian-only, open-air museum. One of the cottages
has been furnished in typical fashion and one of the outbuildings
houses a collection of peat and reed cutting tools and fishing equipment. There is also an arts and craft centre displaying work by local
artists and craftsmen. Nearby, close to the hamlet of Kerbourg, on a
mound beside a windmill, there is a fine *allée couverte*.

Finally, at **Herbignac** at the northern end of the park is the Château
de Ronrouët, an impressive twelfth-century castle partially dismantled in 1618 and set alight during the Revolution. Despite those
attempts at destruction, six towers and a dry moat have survived.
The cannon balls embedded in the wall of one of the towers are not

from a battle, but part of the coat-of-arms of the Rieux family who once held the castle.

St Nazaire was a small fishing port in medieval times, a tiny place bypassed by merchant ships on their way to Nantes. But as ships became larger the journey up the Loire to Nantes became more difficult and the little fishing port became a trading port, and then a centre for shipbuilding. In the Chantiers de l'Atlantique, the Atlantic Shipyard, the French Blue Riband passenger liners *Normandie* and *France* were built. In 1988, the largest cruise liner in the world, the Royal Caribbean Line's *Sovereign of the Seas* was built at the yard. In addition, several battleships and 500,000 ton oil tankers have been launched from St Nazaire. The Ecomusée de St Nazaire, housed in a bright yellow building between the Bassin de St Nazaire and the Loire, explores the development of the town as a port and shipbuilding centre with models of the yards and the great liners and battleships built here. There is also a collection of old shipbuilding tools. Close to the Ecomuseum, and forming part of it, is the submarine *Espadon*, launched at Le Havre in 1957. Here, too, is a terrace, known as the Panorama, from which there is a superb view of the harbour and the Loire, the latter crossed by the 3,356m (3,670yd) suspension bridge that links St Nazaire to St-Brevin-les-Pines.

The *Espadon* lies within the covered lock built by the Germans to give protection to U-boats entering and leaving the submarine base. The shelter not only protected the U-boats from air attack, but allowed a degree of secrecy about fleet movements. The submarine base itself was huge, measuring 300 x 125m (328 x 137yd), its 14 reinforced concrete bays being capable of sheltering 20 U-boats at any one time and including a full repair facility. Despite repeated raids by Allied bombers the base survived the war virtually intact. The base was the target of one of the war's most audacious raids on 27-28 March 1942 when British commandoes attacked it, using the destroyer *Campbelltown* which rammed the lock gates and was later blown up. The raid resulted in dreadful Allied losses, only 242 of the 611 who took part returning to Britain, and many local folk being killed in reprisal. A granite memorial to the dead stands beside the Boulevard de Verdun close to the river.

Following the D-Day Landings the German accompanying force dug in around St Nazaire and the town was virtually destroyed in the fighting that followed. It was a tragic outcome, particularly as the town had been involved in the conflict from the very start, the troop ship *Lancastria* being sunk by dive-bombers in the Loire estuary as it tried to evacuate soldiers of the BEF a few weeks after Dunkirk. Over 3,000 men died when the ship went down.

The town that arose from the debris of 1945 is workmanlike, very much a modern port and town, but there are points of interest for the visitor. In a square beside the aptly named Rue du Dolmen a dolmen and menhir bear witness to the popularity of the Loire's right bank, while the church dedicated to the town's patron saint, St Nazaire, beside Place des Quatre Horloges, built in Gothic style in the nineteenth century and restored in 1945, has excellent stained glass in superb original rose windows. Finally, go to the Jardin des Plantes, a very pleasant garden with fine trees and excellent flower beds, close to the beach of Grand Traict.

From St Nazaire the visitor can take the D100 between the airport and the Loire to reach **Donges**, an oil port and refining centre with a modern church, all concrete and glass, worth a visit for its impressive Calvary and stained glass by Max Ingrand. Now head north to **Pontchâteau**, a pleasant terraced town to the west of which (take the D33 towards Herbignac for 4km [2 miles] and park by the chapel), is the Calvaire de la Madeleine, built by St Louis-Marie Grignion whose birthplace was visited in Montfort. Grignion's original Calvary, erected in 1709, was destroyed during the reign of the Sun King, but was restored in 1821. The original wooden statue of Christ was saved, and is now housed in the small chapel to which pilgrimages are held on Sundays in the summer months. The chapel is decorated with frescoes depicting incidents in St Louis-Marie's life. From it a processional Stations of the Cross leads off, its large statues drawing on local folk lore as well as the story of the Passion.

To the east of Pontchâteau is **Blain**, a light industrial town with a very interesting Musée des Arts et Traditions Populaires. Here, in a building once owned by the Dukes of Rohan, there is a collection of items on the history of the town, from its Roman origins through to modern times, and a reconstruction of how the town looked in the nineteenth century, complete with village square, grocers, bakers, chemists etc. There is even a village policeman. Across the Nantes-Brest canal from the town and its fine museum are the ruins of the Château de la Groulais, once owned by the Dukes of Rohan, but destroyed be Richelieu in 1628. Best preserved of the ruins are the Tour du Pont-Levis, the drawbridge tower, beyond the dry moat, and the Tour de Connetable, the Constable's Tower. Visitors are not allowed into the ruin which has not been stabilised and may, therefore, be unsafe.

North of Blain is the Forêt du Gâvre a huge (4,400 hectares, 10,900 acres) forest of oaks, beech and pine. It is an absolute joy to walk, a series of nine avenues radiating from a central point known as the Belle Étoile. The forest is named for the village of **Le Gâvre** where the

Châteaubriant Castle

Typical marsh boats, Grande Brière

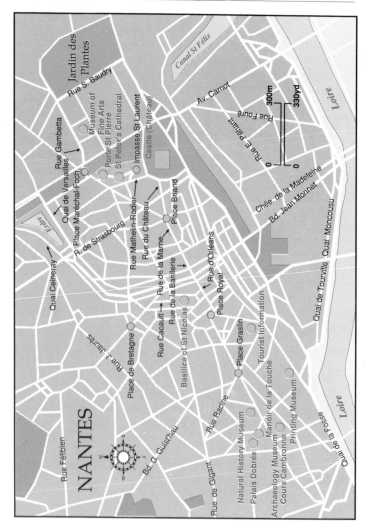

Maison Benoist houses an exhibition on the forest, its flora and fauna. Part of the house is furnished in seventeenth-century style and decorated with a collection of local costumes and *coiffes*. The attic houses a collection of old craft tools.

North-east of Le Gâvre the N171 and, in part, the N137, can be followed to **Châteaubriant**. This town, grouped around its impressive castle and surrounded by fine country, is famous for two stories that illuminate different aspects of love. The first concerns Sybille, who lived in the mid-thirteenth century . So strong was her love for her knight-husband that when he returned from a crusade she ran to embrace him and died of sheer joy while doing so. The second tale took place 300 years later when Jean de Laval, Count of Châteaubriant brought Françoise de Foix to the castle as his wife when she was only 11 years old. He was in love with her, but also so jealous that as she grew into a witty and beautiful young lady he shut her up in the castle refusing to allow her to leave it or to be seen. Rumours of her beauty spread to the king who asked to meet her. Laval ignored him, and when the king insisted on the couple attending Court travelled alone. But the king did manage to lure Françoise away from the castle, one story having it that he bribed a castle servant to give him the code word Laval used to gain access to her. Françoise became the king's mistress, Laval becoming almost insane with jealousy. When the king tired of her he sent her back to Laval who locked her and their daughter up in a room hung with black curtains. The child died, but Françoise lived as a prisoner for ten years until Laval, unable to bear his jealousy any longer, murdered her.

Laval's castle can still be visited, Françoise de Foix's tombstone being sited by the oratory in the Seignorial Palace built especially for her. Other parts of the palace now house town offices and the town library. Across the courtyard from the palace are the keep and sections of old wall from a medieval castle that probably pre-dates Laval's work. Within the walls there is a plaque which commemorates the shooting, on 22 October 1941, of twenty-seven hostages in retaliation for the killing of the Colonel Holtz, the commander of the Nantes German garrison. The commander was killed near Châteaubriant. Beside the N171, which heads east from the town towards Laval, there is a monument at the spot where the executions took place.

South from Châteaubriant is **Nantes**, a larger city than Rennes, and one that is historically Breton, despite now being in Pays de Loire. The city is named for the Namnetes, the Gaullish tribe who had a settlement here on the right bank of the Loire before the arrival of the Romans. After the departure of the Romans the town's position, on the Loire, the border between Brittany and the Frankish province of Anjou, caused it to become an important, if hectic, place. This early importance attracted the attention of Norse raiders who invaded in AD843 catching the townsfolk at church and slaughtering them all, including the clergy. Not until AD939 when Alain Barbe-Torte (Alan of the Crooked Beard), an exiled Breton nobleman, returned from

Britain, were the Normans driven out and Nantes restored to Brittany. Thereafter the town vied with Rennes to be the capital of the Duchy, and it was to here, in 1598, that Henry IV came when the excesses of the Catholic League demanded action. The signing of the Edict of Nantes gave freedom to Protestants and Catholics alike and so put an end to religious conflict, in theory at least. The visit also allowed Henry to see for the first time the power of the Breton dukes. He is reputed to have stood in awe in front of Nantes castle and whistled 'God's teeth' through his own.

With the coming of peace Nantes began a 200-year period of prosperity as its ships traded in sugar and what was euphemistically called ebony. Ebony was the slave trade, ships from Nantes sailing to the African coast to pick up its miserable live cargo, and then sailing to the Antilles to sell on the slaves and to buy cane sugar. The sugar was shipped back to Nantes where it was refined and transported to the rest of France along the Loire, the country's longest river. The slave trade was highly lucrative, the sugar trade merely being, as it were, the icing on the cake. Not until the Revolution did the slave trade end, with financially disastrous results for many Nantes' merchants. That time was a disaster for the average Nantes citizen too. Nantes folk were Catholic and Royalist, and many opposed the Revolution. Consequently, in June 1793 the Paris Convention sent Jean-Baptiste Carrier to the town with orders 'to purge the body politic of all the rotten matters it contains'. Carrier was sadistically good at his job, setting up a Revolutionary Tribunal and executing over 16,000 people in four months. Many were guillotined, but when the prisons overflowed because victims could not be despatched speedily enough, he loaded barges with prisoners and sank them in the Loire. These 'events' were called Les Noyades (The Drownings) and might be considered bad enough, but Carrier plumbed even greater depths with Les Marriages Républicaines in which a man and a women would be stripped naked, tied together and flung into the Loire to drown. At the end of the four months Carrier was recalled to Paris by an outraged Convention, tried for his crimes and guillotined.

The abolition of the slave trade, and the rise of St Nazaire as merchant ships grew larger and the Loire a less attractive waterway as a result, meant that a change of emphasis was required in the city. Gradually it has become a light industrial town and an important centre for the production of food products. The port still operates for vessels of limited tonnage, many of the basic foodstuffs for the food factories being delivered fresh to the city and making use of its large cold storage facilities.

With a city as large and interesting as Nantes exploration should be a leisurely pursuit. Here we offer a single itinerary that visits most of the better city sights, and points out the best way to reach the others. Start at the Jardin des Plantes, a superb garden that includes a wonderful collection of camellias and magnolias, some very fine trees and a collection of wooden sculptures. There is also a statue of Jules Verne. The garden is one of several in the city, the totality being a tribute to the seventeenth-century city merchants who instructed their ships' captains to bring back exotic plants from all over the world. The gardens that were stocked from those plants are one of the city's joys.

Leave the garden at its northern end and turn left along Rue Gambetta to reach the Musée des Beaux Arts, housed in a superb late nineteenth-century building. The collection has works from the thirteenth century through to the present day, the earlier paintings including canvasses by Rubens, de la Tour and Delacroix. The collection of twentieth-century paintings is large and excellent, including a whole room of Kandinsky's Bauhaus work. There are

(Opposite) Nantes economy has prospered due to its shipping trade

The façade of Nantes Cathedral

paintings from the Pont-Aven school, Sisley and Max Ernst, and a room concentrating on the more modern movements, with works by, among others, Vasarely and Léger, the latter being Nantes-born.

Continue along Rue Gambetta and then cross Rue Sully into Place Maréchal-Foch once, and occasionally still, called Place Louis XVI because of the column erected to the king in 1790. To the right now, a pleasant garden walk leads to Quai Ceineray. This is named for the architect who built the houses that create the square, and must be crossed to reach the River Erdre. Across the river is Quai de Versailles which leads to the Ile de Versailles, an old section of marshland that has been reclaimed to form a Japanese garden with rockeries and waterfalls. From the Quai boat trips on the Erdre can be made, while the Maison de l'Erdre has displays on the river's wildlife.

In Place Maréchal-Foch, to the left, is Port St Pierre a fifteenth-century town gate built on the site of a third-century gate into the Roman town. Beyond is the city's cathedral. The cathedral is a very austere building externally, but inside the soaring height — the vaults are 37½m (123ft) high, the height being possible because the building is in limestone rather than granite — and modern stained glass make it much friendlier. In the south transept, beautifully lit by a huge window, is the tomb of François II, worked in the early sixteenth century and one of the masterpieces of Breton Renaissance art. The tomb was the work of the Breton sculptor Michel Colombe, and only escaped destruction during the Revolution because the town architect courageously hid it in sections. It was re-constructed in 1817. The tomb, with its black and white marble, and the astonishing figures of the four Cardinal Virtues (look for Prudence, a double-faced figure, one face a young girl signifying the future, the other an old man representing the past) is magnificent. In the north transept the tomb of General Lamoricière is also excellent.

From the cathedral's southern side, take Impasse St Laurent to reach Rue Mathelin-Rodier. Here, at No 3, the Maison de Guigny, the Duchess of Berry hid in 1832. The duchess was mother of the infant heir to the French throne, and returned to France from Scotland in that year to foment a rebellion that would, she hoped, restore the monarchy. Recalling Nantes' Royalist sympathies she hid here, but failed to raise any enthusiasm for a revolt. Ultimately she was betrayed by a servant and police arrived at the house. With a maid and two men (her clerk and her secretary) she hid in a secret room beside the chimney. The police failed to discover her, and believing she had left the house, but for just a short while, left a small force in the house to await her return. The men were cold and lit a fire and, after a time, it was so hot in the hiding place that the women's dresses caught fire. The fire was smothered and, thankfully, the police fell asleep, their fire going out. However, when morning came the police re-lit the fire, and this time the duchess and her companions were forced out of hiding, near to death from heat and fumes. The duchess went to prison, but released when it was discovered she had re-married after her child's birth, a marriage that annulled his claim to the throne.

Rue Mathelin-Rodier leads to the Château des Ducs de Bretagne. The castle was begun by Duke François II in 1466 and completed by his daughter Anne, though the site it occupies was an old one: the remains of an earlier castle and a Roman fort can still be seen. Inside the moat, crossed by drawbridge, the castle is virtually complete — one tower, used as a powder magazine, blew up in 1800 — and surrounds the old Ducal Palace. Within the castle there are three domestic buildings, the first palace, now called the Governor's Lesser Palace, the work of François I, the Saddlery and the Governor's Major Palace, the work of François II and his daughter. The Major Palace stands in front of the Tour de Boulangerie (Bakery Tower), occasionally called the Tour d'Enfer (Tower of Hell) as it was the medieval prison. Its walls still carry graffiti from that time. To the side of the palace is the beautiful Tour de la Couronne d'Or (Golden Crown Tower). At the foot of the tower is the castle well, its elegant wrought-iron cover the shape of the Ducal crown.

The Major Palace houses the Musée d'Art Populaire Régional, which houses a collection of costumes and *coiffes* from all over Brittany, as well as other collections of Breton furniture, old maps of the dukedom, pottery and wrought ironwork. In the Saddlery there is a second museum, the Musée des Salorges, devoted to the sea, with three ships' figureheads, a collection of model ships, and another of old navigational instruments. Behind the Saddlery is the sixteenth-century Tour de Fer à Cheval (Horseshoe Tower) which houses a most interesting collection of work by contemporary weavers who prove that weaving can produce excellent art.

From the castle, walk towards the city, taking Rue du Château to Place Briand and continuing along Rue de la Marne and Rue de la Barillerie to pass, to both the left and the right, the Plateau Ste Croix with some excellent half-timbered houses. From Place Royal a de-tour northward (to the right) passes the Basilica of St Nicolas to reach Place de Bretagne, the centre of the city, where the old and new architectures meet. In the streets around Place Royal are some fine eighteenth-century houses, built on the profits of sugar and ebony. There are good houses from this period in Rue Crébillon ahead, which leads into Place Graslin. Ahead now is a small complex of buildings. The Musée d'Histoire Naturelle has fine collections of shells and skeletons, and a vivarium of reptiles from all over the world. The Palais Dobrée is a nineteenth-century mansion built by a Nantes shipowner and has a collection of medieval statuary and religious artefacts including a reliquary holding the heart of the Duchess Anne. The Manoir de la Touche, also known as Jean V's house because Duke Jean V died here in 1442, has a collection of items from the time of the Revolution. Finally, the Musée d'Archéologie Régional has collections of Egyptian, Greek and Etruscan artifacts as well as some local Gallo-Roman and Norse items.

From Place Graslin, or from the museum complex, Cours Cambronne, an elegant street with fine eighteenth and nineteenth-century houses is reached. South of here is the Musée de l'Imprimerie, a printing museum with a collection of old printing machines and a gallery of lithographs and illuminated manuscripts. The museum stands on the Quai de la Fosse, on the Madeleine arm of the Loire — the Loire splits into two at the city, forming the Ile Beaulieue. Moored on the river is the French Naval ship *Maillé-Brézé*, an anti-submarine support ship which can be visited. Close by is the Musée Jules Verne, dedicated to the science fiction writer who was a native of Nantes. The museum has a remarkable collection of memorabilia and first editions.

Close to the Jules Verne Museum is the Belvédère de Ste Anne, a viewpoint of Nantes and the river, a panorama dial helping point out the details of the view.

Additional Information

Places to Visit

Batz-sur-Mer
St Guénolé's Church Bell Tower
Open: mid-June to mid-September daily 10am-12noon, 3-6.30pm.
Mid-September to mid-June daily 9am-4pm.
☎ 40 238679

Saltmarsh Museum
Open: June to September daily 10am-12noon, 3-7pm. October to May Saturday, Sunday 3-7pm.
☎ 40 238279

Blain
Museum of Popular Arts and Traditions
Open: Easter to September daily except Monday 2-6pm. October to Easter Saturday, Sunday 2-6pm.
☎ 40 871511

Careil
Castle
Open: June to September daily 10.30am-12noon, 2.30-6pm.
☎ 40 602299

Châteaubriant
Castle
Open: mid-June to mid-September
Monday,Wednesday to Saturday
10am-12noon, 2-7pm. Sunday
10am-12noon.
☎ 40 282090

Guérande
History Museum
Open: Easter to September daily
9am-12noon, 2-7pm.
☎ 40 429652

Herbignac
Ranrouët Castle
Open: June to September Monday
to Saturday 3-6pm. Sunday 9am-
12.30pm, 3-7pm.
☎ 40 668501

Ile de Fédrun
Park Administrative Services Office
Open: mid-September to March
Monday to Friday 9am-12.30pm, 2-
5.30pm.
☎ 40 884272

Bride's House
Open: all year daily 10am-7pm.

Brière Thatched Cottage
Open: June to September daily
10am-12.30pm, 3-7pm.
☎ 40 884272

Kerhinet
Open: June to September daily
10am-12.30pm, 3-7pm.
☎ 40 619406

La Chapelle-des-Marais
Park Information Centre
Open: April to mid-June Monday to
Saturday 2.30-6.30pm. Mid-June to
mid-September daily 10am-12.30pm,

3-7pm. Mid-September to March
Wednesday 2.30-6.30pm.
☎ 40 668501

Clogmaker's House
Open: July to mid-September daily
9am-12.30pm, 3-7pm. Mid-
September to June Wednesday 3-
7pm.
☎ 40 668501

Town Hall
Open: all year Monday to Wednesday 9am-12noon, 2-5pm. Thursday
to Saturday 9am-12noon.

Le Croisic
Côte d'Amour Aquarium
Open: July, August daily 10am-
8pm. September, October and April
to June daily 10am-12noon, 2-6.30pm.
November to March daily except
Monday 10am-12noon, 2-6pm.
☎ 40 230244

Naval Museum
Open: Easter, May to September
Monday,Wednesday to Saturday
10am-12noon, 3-7pm.
☎ 40 629117

Le Gâvre
Maison Benoist
Open: July to September daily 2.30-
6.30pm. October to June Sunday
2.30-6.30pm.
☎ 40 512618

Nantes
Museum of Fine Arts
10 Rue Georges Clemenceau
Open: all year Monday, Wednesday
to Saturday 10am-12noon, 1-
5.45pm. Sunday 11am-5pm
☎ 40 416565

Boat trips on the Erdre
Cruises take 3 or 4 hours and meals
are served on board. There is also a
guide. For details
☎ 40 202450

Maison de l'Erdre
Ile de Versailles
Open: all year Tuesday to Saturday
1-7pm. Sunday 1-6pm.
☎ 40 470451

Ducal Castle and Museums
Castle: July, August daily 10am-7pm
Open: September to June daily
except Tuesday 10am-12noon, 2-6pm.
Museums open: July, August daily
10am-12noon, 2-6pm. September to
June daily except Tuesday 10am-
12noon, 2-6pm.
☎ 40 471815

Natural History Museum
12 Rue Voltaire
Open: all year Tuesday to Saturday
10am-12noon, 2-6pm. Sunday 2-6pm.
☎ 40 733003

*Thomas Dobrée Mansion, Touche
    Manor and Regional Archeology
    Museum*
Place Jean V
Open: all year daily except Tuesday
10am-12noon, 2-6pm.
☎ 40 697608
A combined ticket is available for
the Natural History Museum,
Dobrée Mansion, Touche Manor
and Regional Archeological
Museum.

Printing Museum
24 Quai de la Fosse
Open: all year except August
Tuesday to Friday 2-6pm.
Wednesday, Saturday 10am-
12noon, 2-5pm. Guided tour every
day at 2.30pm.
☎ 40 732655

Maillé-Brézé
Quai de la Fosse
Open: April to September daily
except Monday 2-5pm. October to
March Wednesday, Sunday 2-5pm.
☎ 40 695715

Jules Verne Museum
3 Rue de l'Hermitage
Open: all year daily except
Tuesday 10am-12.30pm, 2-5pm.
☎ 40 891188

Post Office and Telecommunications
Place de Bretagne
Market Day: Saturday
Car Hire: all major and French hire
companies represented. Ask at the
tourist office for details.

Rosé
Lock Keeper's Cottage
Open: June to September daily
10am-12.30pm, 3-7pm.
☎ 40 911780

Nature Reserve
Open: May to October daily 9am-
6pm.
☎ 40 911780

Saillé
Saltworkers' House
Open: May to September daily
10am-12noon 2-5pm. Guided tours
of the saltmarshes are offered from
the house at 5pm on Monday,
Wednesday and Friday, weather
permitting.
☎ 40 249671 or 40 243444

St Lyphard
Church Tower
Open: Easter to September daily
10.30-11.30am, 2-6pm.
Guided tours only.
☎ 40 914134

St Nazaire
Ecomuseum, Espadon and Panorama
Open: June to September daily
9.30am-7pm. October to May daily
except Tuesday 10am-12noon, 2-6pm.
☎ 40 668216 or 40 667966
Note: There are a variety of tickets
that allow entrance to the three sites
in various combinations, but because
of the limited space reservations
must always be made for visits to
Espadon.

Tourist Information Centres

**Comité Départemental du
   Tourisme de Loire-Atlantique**
Maison du Tourisme
Place du Commerce
44000 Nantes
☎ 40 895077

Châteaubriant
22 Rue de Couéré
44110
☎ 40 282090

Guérande
1 Place du Marché-aux-Bois
44350
☎ 40 249671

La Baule
8 Place de la Victoiré
44500
☎ 40 243444

Le Croisic
Place de la Gare
44490
☎ 40 230070

Nantes
Maison du Tourisme
Place du Commerce
44000
☎ 40 470451

St Nazaire
Place François Blanchot
BP 178 44613
☎ 40 224065

Brittany: Fact File

Accommodation

Tourist hotels are classified officially by the government in 'star' categories which range from 'four-star L' through three intermediate grades, to 'one star', which is of moderate, but quite adequate, comfort. These are objective ratings based on facilities in relation to the number of bedrooms. They are not in themselves recommendations of quality.

All hotels are required to show their room rates, remember that the rate will be for the room, and not per person, and a menu if they have a restaurant, in their reception area. It is normal practice to visit the room before finally agreeing to take it, though this practice is not always followed, especially if you have booked your room from the local Tourist Information Centre and it is the last one in town. The Tourist Information Centre will usually charge you the price of the phone call to enquire/book the room, but that is a small price to pay. In most hotels breakfast will not be included in the price of the room. Check to make sure, and if it is not ask what breakfast will cost: you may well find that it will be cheaper to go to a local café or bar.

In advance of your stay it may also be worthwhile obtaining a copy of *Logis et Auberges de France*, from the French Government Tourist Office in your own country. This is an association of family-run hotels which offer good service and food at the lower end of the price spectrum.

Many other more modest, non-tourist, hotels exist in most towns and villages, as do furnished room and flats to let. Properly equipped country houses, villas, cottages and farms (or self-contained parts of them) can be rented as holiday homes (*gîtes*). *Gîtes* are usually rented by the week and are competitively priced, so much so that you will need to book early. All *gîtes* are inspected annually and are invariably in excellent condition. As they are usually in superb rural settings they offer a peaceful base, though having your own transport is likely to be a necessity.

Well-equipped camp and caravan sites, sometimes in very lovely settings, can be found almost everywhere. As with the hotels there is a star system, the lowest grade (no stars) being very basic, the highest (4 star) often being equipped with shops, restaurants, swimming pools, tennis courts and so on. There will also be marked out pitches, rather than the free-for-all of the lower grades, and hot showers. A camping carnet is useful as some sites give a discount to carnet holders. Those sites which require the camper to surrender his passport will usually accept the carnet instead, which is also useful if you suddenly need to cash travellers' cheques. The better sites, that is those closest to the beach, or those with the best facilities, are often full at peak times. To ensure that you will have a pitch it is best to book in advance. The Brittany Chamber of Commerce, and the French Government Tourist Office in your home country will have details of all sites.

More adventurous travellers could use a canal boat as a floating hotel (See Travel) or try a horse-drawn caravan or *roulotte*. Such caravans might limit the sights that can be visited, but are very romantic. If you are interested contact:-
In Finistère Roulottes de Bretagne
Gare de Locmaria-Berrien
29218 Huelgoat
☎ 98 997328

In Morbihan Attelages Morbinhannais
Ker Samuel
56610 Le Saint
☎ 97 230616

Annual Events and Festivals

Brittany has a great number of worthwhile events. Only the major ones are listed here, though some others are mentioned in the text:

Pardons
Tréguier: The Pardon of St Yves (Pardon des Pauvres) on the third Sunday in May.
St Jean-du-Doigt: The Pardon of St Jean on the Sunday closest to 24 June.
Ste Anne-d'Auray: The Pardon of Ste Anne on the last

weekend in July.

Dinard: The Pardon of the Sea on the third Sunday in August.

Ste Anne-la-Palud: The Pardon of Ste Anne-la-Palud on the last Sunday in August.

St Fiacre: The Pardon of St Fiacre on the last Sunday in August.

Le Folgoët: The Pardon of the Woodland Fool on the first Sunday in September.

Carnac: The Pardon of St Cornély on the second Sunday in September.

Josselin: The Baker's Pardon on the second Sunday in September.

Festivals

St Malo: Festival of Rock Music at the end of February.
Jazz Festival during the first weekend in August

Rennes: Les Tombées de la Nuit - Création Bretonne (a series of night-time concerts and floodlit tableaux) at the end of June and the beginning of July. Rock Festival during the first fortnight in December.

Nantes: Carnival and arts festival in early July.

Pont-l'Abbe: Festival of Embroidery on the second Sunday in July.

Lamballe: Festival of Ajonc d'Or (the Golden Gorse, a folklore festival) on the second Sunday of July.

Paimpol: Festival of Newfoundland and Iceland on the third Sunday of July.

Fouesnant: Apple Festival on the third Sunday of July.

Dinan: International Music Festival at the end of July.

Quimper: The Cornouaille Festival (of Breton culture) during the week preceding the fourth Sunday of July.

Lannion: Music Festival. Various events during July and August.

Redon: Festival of the Abbey (a festival of theatre, music and dance) from mid-July to mid-August.

Morlaix: Les Mercredis de Morlaix (a series of festivals and fairs) on Wednesdays in July and August.

Pont Aven: Festival of Ajonc d'Or (the Golden Gorse, a folklore festival) on the first Sunday of August.

Lorient: Celtic Festival (cultural events by groups from all Celtic areas) during the first fortnight in August.

Plomodiern/Ménez-Hom: Folklore Festival on the 15 August, held in the village and on the peak behind it.

Châteauneuf-de-Faou: International Festival of Folk Dancing on 15 August.

Guingamp: Festival of Breton music and dance during the weekend of mid-August.

Cap Sizun: Heather Festival on the second Sunday in August.

St Briac: Fêtes des Mouettes (the Seagull Festival with processions of Breton dancers and traditional Breton bands, some at night) on the second Sunday in August.

Concarneau: Festival of the Blue Nets (after Quimper's Cornouaille Festival the most important event in the calendar of Breton cultural events) on the third Sunday of August.

Carnac: Festival of the Menhirs on the third Sunday in August.

Fougères: the Festival of Livre Vivant (an historical pageant with *son et lumière*) at the end of August/beginning of September.

Arrival and Customs

No visa is required for holders of British, American and Canadian passports. Normal EEC customs regulations apply for those travelling from Britain. Normal European regulations apply for those travelling from North America.

Climate

The Breton climate is a maritime one, similar to that of southern Britain, especially Cornwall, though warmer, sunnier and a little more reliable in summer, and with fewer frosts in winter, though it also tends to be wetter in winter. The average temperature in July and August is about 21°C (70°F), and a little warmer in the south than in the north. Near the sea, especially on the western coast, there is likely to be a breeze, even on the best of days.

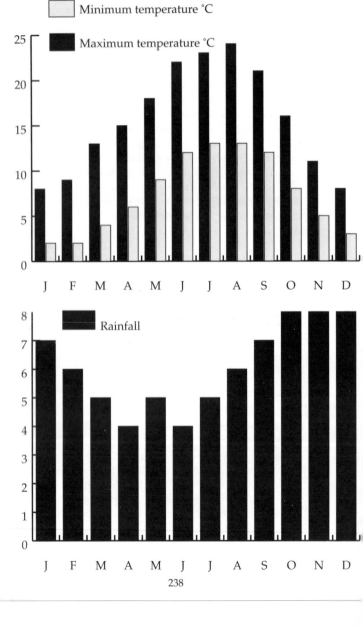

Currency and Credit Cards

All major credit cards (Access, Visa, American Express etc) are taken at most large restaurants, hotels, shops and garages. Eurocheques and traveller's cheques are also accepted. Banks are normally open from 8.30am-12noon, 1.30-4.30pm Monday to Friday only.

The French unit of currency is the French *franc*. There are no restrictions on the import of French or foreign currency. The export of currency valued at up to 5,000 French *francs* in any currency (including French francs) is permitted. Amounts worth in excess of 5,000 French *francs* may be exported, providing that the money has been declared on entry. The French *franc* (abbreviated for FF) is divided into 100 *centimes*. Current coins include 5, 10, 20 and 50 *centime* pieces as well as 1, 2, 5 and 10 *franc* pieces. Bank notes come in denominations of 20, 50, 100, 200 and 500 *francs*.

Disabled Visitors

Not all of the sites listed in this guide are accessible to disabled visitors. A list of those that are, not only in Brittany, but in the whole of France, can be found in the publication *Touristes quand même! Promenades en France pour les voyageurs handicapés*. This excellent guide can be obtained from:

Comité National Français de Liaison pour la Réadaptiondes Handicapés
38 Boulevard Raspail
75007 Paris

The guide will be of interest not only to those with a physical handicap, but to the visually handicapped and visitors with a hearing difficulty.

Electricity

Electricity operates at 220v ac, 50 Hertz (cycles/sec) in most places. Some small areas are still at 110v ac. Adaptors will be needed by those people who do not use continental two-pin plugs at home.

Health Care

British travellers have a right to claim health services in France by virtue of EEC regulations. Form E111, available from Post Offices, should be obtained to avoid complications. American and Canadian visitors will need to check the validity of their personal health insurances to guarantee they are adequately covered.

For emergency assistance, dial 19 in all towns. In country areas it may be necessary to phone the local *gendarmerie* (police).

Pharmacies, clearly marked with a green cross, can usually deal with minor ailments or advise people where to go if any additional help is needed.

Language

There are sufficient phrase books on the market to render a glossary of useful French words and expressions superfluous. However, a glossary of Breton words is included here to help the visitor understand a little more about the countryside, as it explains some frequently seen names, and the occasional Breton event.

aber — estuary
bihan — small
biniou — Breton bagpipe
bombarde — Breton oboe
bragou — breeches
braz — large
brocante — antiques
chupen — embroidered waistcoat
coiffe — head-dress
criée — fish market
far — pudding
festou noz — night festival
giz — costume
goat — wood
(also occasionally rendered at coat, goët or hoët)
haras — stud farm
kenavo — goodbye
ker — village or house
lann — consecrated ground (usually the site of a church)

men — stone
mor — sea
pleu — parish
(also rendered as pl, ploë, plou or plé, and usually
followed by a saint's name)
yermat — good health

Maps

There are a number of maps of Brittany of which the best are
the Michelin 1: 200,000 (1 centimetre to 2 kilometres, about 1
inch to 3 miles) and the RAC map at the resolutely Imperial
scale of 1 inch to 4 miles. The Michelin is Sheet 230 in their
series, the RAC sheet being identifed solely as Brittany. For
route planning and general motoring these maps are excellent. Those wanting more detail, or to find off-the-beaten-
track spots and roads, will find the IGN (Institut Géographique
National) series invaluable. The Series Verte, at 1: 100,000
has all the information most visitors will need. Brittany is
covered by 5 sheets, Nos. 13, 14, 15, 16 and 24, though the
eastern edges of Ille-et-Vilaine and Loire-Atlantique do creep
on to Sheets 17 and 25 respectively. More detail, especially of
things of interest, such as the position of megalithic remains,
are to be found on IGN's 1: 50,000 series. There are too many
of these to number, but those looking for the stones around
Carnac will find Sheet 501, which covers that area, together
with the Gulf of Morbihan and Belle Ile, especially useful. It
should be noted that neither of these series are very good at
identifying footpaths other than the national series of GR
paths. For information on local walking it is best to consult
the Tourist Information Centre which will either have leaf-
lets, or details of local guides.

Measurements

France uses the metric system. Conversions are:
1 kilogram (1,000 grams) = 2.2 lb
1 litre = 1¾ pints
4.5 litres = 1 gallon
1.6 km = 1 mile
1 hectare = 2½ acres (approx)

Post and Telephone Services

Stamps (*timbres*) are available from post offices, which are normally open from 8am-7pm Monday to Friday and 8am-12noon on Saturday. In some smaller towns and villages, the post office may be shut for lunch, both the timing and the duration of the break being a local custom.

Telephones in France take cards rather than coins or tokens. These are available from kiosks and bars. The dial codes from France are:

Great Britain 19 44
Canada 19 1
USA 19 1

Remember to leave out the first zero of your home country number eg to dial the French Government Tourist Office in London (071 491 7622) from France, dial 19 44 71 491 7622.

Public Holidays

New Year's Day
Easter Monday
May Day
Ascension Day
V.E. Day — 8 May
Whit Monday
Bastille Day — 14 July
Assumption Day — 15 August
All Saints' Day — 1 November
Armistice Day — 11 November
Christmas Day

Shopping

The *charcuterie* is the pork butcher, though the modern shop sells a wider range of food than the name implies. Here you will find all sorts of cooked meats and pâte, quiches, pizzas and local specialities.

The *boucherie* is the butcher's shop. Here uncooked sausage will be sold, cooked sausage being found at the *charcuterie*, together with other uncooked meat, including poultry.

The *poissonerie* (fish shop) is more in evidence in Brittany than in most other French provinces. Here you will be able to buy all manner of fish, as well as the langoustines, mussels and oysters for which the area is famous. In villages by the sea it is also worth trying the local fish market, or the quayside stalls where fresh fish and shellfish will be on sale at the lowest available prices.

The *boulangerie* is the pride of most French towns, a morning procession of shoppers armed with *baguettes*, the typical French stick bread, leaving every day, including Sunday. As you will soon find, the bakery will sell much more than *baguettes*, *croissants*, *brioches*, and a vast assortment of loaves also being available. There will be no cakes, however. For those you must visit the *pâtisserie* which specialises in cakes and pastries. They will be mouth-wateringly tempting, but expensive.

The final shop is the *epicerie* or *alimentation*, or grocery. If the town has no *fromagerie* (cheese shop) this is where you will buy cheese, as well as more general foods. The *epicerie* has been hardest hit by the growth in supermarkets and hypermarkets. These are more convenient — and a visit to the out-of-town hypermarket, likely to a vast place, is an education in itself — and sell a good range of food, but have nothing of the character of the shops they have replaced.

Shopping Hours

Food shops are usually open from 8am-6/6.30pm, while other shops are open from 9/10am-6/6.30pm. The half day closing varies, but is usually Monday. In some towns shops other than food shops close all day on Monday. Lunchtime closing is usually from 12noon until 2pm, though supermarkets stay open throughout the day. Supermarkets also tend to stay open longer at night, usually closing at 8pm.

Sports and Pastimes

Brittany is an ideal activity holiday destination, being blessed with a good mix of country, and wide open spaces. Not surprisingly for a country which is the home of the world's greatest cycle race, and being relatively flat, the region is very popular with cyclists. For general information contact:

Fédération Française de Cyclotourisme
8 Rue Jean-Marie-Jégo
75013 Paris
☎ 45 803021

Contact the local tourist office for details of cycle hire and organised cycle trips, usually held on Sundays with the assistance of the local cycling club.

The walker is well catered for, several GR's (*Grand Randonnée* or long-distance footpath) criss-crossing the region. The best of these is a matter of personal preference, but GR34 which traverses the northern coast must be a strong contender. For information on the entire French GR system contact:

Fédération Française de la Randonnée Pédestre
Comité de Promotion des Sentiers de Grande Randonnées
64 Rue de Gergovie
75014 Paris
☎ 45 453102

Locally, walking groups produce topo-guides to the *Petits Randonnée*, which will give an enjoyable half-day's circular route. The openness of the country that has benefitted the walker has also been used to advantage by horse-riders, and a series of equestrian pathways also exists. For information on these contact (for the whole of France):

Fédération des Randonneurs Équestres
16 Rue des Apennins
75017 Paris
☎ 45 262323

The local tourist office will be able to help you with these, as well as details of local riding stables.

Golf is becoming increasingly popular in France and Brittany has some very good courses. Again the local tourist office will be happy to provide details. The office will also provide details for those who wish to use swimming pools rather than the sea, or to play tennis.

The opportunities the coast of Brittany offers the sailor have been mentioned many times in the text, but warrant a further mention here. Though the winds around Brittany are less dependable than those elsewhere, they are usually lively and as a result the coastal waters offer some of Europe's best sailing for the windsurfer and dinghy helmsman: board and boat hire and tuition is available in virtually every port and coastal village. A word of caution is necessary however. The coastline is often rocky and very hostile to those attempting to land away from the beaches and ports, as a result of which sailors who get into difficulties can face a daunting challenge when trying to get ashore. Do make sure your skill level is equal to the coast and the weather, do check the weather forecast beforehand, and do have a word with some of the locals about the tides and currents you might experience.

Finally, a few words about that most uniquely French game, *boules* or *pétanque*. The object of the game, which is played in virtually every market square, and on any other available flat surface, is to land your heavy metal *boule* closest to the *cochonnet* (little pig, or jack). The throws, executed with a backward flip of the wrist are either *pointe*, a skilful placing of the *boule* near the jack, or *tir*, a harder throw directed at the opponent's *boule*, the aim being to knock it out of the way. There are several local versions of the game, but at its purest the player whose *boule* is not closest to the jack has the next turn, until all *boules* have been thrown. Whoever is nearest the jack at that stage wins.

Tipping

Tips (*pourboires*) are given as in your home country but in France they also apply to guides at both châteaux and museums.

Tourist Offices

The main French tourist offices are:
UK
178 Piccadily
London W1V 0AL
☎ 071 491 7622

Brittany Chamber of Commerce
31 Seward Street
London EC1V 3PA
☎ 071 490 5579

USA
610 Fifth Avenue Suite 222
New York
NY 10020-2452
☎ 212 757 1683

Canada
1981 Avenue McGill College
Tour Esso Suite 490
Montreal
Quebec H3 A2 W9
☎ 514 288 4264

The main tourist offices for the Breton *départements* are known as the CDT (Comite Départemental du Tourisme). However they are not open to the visitor, except by post or by telephone. Within the *départements* the main town offices are called Syndicates d'Initiative. Both are listed in each chapter.

Travel

HOW TO GET THERE

Brittany Ferries operate services direct to Brittany from Britain (Plymouth to Roscoff and Portsmouth to St Malo) and Ireland (Cork to Roscoff). They also operate services from Poole to Cherbourg and Portsmouth to Caen which will be of interest to those visiting eastern Brittany. The crossing times are long in comparison to those at the eastern end of the Channel, but the boats are superbly equipped with adequate seating for all passengers. There are cabins, which are handy on day crossings as well as at night, and large numbers of reclining seats. In addition, Sealink have a Weymouth to Cherbourg ferry, and both Sealink and P&O operate from Portsmouth to Cherbourg.

Those crossing the channel to one of the ports of Pas de Nord should follow the autoroute to Paris, heading west from there on the A11. This autoroute splits at Le Mans, the A11 heading south-west to Nantes, with the A18 continuing eastwards to the Breton border near Rennes.

Paris is connected to Rennes, Brest and other cities on the south and west coasts by good train services, including the fast and efficient TGV service.

Quimper, Brest, Rennes and Nantes are all served by Air France flights from Paris. Nantes is also reached by Air France from Heathrow, and by Britair from Cork. Britair also fly from Gatwick to Quimper, Brest and Rennes.

WHEN YOU ARE THERE

Car Hire
Car hire is available from many companies, including all the well-known major European ones, and from all the big towns (ask at the local Tourist Information Centre) the airports and all large railway stations.

Rules of the Road
The speed limits currently applied to French roads are:

In dry conditions:	In the wet:
Autoroutes 130kph (81mph)	110kph (68mph)
National (N) roads 110kph (68mph)	90kph (56mph)
Other roads 90kph (56mph)	80kph (50mph)
In towns 60kph (37mph)	60kph (37mph)

Please Note: There is a new minimum speed limit of 80kph (50mph) for the outside lane on autoroutes during daylight, on level ground and with good visibility. In France you must drive on the right-hand side of the road. No driving is permitted on a provisional licence and the minimum age to drive is 18. Stop signs mean exactly that, the vehicle must come to a complete halt. It is compulsory for front seat passengers to wear seat belts and children below the age of 10 are not allowed to travel in the front seats. All vehicles must carry a red warning triangle and a spare headlamp bulb. There are strict, and very strictly interpreted, laws on speeding and drink-driving. The former will usually result in an on-the-spot fine, while the latter will usually result in confiscation of the car.

In built-up areas, the motorist must sometimes give way to anybody coming out of a side-turning on the right. This is indicated by the sign *priorité à droite*. However, this rule no longer applies at roundabouts which means vehicles already on the roundabout have right of way (*passage protégé*). All roads of any significance outside built-up areas have right of way.

Car Parking

Car parking is no easier in French towns than it is in most other large European cities. The by-laws vary from town to town and, occasionally, from day to day. To be safe it is best to use car parks. Check before leaving your parked car: it is common practice to take your ticket with you, to pay as you return and to use the stamped ticket or token to raise the exit barrier. If you drive to an exit and then discover this rule, it is likely that you will have a queue of cars behind you when you are trying to work out what has gone wrong or are trying to reverse. Since tokens are time-limited, the queue is unlikely to be sympathetic.

Trains

Brittany has reasonable train services in the east-west direction, but not in the north-south direction. If you intend to use public transport for your trip, check on the availability of services beforehand, and consider using buses as well as trains.

Canals

Brittany has about 600km (372 miles) of navigable canals and rivers which offer endless possibilities for relaxing travel. Several companies in Britain offer package holidays on the water, and there are many local companies in Brittany who offer a similar service. The largest is:

Chemins Nautiques Bretons
Le Port Lyvet
La Vicomté-sur-Rance
22690 Pleudihen
☎ 96 832871

INDEX

MPC

A Note to the Reader

Thank you for buying this book, we hope it has helped you to plan and enjoy your visit. We have worked hard to produce a guidebook which is as accurate as possible. With this in mind, any comments, suggestions or useful information you may have would be appreciated.

Please send your letters to:
The Editor
Moorland Publishing Co Ltd
Moor Farm Road West
Ashbourne
Derbyshire
DE6 1HD

The Travel Specialists

Visitor's Guides

Tour & Explore with MPC Visitor's Guides

Austria
Austria: Tyrol &
  Vorarlberg

Britain:
Cornwall & Isles of
  Scilly
Cotswolds
Devon
East Anglia
Guernsey, Alderney
  and Sark
Hampshire & Isle of
  Wight
Jersey
Kent
Lake District
Scotland: Lowlands
Somerset, Dorset &
  Wiltshire
North Wales and
  Snowdonia
North York Moors,
  York & Coast
Northumbria
Northern Ireland
Peak District
Sussex
Yorkshire Dales &
  North Pennines

Crete
Cyprus
Denmark
Egypt
Finland
Florida

France:
Alps & Jura
Corsica
Dordogne
Loire
Massif Central
Normandy Landing
  Beaches
Provence & Côte
  d'Azur

Germany:
Bavaria
Black Forest
Rhine & Mosel
Southern Germany
Northern Germany

Iceland

Italy:
Florence & Tuscany
Italian Lakes
Northern Italy

Mauritius,
  Rodrigues &
  Reunion

Peru

Spain:
Costa Brava to Costa
  Blanca
Mallorca, Menorca,
  Ibiza &
  Formentera
Northern & Central
  Spain
Southern Spain &
  Costa del Sol

Sweden
Switzerland
Tenerife
Turkey
Yugoslavia: The
  Adriatic Coast

World Traveller
*The new larger format
Visitor's Guides*

Czechoslovakia
France
Holland
Norway
Portugal
USA

MPC Guides

Explore the World with the Best in Travel Guides

Off the Beaten Track
Austria
Britain
France
Greece
Italy
Portugal
Scandinavia
Spain
Switzerland
West Germany

Spectrum Guides
African Wildlife Safaris
Kenya
Maldives
Pakistan
Seychelles
Tanzania
Zimbabwe

Insider's Guides
Australia
Bali
California
Eastern Canada
Western Canada
China
Florida
Hawaii
Hong Kong
India
Indonesia
Japan
Kenya
Malaysia & Singapore
Mexico
Nepal
New England
Spain
Thailand
Turkey
Russia

A complete catalogue of all our travel guides to over 125 destinations is available on request